Pluricentricity and Pluriareality

Studies in Language Variation (SILV)
ISSN 1872-9592

The series aims to include empirical studies of linguistic variation as well as its description, explanation and interpretation in structural, social and cognitive terms. The series covers any relevant subdiscipline: sociolinguistics, contact linguistics, dialectology, historical linguistics, anthropology/anthropological linguistics. The emphasis will be on linguistic aspects and on the interaction between linguistic and extralinguistic aspects – not on extralinguistic aspects (including language ideology, policy etc.) as such.

For an overview of all books published in this series, please see *benjamins.com/catalog/silv*

Editors

Peter Auer
Universität Freiburg

Frans Hinskens
Meertens Instituut &
Radboud Universiteit
Nijmegen

Paul Kerswill
University of York

Editorial Board

Suzanne Aalberse
Universiteit van Amsterdam

Arto Anttila
Stanford University

Gaetano Berruto
Università di Torino

Jenny Cheshire
University of London

Katie Drager
University of Hawai'i at Mānoa

Katarzyna Dziubalska-Kołaczyk
Adam Mickiewicz University in Poznań

Jürg Fleischer
Philipps-Universität Marburg

Peter Gilles
University of Luxembourg

Brian D. Joseph
The Ohio State University

Johannes Kabatek
Universität Zürich

Pia Quist
University of Copenhagen

Anne-Catherine Simon
Université catholique de Louvain

Sali A. Tagliamonte
University of Toronto

Øystein Alexander Vangsnes
UiT The Arctic University of Norway

Juan A. Villena Ponsoda
Universidad de Málaga

Volume 32

Pluricentricity and Pluriareality
Dialects, Variation, and Standards
Edited by Philipp Meer and Ryan Durgasingh

Pluricentricity and Pluriareality

Dialects, Variation, and Standards

Edited by

Philipp Meer
University of Münster

Ryan Durgasingh
Ruhr University Bochum & University of Münster

John Benjamins Publishing Company
Amsterdam / Philadelphia

TM The paper used in this publication meets the minimum requirements of the American National Standard for Information Sciences – Permanence of Paper for Printed Library Materials, ANSI Z39.48-1984.

DOI 10.1075/silv.32

Cataloging-in-Publication Data available from Library of Congress:
LCCN 2024049373 (PRINT) / 2024049374 (E-BOOK)

ISBN 978 90 272 1915 2 (HB)
ISBN 978 90 272 4623 3 (E-BOOK)

© 2025 – John Benjamins B.V.
No part of this book may be reproduced in any form, by print, photoprint, microfilm, or any other means, without written permission from the publisher.

John Benjamins Publishing Company · https://benjamins.com

Table of contents

Acknowledgements   VII

CHAPTER 1. Modeling variation: Pluricentricity and pluriareality — The debate surrounding both models, and potentials for their complementarity   1
   Philipp Meer & Ryan Durgasingh

CHAPTER 2. Pluriareal languages and the case of German   15
   Stephan Elspaß

CHAPTER 3. Conceptualization of German from an Austrian perspective: Empirical evidence from Austrian schools   45
   Jutta Ransmayr

CHAPTER 4. Regiocentric use and national indexicality: Enregisterment as a theoretical integration for standard German   66
   Konstantin Niehaus

CHAPTER 5. Pluricentricity versus pluriareality? Areal patterns in the English-speaking world   90
   Edgar W. Schneider

CHAPTER 6. The pluricentricity vs. pluriareality debate: What postcolonial diffusion and transnational language contact can tell us   118
   Sarah Buschfeld

CHAPTER 7. A Scottish perspective on the pluricentricity/pluriareality debate   141
   Andreas Weilinghoff

CHAPTER 8. Revising the *Algemene Nederlandse Spraakkunst*: A pluricentric approach to diatopic variation in the grammar of Standard Dutch?   165
   Arne Dhondt, Timothy Colleman & Johan De Caluwe

CHAPTER 9. Pluricentricity AND pluriareality: Building the case for complementarity   187
   Ryan Durgasingh & Philipp Meer

Index   197

Acknowledgements

We owe our gratitude to the many people and organizations who have supported this work from its origins as a conference to the now published volume. To begin, we would like to thank the Graduate School Empirical and Applied Linguistics at the University of Münster for entrusting us with the responsibility of spearheading its graduate conference in 2019, and for all of its generous logistical and financial support to that end. The international conference, "Pluricentricity versus Pluriareality: Models, Varieties, Approaches", was also made a success through the support of several professors, our fellow graduate students at the time, student volunteers, and many others, including: Gunter De Vogelaer, Dagmar Deuber, Christine Dimroth, Anika Gerfer, Christian Gewering, Ulrike Gut, Eva Hänsel, Ka Man (Darlene) Lau, Dejan Matic, Christina Nelson, Jan-Philipp Pflügl, Juliane Schopf, Muhammad Shakir, Katrin Thelen, and Mats Väisänen. We thank them all. We would further like to acknowledge funding we received from the International Office of the University of Münster.

We gratefully acknowledge all of our conference presenters who expertly addressed the knotty issues of variation in standards, and especially thank our plenary speakers for lively talks which impacted our thinking regarding this volume: Stefan Dollinger, Stephan Elspaß, Rudolf Muhr, and Edgar W. Schneider. To these plenary speakers and Sarah Buschfeld, who also helped us to sum-up the conference theme while spurring us to rethink the "versus" of its title in our final roundtable, we offer our enduring thanks for their insights and guidance.

When, in the early days after the conference, we decided to reach out to potential contributors with the idea for this book, we were met with enthusiasm by our present authors. Their commitment over the course of the intervening years — through the ups-and-downs of usual life, work pressures, and the uncertainties of a global pandemic — kept us grounded and inspired us to push through to the end. Needless to say, this book would not exist without them.

We acknowledge, too, the various ways in which John Benjamins and its "Studies in Language Variation" series editors have helped to shape and guide this work. Peter Auer, Frans Hinskens, and Paul Kerswill's timely reviews, patience, and overall collegiality made it possible for us and our contributors to shape and refine this volume.

To Fahimah Ali, who came in at the last stretch to lend us her sharp eye for copyediting and referencing, we give our thanks and best wishes for her ongoing academic journey.

Finally, while these acknowledgments have foregrounded this book, the reality is that the volume really came together in the background of life. As such, we cannot thank our families and friends enough for the innumerable ways in which their care and support have given us the strength and space necessary to pull it all together. To them, we offer our highest esteem.

CHAPTER 1

Modeling variation
Pluricentricity and pluriareality —
The debate surrounding both models,
and potentials for their complementarity

Philipp Meer[1,2] & Ryan Durgasingh[1,3]
[1] University of Münster, Germany | [2] University of Campinas, Brazil |
[3] Ruhr University Bochum

The question of how to conceptualize variation in languages with more than one standard variety, such as English, Dutch, or German, has been a central one to variation linguistics. Variation in these languages is sometimes modeled according to two opposed approaches: pluricentricity and pluriareality, though not uncontroversially. The present chapter first introduces the pluricentricity/pluriareality debate and then identifies several aspects that warrant a more extensive and thorough discussion of their potential complementarity. It then introduces the volume, which is the first of its kind to consolidate pluricentric and pluriareal perspectives on modeling standard language variation in a systematic manner. A major contribution of the volume lies in the fact that most chapters seek to integrate both concepts in modeling variation.

Keywords: pluricentricity, pluriareality, language standardization, language variation, German, English, Dutch, World Englishes, epicenter, national varieties

1. Introduction

The question of how to model variation in languages with more than one standard variety has been a central one to variation linguistics and sociolinguistics. Related research has, to some degree, taken place in these linguistic disciplines more generally, but certain discussions have largely played a role in research on particular languages, including English and especially German linguistics. While there is agreement that languages such as Dutch, English, German, Portuguese, or Spanish are by no means homogenous, even at the level of standard usage, disagreement exists as to how this heterogeneity may be ideally conceptualized. Linguistic variation in these languages is sometimes modeled according to two opposed approaches: *pluricentricity* and *pluriareality* (e.g. Clyne 1992; Leitner 1992; Muhr 1997; Scheuringer 1996; Auer 2014; Hundt 2013; Niehaus 2015; Elspaß et al. 2017; Dollinger 2019a). The former is commonly adopted in English linguistics (at least implicitly) — especially in the World Englishes paradigm (Kachru 1985; Schneider, E.W. 2007; Buschfeld & Kautzsch 2020; Nelson et al. 2020; Schreier et al. 2020) — as well as Dutch linguistics (Ruette et al. 2014; Speelman et al. 2014) and other philologies; the latter has so far largely played a role in German linguistics only (Scheuringer 1996; Pohl 1997; Ammon 1998; Elspaß & Niehaus 2014; Elspaß & Kleiner 2019).

Pluricentricity describes a situation wherein a single language has several national standard varieties which interact with each other and are used for official purposes within their national contexts (Clyne 1992). Specifically, the term refers to "languages with several interacting centres, each providing a national variety with at least some of its own (codified) norms" (Clyne 1992:1). Pluriareality, on the other hand, questions the notion of (exclusively) national standards, and aims to model linguistic variation independently of national and political borders, especially in contiguous areas (e.g. Scheuringer 1996; Niehaus 2015; Elspaß & Dürscheid 2017; Elspaß et al. 2017). More explicitly, in analogy to Clyne (1992:1), pluriareality describes "a language [that] has more than one standard variety with its own norms of usage", with potentially "more than one standard variety within a nation" that may, in some cases, "transcend national borders" (Elspaß, this volume:21).

Both pluricentricity and pluriareality have in common that they are directed against ideas of relatively homogenous standard languages (Milroy 2001). In German linguistics, pluricentricity and subsequently pluriareality were popularized at the end of the 20th century in reaction to earlier notions of standardness in the German-speaking countries in Europe that were heavily centered on standard (northern) German German (Moser 1959; see Kloss 1978, Clyne 1992; Ammon 1995, 1998; Pohl 1997). In line with these developments, the idea of Dutch as a pluricentric language has become mainstream over a formerly exonormative orientation toward Netherlandic Dutch, even outside the Netherlands (Ruette et al. 2014:104). Similarly, in English linguistics, from the 1980s onwards, there has been a growing academic discussion on the diversity of English worldwide and recognition of the decreasing influence of historical input varieties, especially British English(es), in former colonies (Platt & Weber 1980; Pride 1982; Platt et al. 1984; Kachru 1985). However, apart from Clyne (1992), Leitner (1992), Hundt (2013), Schneider, E.W. (2014), a few others, and more recently Dollinger (2019a, b), research in this context has largely not included extensive references to pluricentricity; pluriareality has not yet been adopted into English linguistics, but related ideas and concepts have also been discussed there (see below). From a sociolinguistic perspective, both models further have in common that they recognize the coexistence of different standard varieties on a par. Lastly, both attribute attention to standard language usage especially and share a particular focus on geographically conditioned variation.

However, pluricentricity and pluriareality fundamentally disagree on the status and importance of national borders and nation states in mapping language variation. While pluricentricity emphasizes the importance of national borders and nation states in understanding and determining the existence or emergence of different (standard) varieties (e.g. Ebner 2014: 8; Dollinger 2019a: 44; 2019b: 100), pluriareality notes the potential risk of overemphasizing political aspects in conceptualizing variation at the standard level. It was on this basis that the pluriareality model was introduced into German linguistics (e.g. Scheuringer 1996). Instead, pluriareality emphasizes the underlying importance of (traditional) dialect boundaries on variable standard usage in the German language (Wolf 1994; Pohl 1997: 69).

In German linguistics, the question of national borders and nation states in the modeling of variation (and its potential socio-political implications) has featured prominently in heated academic debates, often in the context and concerning the status of Austrian German. So far, however, these arguments have not always been fully nuanced and constructive. While this debate has essentially been limited to German linguistics, conceptually related discussions have also occurred in English linguistics. In regions like the Caribbean (Allsopp 1996; Devonish & Thomas 2012; Deuber 2013; Hänsel & Deuber 2019; Deuber et al. 2021), the South Pacific (Biewer 2015), or West Africa (Gut 2012), the possibility of overarching regional standardization tendencies has been discussed, often with complex findings and indications of both national and some regional tendencies. Sizable and systematic empirical research on these aspects, however, is often not yet fully available. At the same time, although World Englishes is traditionally focused on the development of Englishes in different postcolonial nations, issues of methodological nationalism and the importance of transnational perspectives, contact, mobility, and influences have been emphasized, especially more recently (Mair 2013, 2021; Buschfeld et al. 2018; Schneider, B. 2019; Bolander 2020; Meer & Deuber 2020; Starr 2021; Tseng & Hinrichs 2020). A systematic as well as nuanced and constructive discussion of pluricentricity and pluriareality is thus of relevance not only for German linguistics, but variation linguistics more generally, including research on the modeling of variation in languages such as English and Dutch.

In fact, apart from disagreement on the importance of nation states, pluricentricity and pluriareality have distinct underlying foci and provide different perspectives that warrant a more extensive and thorough discussion of their potential complementarity. However, to date, potentials for an integration of both models have not yet been systematically explored. Rather than viewing the models in strict opposition to each other, both could potentially be seen as adding different layers to our understanding of (standard) variation that allow its modeling to approximate more closely the complex and multidimensional nature of linguistic reality, as we layout below.

- Firstly, both models weigh the importance of language production and perception to different degrees in capturing and conceptualizing linguistic variation (see also Ransmayr, this volume; Niehaus, this volume; Schneider, this volume). Pluricentricity takes into account findings on (standard) language production and usage patterns but also attributes particular importance to aspects such as (national) identity, prestige, metalinguistic awareness, and attitudes toward varieties (e.g. Clyne 1992; Muhr 2012, 2018: 35; Hundt 2013; Schmidlin et al. 2017: 16) — aspects that are broadly linked to perception. While pluriareality also generally acknowledges the relevance of whether potential (national and/or intra-/transnational) standards are recognized and accepted by their speakers (Elspaß, this volume; Niehaus, this volume; see also Vergeiner et al. 2021), it has primarily focused on observable areal distribution patterns at the level of standard language production (e.g. Niehaus 2015; Elspaß & Dürscheid 2017; Elspaß & Kleiner 2019). However, neither pluricentricity nor pluriareality are solely concerned with production or perception; the models simply deviate in their relative treatment of both aspects. Pluricentricity additionally highlights asymmetries, hierarchies, and dependencies between varieties (Clyne 1995: 21; Scharloth 2005; Mair 2013; Tupas 2015), while pluriareality is more concerned with a descriptive account of variation (Elspaß & Dürscheid 2017: 88–93).
- Secondly, while both models generally draw on usage-based approaches to variation, they differ in the ways varieties are operationalized. Pluricentricity places greater emphasis on the concept of the nation in investigating patterns of variation and mutual influences between different (standard) varieties, often in an a priori manner. For instance, in World Englishes, potential influences from "larger" on "smaller" neighboring varieties — e.g. from Indian on Bangladeshi English or Australian on Fiji English, sometimes termed "epicentric" influences (Hundt 2013; Schneider, E.W. 2014, see below) — or regional similarities/differences more generally are mostly investigated with focus on the national level. These analyses typically rely on (sub)corpora compiled for different national varieties of English and studies of attitudes and perceptions of these, including in contiguous areas (see e.g. Hoffmann et al. 2011;

Bernaisch 2012; Bernaisch & Koch 2016; Gries & Bernaisch 2016; Heller et al. 2017 on the South Asian context).[1] Pluriareality, in turn, strongly relies on (i) a bottom-up approach to modeling variation that largely draws on regional corpora that transcend national borders (in contiguous areas) and take into account sub-national localities, and (ii) data-driven techniques that aim to establish patterns based on an (aggregate) analysis of a large number of linguistic features.

- Thirdly, the idea of potential complementarity is strengthened by the existence of terminologically and conceptually related models and concepts. Although predominantly concerned with the national level, pluricentricity — not generally unlike pluriareality — acknowledges the possible existence of sub-national (standard) varieties, a situation which is referred to by terms such as "regional pluricentricity" (Reiffenstein 2001: 88), "regionally pluricentric" (Auer 2014: 44), or "second level pluricentricity" (Muhr 2018: 40–42). According to Muhr (2018: 40), the second level of pluricentricity describes "regional variation within NVs [national varieties]", which is understood to encompass "pan-regional linguistic features that are also charged with aspects of (regional or pan-regional) identity", especially in geographically larger countries. However, unlike in the case of pluriareality, transnational variation is not in particular focus (ibid.). While higher degrees of transnational variation are seen as a pluriareal argument against (exclusively) national standards at the level of production, pluricentrists often highlight perceptual differences of transnational linguistic variants and their association with distinct national social meanings (e.g. Muhr 2018: 39). A potential link between these opposing views in the context of diverging patterns of (standard) language use, social indices, and perception may be the role of enregisterment (Agha 2007; Auer 2014; see Niehaus, this volume, for details).
- Fourthly, unlike pluriareality, pluricentricity — at least in those frequent cases when essentially equated with *plurinationality* — does not typically scrutinize the issue of "radiation" in greater detail, i.e. the possible influence and spread from an assumed center to its associated periphery, as the term may be taken to suggest (Auer 2014: 22). However, in English linguistics, center-periphery

---

1. This is partially related to the facts that (i) corpora that comprise smaller regions within different postcolonial nations in contiguous areas are largely not available (but see e.g. Yurchenk et al. 2021) and (ii) English, unlike German or Dutch in Europe for instance, is often spoken in dispersed territories, even within the same region, and investigations into similarities/differences between varieties at the regional level, with a view to both production and perception, can be conducted in a (at least somewhat) more straightforward manner (see e.g. Deuber 2014; Meer et al. 2019; Deuber et al. 2021; Hänsel et al. 2022; Meer et al. 2023; Meer & Durgasingh 2024 on standard varieties in the anglophone Caribbean).

readings of pluricentricity and the issue of linguistic *epicenters* have received some attention (Leitner 1992; Hoffmann et al. 2011; Hundt 2013; Schneider, E.W. 2014; Gries & Bernaisch 2016; Heller et al. 2017; Peters et al. 2019; Hackert 2022; see also Schneider, this volume; Buschfeld, this volume). Most of this research has focused on the question of emerging epicenters, i.e. postcolonial varieties that (i) have endonormatively stabilized (in the sense of Schneider, E.W. 2007) and (ii) "serve as a model of English" for (neighboring) countries (Hundt 2013: 185). Thus, there seems to be a higher degree of conceptual overlap between pluriareality and pluricentricity than is traditionally acknowledged — at least when widening the view to these center-periphery readings of pluricentricity in English linguistics. Notwithstanding similarities (see also Elspaß, this volume), as mentioned above, research on linguistic epicenters in World Englishes is still fundamentally grounded at the level of national varieties, and exclusively bottom-up approaches to mapping variation in a pluriareal sense are rare (or even absent). There may thus be potential for mutual gains by uniting perspectives from (center-periphery) pluricentricity and pluriareality across research on different languages.

Scrutinizing aspects such as those above, the present volume is the first of its kind to consolidate pluricentric and pluriareal perspectives on modeling standard language variation in a systematic and extensive manner. The volume comprises papers and keynote addresses given at the "International Conference on Pluricentricity vs. Pluriareality: Models, Varieties, Approaches" at the University of Münster in 2019 as well as additional contributions. The volume combines perspectives from leading scholars and early-career researchers from German, English, and Dutch linguistics on the pluricentricity/pluriareality debate. A major contribution of the volume lies in the fact that most chapters argue for a "Third Way" in the debate, seeking to integrate both concepts in modeling variation. The chapters argue that these concepts are potentially interrelated or complementary, rather than strictly opposed to each other, as has often been indicated in previous research. Moreover, several chapters set out to explore the applicability and usefulness of pluriareality in English linguistics and, in so doing, provide new perspectives for the World Englishes paradigm. Lastly, some of the contributions also suggest going beyond the traditional realms of the pluricentricity/pluriareality debate and its focus on variation at the standard level to take into account linguistic complexity in a globalized world to a greater extent. These aspects include variation at the intersection of standard/nonstandard usage, multilingualism, or scenarios that involve more than one epicenter, to name but a few (see Buschfeld, this volume; Schneider, this volume; see also Hundt 2013; Hackert 2022)

The volume has a wide methodological scope. The chapters make use of a range of approaches, extending from corpus linguistics (including corpus phonetics) to language attitude research, sociolinguistics, and dialectology, as well as mixed-method approaches. Theoretically oriented chapters are also included. The combination of different methods and sources of data allows for an informed and objective discussion in the so far heated debate and enables the chapters to elaborate on several of the above-mentioned aspects pertaining to the potential complementarity of pluricentricity and pluriareality.

2. Overview of individual contributions

The book is structured into four sections. **Section I** takes us to variational research on the German language — the context in which the pluricentricity/pluriareality debate originated. The section begins with a paper by Stephan Elspaß on "Pluriareal languages and the case of German" (**Chapter 2**). The chapter starts with a discussion of the main tenets and assumptions of pluricentricity and pluriareality, then moves on to examine their viability in modeling variation in standard German in Europe, drawing on conceptual aspects and a large variety of corpus-based data. With a particular focus on patterns of language production, Elspaß argues that the pluriareal model seems to be more suitable to describe variation in standard German. More generally, the author suggests that pluricentricity and pluriareality should be seen as complementary insofar as each is likely to be more appropriate for different kinds of standard language scenarios: pluricentricity in the case of varieties across dispersed territories, pluriareality in contiguous areas.

Chapter 3 by Jutta Ransmayr shifts the focus to the perception of standard varieties of German. Her contribution, titled "Conceptualization of German from an Austrian perspective: Empirical evidence from Austrian schools," presents the findings of a large-scale survey among upper secondary school students and teachers of German in Austria concerning their metalinguistic awareness and perception of (standard) German. The results show that most students, and especially teachers, conceptualize German in accordance with the pluricentric model. At the same time, teachers' perceptions also include pluriareal aspects, such that an Austrian standard is recognized while intra-Austrian and transnational variation and similarities are acknowledged. Ransmayr argues that pluricentric and pluriareal views need not be contradictory and may, in fact, build on each other: meticulous pluriareal accounts of the distribution of variants may be used as a foundation for further pluricentric exploration and theorizing of aspects beyond geographical variation.

The last paper in this section, "Regiocentric use and national indexicality: Enregisterment as a theoretical integration for standard German" (**Chapter 4**), by Konstantin Niehaus, suggests a link between issues of language production and perception in the pluricentricity/pluriareality debate in the German context by drawing on language ideologies and the concept of enregisterment (Agha 2007). After a brief literature review, Niehaus proposes a new theoretical framework for modeling standard German (and potentially standards in other languages) that combines the pluriareal concept of areas in terms of high (aggregate) density in frequency of variants with the issue of social meaning of variation, which is often emphasized in pluricentric accounts. On this basis, the author provides an outlook for further research and identifies reciprocal aspects to scrutinize further in pluricentric and pluriareal thinking.

Section II provides perspectives from the English-speaking world. In his contribution, "Pluricentricity versus pluriareality? Areal patterns in the English-speaking world" (**Chapter 5**), Edgar W. Schneider introduces and critically discusses the notions of pluricentricity and pluriareality, arguing that the former may be seen as "ambiguous" and the latter as "controversial." Based on a large variety of different (corpus) data, Schneider investigates the viability of the pluricentric and pluriareal approaches in modeling variation in English worldwide. The results show (i) little evidence of distinct national varieties in terms of specific features but cross-varietal differences in general usage tendencies, (ii) mostly preliminary or, at times, inconclusive indications concerning epicentric influence in neighboring varieties, and (iii) considerable evidence of overlap in areal language production patterns within and across national borders. Ultimately, Schneider argues that pluricentricity and pluriareality need not exclude each other but may capture different aspects of the complexity of English worldwide, with varying emphases on patterns in perception and production, respectively.

Chapter 6, "The pluricentricity vs. pluriareality debate: What postcolonial diffusion and transnational language contact can tell us" by Sarah Buschfeld provides another Anglophone perspective. Drawing on English in Singapore and Namibia as well as Southeast Asia and Southern Africa more generally, Buschfeld shows that both pluricentricity and pluriareality contribute to understanding the types and degrees of variation observed in these linguistically diverse contexts. At the same time, the author reminds us of potential limitations of both models, such as a relatively narrow focus on standard language productions.

Section II closes with a contribution by Andreas Weilinghoff in "A Scottish perspective on the pluricentricity/pluriareality debate" (**Chapter 7**). Weilinghoff presents the findings of a meticulous corpus phonetic analysis of the Scottish Vowel Length Rule (SVLR), an alternation pattern in vowel duration traditionally associated with Scottish English(es). The results show that variation in the SVLR in Scottish Standard English is primarily conditioned by language-internal (prosodic) factors; the SVLR seems to operate relatively homogenously at a national level and mostly independently of geographical factors. At the same time, previous studies have shown that the SVLR can also be found in Northern England. Based on these observations, Weilinghoff suggests that an oppositional view of both models is not productive and may, in some cases, distract from the role of other, non-geographical variables in influencing variation.

Section III examines pluricentricity and pluriareality from the viewpoint of Dutch linguistics. In **Chapter 8**, "Revising the *Algemene Nederlandse Spraakkunst*: A pluricentric approach to diatopic variation in the grammar of standard Dutch?", Arne Dhondt, Timothy Colleman, and Johan De Caluwe investigate whether the pluricentric perspective taken in the main reference grammar for Dutch, with its focus on national standard varieties, aligns with actual language use. Using Belgian and Netherlandic newspaper corpora, the authors compare the regional distribution of grammatical variants with those described in the grammar. Their findings show that the patterns of distribution do not always coincide with national borders. While this finding, as the authors indicate, could technically be interpreted in favor of pluriareality, Dhondt, Colleman, and De Caluwe argue that the observed patterns are not necessarily at odds with a pluricentric view either, especially when focusing on general usage tendencies rather than the question of variety-exclusive variants.

Section IV aims to bring the arguments of the previous chapters together. In **Chapter 9**, "Pluricentricity AND pluriareality: Building the case for complementarity," Ryan Durgasingh and Philipp Meer discuss the insights and findings of the individual contributions in light of the previous pluricentricity/pluriareality debate, and ultimately aim to evaluate the question of whether and in which ways pluricentricity and pluriareality may be seen as complementary to each other.

References

Agha, Asif. 2007. *Language and social relations*. Cambridge: Cambridge University Press.
Allsopp, Richard. 1996. *Dictionary of Caribbean English usage*. Oxford: Oxford University Press.
Ammon, Ulrich. 1995. *Die deutsche Sprache in Deutschland, Österreich und der Schweiz*. Berlin: De Gruyter.
Ammon, Ulrich. 1998. Plurinationalität oder Pluriarealität? Begriffliche und terminologische Präzisierungsvorschläge zur Plurizentrizität des Deutschen — mit Ausblick auf ein Wörterbuchprojekt. In Peter Ernst & Franz Patocka (eds.), *Deutsche Sprache in Raum und Zeit*, 313–323. Wien: Edition Praesens.

Auer, Peter. 2014. Enregistering pluricentric German. In Augusto S. d. Silva (ed.), *Pluricentricity: Language variation and sociocognitive dimensions*. Berlin: De Gruyter.

Bernaisch, Tobias. 2012. Attitudes towards Englishes in Sri Lanka. *World Englishes* 31(3). 279–291.

Bernaisch, Tobias & Christopher Koch. 2016. Attitudes towards Englishes in India. *World Englishes* 35(1). 118–132.

Biewer, Carolin. 2015. *South Pacific Englishes: A sociolinguistic and morphosyntactic profile of Fiji English, Samoan English and Cook Islands English*. Amsterdam: Benjamins.

Bolander, Brook. 2020. World Englishes and transnationalism. In Daniel Schreier, Marianne Hundt & Edgar W. Schneider (eds.), *The Cambridge Handbook of World Englishes*, 676–701. Cambridge: Cambridge University Press.

Buschfeld, Sarah & Alexander Kautzsch (eds.). 2020. *Modelling world Englishes: A joint approach to postcolonial and non-postcolonial varieties*. Edinburgh: Edinburgh University Press.

Buschfeld, Sarah, Alexander Kautzsch & Edgar W. Schneider. 2018. From colonial dynamism to current transnationalism: A unified view on postcolonial and non-postcolonial Englishes. In Sandra C. Deshors (ed.), *Modelling World Englishes in the 21st century: Assessing the interplay of emancipation and globalization of ESL varieties*, 15–44. Amsterdam: Benjamins.

Clyne, Michael G. (ed.). 1992. *Pluricentric languages: Differing norms in different nations*. Berlin: De Gruyter.

Clyne, Michael G. 1995. *The German language in a changing Europe*. Cambridge: Cambridge University Press.

Deuber, Dagmar. 2013. Towards endonormative standards of English in the Caribbean: A study of students' beliefs and school curricula. *Language, Culture and Curriculum* 26(2). 109–127.

Deuber, Dagmar. 2014. *English in the Caribbean: Variation, style and standards in Jamaica and Trinidad*. Cambridge: Cambridge University Press.

Deuber, Dagmar, Stephanie Hackert, Eva C. Hänsel, Alexander Laube, Mahyar Hejrani & Catherine Laliberté. 2021. The norm orientation of English in the Caribbean: A comparative study of newspaper writing from ten countries. *American Speech*. Advance online publication. 1–40.

Devonish, Hubert & Ewart A. T. Thomas. 2012. Standards of English in the Caribbean. In Raymond Hickey (ed.), *Standards of English: Codified varieties around the world*, 179–197. Cambridge: Cambridge University Press.

Dollinger, Stefan. 2019a. *The Pluricentricity Debate*. London: Routledge.

Dollinger, Stefan. 2019b. Debunking "pluri-areality": On the pluricentric perspective of national varieties. *Journal of Linguistic Geography* 7(2). 98–112.

Ebner, Jakob. 2014. Österreichisches Deutsch: Ein Klärungsversuch. In Bundesministerium für Bildung (ed.), *Österreichisches Deutsch als Unterrichts – und Bildungssprache*, 7–9. Vienna.

Elspaß, Stephan & Christa Dürscheid. 2017. Areale grammatische Variation in den Gebrauchsstandards des Deutschen. In Marek Konopka & Angelika Wöllstein-Leisten (eds.), *Grammatische Variation: Empirische Zugänge und theoretische Modellierung*, 85–104. Berlin: De Gruyter.

Elspaß, Stephan, Christa Dürscheid & Arne Ziegler. 2017. Zur grammatischen Pluriarealität der deutschen Gebrauchsstandards — oder: Über die Grenzen des Plurizentrizitätsbegriffs. *Zeitschrift für deutsche Philologie* 136. 69–91.

Elspaß, Stephan & Stefan Kleiner. 2019. Forschungsergebnisse Zur Arealen Variation Im Standarddeutschen. In Joachim Herrgen & Jürgen E. Schmidt (eds.), *Deutsch: Sprache und Raum — ein Internationales Handbuch der Sprachvariation*, 159–184. Berlin: De Gruyter.

Elspaß, Stephan & Konstantin Niehaus. 2014. The standardization of a modern pluriareal language: Concepts and corpus designs for German and beyond. *Orð og tunga* 16. 47–67.

Gries, Stefan T. & Tobias Bernaisch. 2016. Exploring epicentres empirically: Focus on South Asian Englishes. *English World-Wide* 37(1). 1–25.

Gut, Ulrike. 2012. Standards of English in West Africa. In Raymond Hickey (ed.), *Standards of English: Codified varieties around the world*, 213–228. Cambridge: Cambridge University Press.

Hackert, Stephanie. 2022. The epicentre model and American influence on Bahamian Englishes. *World Englishes* 41(3). 361–376.

Hänsel, Eva C. & Dagmar Deuber. 2019. The interplay of the national, regional, and global in standards of English: A recognition survey of newscaster accents in the Caribbean. *English World-Wide* 40(3). 241–268.

Hänsel, Eva C. Michael Westphal, Philipp Meer & Dagmar Deuber. 2022. Context matters: Grenadian students' attitudes towards newscasters' and teachers' accents. *Journal of Pidgin and Creole Languages* 37(1). 16–52.

Heller, Benedikt, Tobias Bernaisch & Stefan T. Gries. 2017. Empirical perspectives on two potential epicenters: The genitive alternation in Asian Englishes. *ICAME Journal* 41(1). 111–144.

Hoffmann, Sebastian, Marianne Hundt & Joybrato Mukherjee. 2011. Indian English — An emerging epicentre? A pilot study on light verbs in web-derived corpora of South Asian Englishes. *Anglia* 129(3–4). 258–280.

Hundt, Marianne. 2013. The diversification of English: Old, new and emerging epicentres. In Daniel Schreier & Marianne Hundt (eds.), *English as a contact language*, 182–203. Cambridge: Cambridge University Press.

Kachru, Braj B. 1985. Standards, codification and sociolinguistic realism: The English language in the outer circle. In Randolph Quirk & H. G. Widdowson (eds.), *English in the world: Teaching and learning the language and literatures*, 11–30. Cambridge: Cambridge University Press.

Kloss, Heinz. 1978. *Die Entwicklung neuer germanischer Kultursprachen seit 1800*, 2nd edn. Düsseldorf: Schwann.

Leitner, Gerhard. 1992. English as a pluricentric language. In Michael G. Clyne (ed.), *Pluricentric languages: Differing norms in different nations*, 179–237. Berlin: De Gruyter.

Mair, Christian. 2013. The world system of Englishes: Accounting for the transnational importance of mobile and mediated vernaculars. *English World-Wide* 34(3). 253–278.

Mair, Christian. 2021. World Englishes: From Methodological Nationalism to a Global Perspective. In Britta Schneider, Theresa Heyd & Mario Saraceni (eds.), *Bloomsbury World Englishes Volume 1: Paradigms*, 27–45: Bloomsbury Academic.

Meer, Philipp & Dagmar Deuber. 2020. Standard English in Trinidad: Multinormativity, translocality, and implications for the Dynamic Model and the EIF Model. In Sarah Buschfeld & Alexander Kautzsch (eds.), *Modelling world Englishes: A joint approach to postcolonial and non-postcolonial varieties*, 274–297. Edinburgh: Edinburgh University Press.

Meer, Philipp & Ryan Durgasingh. 2024. Sociophonetic and morphosyntactic variation in Caribbean creoles and Englishes. In Kingsley Bolton (ed.), *The Wiley Blackwell Encyclopedia of World Englishes*. Hoboken, NJ: Wiley.

Meer, Philipp, Robert Fuchs, Dagmar Deuber, Véronique Lacoste & Eva C. Hänsel. 2023. Prosodic variation of English in Dominica, Grenada, and Trinidad. *World Englishes* 42(1). 48–72.

Meer, Philipp, Michael Westphal, Eva C. Hänsel & Dagmar Deuber. 2019. Trinidadian secondary school students' attitudes toward accents of Standard English. *Journal of Pidgin and Creole Languages* 34(1). 83–125.

Milroy, James. 2001. Language ideologies and the consequences of standardization. *Journal of Sociolinguistics* 5(4). 530–555.

Moser, Hugo. 1959. Neuere und neueste Zeit. Von den 80er Jahren des 19. Jahrhunderts zur Gegenwart. In Friedrich Maurer & Friedrich Stroh (eds.), *Deutsche Wortgeschichte* (Vol. 2). Berlin: De Gruyter.

Muhr, Rudolf. 1997. Zur Terminologie und Methode der Beschreibung plurizentrischer Sprachen und deren Varietäten am Beispiel des Deutschen. In Rudolf Muhr & Richard Schrodt (eds.), *Österreichisches Deutsch und andere nationale Varietäten plurizentrischer Sprachen in Europa: Empirische Analysen*, 40–67. Vienna: Hölder-Pichler-Tempsky.

Muhr, Rudolf. 2012. Linguistic dominance and non-dominance in pluricentric languages: A typology. In Rudolf Muhr (ed.), *Non-dominant varieties of pluricentric languages: Getting the picture*, 23–48. Frankfurt: Peter Lang.

Muhr, Rudolf. 2018. Misconceptions about pluricentric languages and pluricentric theory – an overview of 40 years. In Rudolf Muhr & Benjamin Meisnitzer (eds.), *Pluricentric languages and non-dominant varieties worldwide: New pluricentric languages – old problems*, 17–56. Frankfurt: Peter Lang.

Nelson, Cecil L. Z. G. Proshina, Daniel R. Davis, Braj B. Kachru & Yamuna Kachru (eds.). 2020. *Handbook of world Englishes*, 2nd edn. Hoboken, NJ: Wiley-Blackwell.

Niehaus, Konstantin. 2015. Areale Variation in der Syntax des Standarddeutschen: Ergebnisse zum Sprachgebrauch und zur Frage Plurizentrik vs. Pluriarealität. *Zeitschrift für Dialektologie und Linguistik* 82(2). 133–168.

Peters, Pam, Adam Smith & Tobias Bernaisch. 2019. Shared Lexical Innovations in Australian and New Zealand English. *Dictionaries: Journal of the Dictionary Society of North America* 40(2). 1–30.

Platt, John, Heidi Weber & Ho M. Lian. 1984. *The New Englishes*. London: Routledge.

Platt, John T. & Heidi Weber. 1980. *English in Singapore and Malaysia: Status, features, functions*. Oxford: Oxford University Press.

Pohl, Heinz D. 1997. Gedanken zum Österreichischen Deutsch (als Teil der „pluriarealen" deutschen Sprache). In Rudolf Muhr & Richard Schrodt (eds.), *Österreichisches Deutsch und andere nationale Varietäten plurizentrischer Sprachen in Europa: Empirische Analysen*, 67–87. Vienna: Hölder-Pichler-Tempsky.

Pride, John (ed.) (1982). *New Englishes*. Rowley, MA: Newsbury House.

Reiffenstein, Ingo. 2001. Das Problem der nationalen Varietäten. Rezensionsaufsatz zu Ulrich Ammon: Die deutsche Sprache in Deutschland, Österreich und der Schweiz. Das Problem der nationalen Varietäten, Berlin/New York 1995. *Zeitschrift für deutsche Philologie* (1). 78–89.

Ruette, Tom, Dirk Speelman & Dirk Geeraerts. 2014. Lexical variation in aggregate perspective. In Augusto S. d. Silva (ed.), *Pluricentricity: Language variation and sociocognitive dimensions*. Berlin: De Gruyter.

Scharloth, Joachim. 2005. Asymmetrische Plurizentrizität und Sprachbewusstsein: Einstellungen der Deutschschweizer zum Standarddeutschen. *Zeitschrift für germanistische Linguistik* 33(2–3).

Scheuringer, Hermann. 1996. Das Deutsche als pluriareale Sprache: Ein Beitrag gegen staatlich begrenzte Horizonte in der Diskussion um die deutsche Sprache in Österreich. *Die Unterrichtspraxis / Teaching German* 29(2). 147–153.

Schmidlin, Regula, Eva Wyss & Winifred Davies. 2017. Plurizentrik revisited — aktuelle Perspektiven auf die Variation der deutschen Standardsprache. In Winifred Davies, Annelies Häcki Buhofer, Regula Schmidlin, Melanie Wagner & Eva Wyss (eds.), *Standardsprache. zwischen Norm und Praxis: Theoretische Betrachtungen, empirische Studien und sprachdidaktische Ausblicke*, 8–20. Tübingen: Narrr.

Schneider, Britta. 2019. Methodological nationalism in linguistics. *Language Sciences* 76. 101169.

Schneider, Edgar W. 2007. *Postcolonial English: Varieties around the world*. Cambridge: Cambridge University Press.

Schneider, Edgar W. 2014. Global diffusion, regional attraction, local roots? Sociocognitive perspectives on the pluricentricity of English. In Augusto S. d. Silva (ed.), *Pluricentricity: Language variation and sociocognitive dimensions*. Berlin: De Gruyter.

Schreier, Daniel, Marianne Hundt & Edgar W. Schneider (eds.). 2020. *The Cambridge Handbook of World Englishes*. Cambridge: Cambridge University Press.

Speelman, Dirk, Leen Impe & Dirk Geeraerts. 2014. Phonetic distance and intelligibility in Dutch. In Augusto S. d. Silva (ed.), *Pluricentricity: Language variation and sociocognitive dimensions*. Berlin: De Gruyter.

Starr, Rebecca L. 2021. Transnational dialect contact and language variation and change in World Englishes. In Alexander Onysko (ed.), *Research Developments in World Englishes*, 149–172. London: Bloomsbury.

Tseng, Amelia & Lars Hinrichs. 2020. Mobility and the English language. In Bas Aarts, April M. S. McMahon & Lars Hinrichs (eds.), *The handbook of English linguistics*, 2nd edn. 637–652. Hoboken NJ: Wiley.

Tupas, T. R. F. (ed.). 2015. *Unequal Englishes: The politics of Englishes today*. New York, NY: Palgrave Macmillan.

Vergeiner, Philip C. Elisabeth Buchner, Eva Fuchs & Stephan Elspaß. 2021. Weil STANDARD verständlich ist und DIALEKT authentisch macht. In Toke Hoffmeister, Markus Hundt & Saskia Naths (eds.), *Laien, Wissen, Sprache*, 417–442. Berlin: De Gruyter.

Wolf, Norbert R. 1994. Österreichisches zum österreichischen Deutsch. Aus Anlaß des Erscheinens von: Wolfgang Pollak: Was halten die Österreicher von ihrem Deutsch? Eine sprachpolitische und soziosemiotische Analyse der sprachlichen Identität der Österreicher. *Zeitschrift für Dialektologie und Linguistik* 61(1). 66–76.

Yurchenko, Asya, Sven Leuckert & Claudia Lange. 2021. Comparing written Indian Englishes with the new Corpus of Regional Indian Newspaper Englishes (CORINNE). *ICAME Journal* 45(1). 179–205.

CHAPTER 2

Pluriareal languages and the case of German

Stephan Elspaß
Paris-Lodron-Universität Salzburg, Austria

In the sociolinguistic discourse on standard language varieties, linguists working on standard varieties in contiguous language areas, such as in the German-speaking countries, have proposed and expanded the model of pluriareality to account for perceived deficiencies in the increasingly plurinational conception of pluricentricity. This paper first discusses the basic assumptions and characteristics of both models and then demonstrates that the model of pluriareality appears to be more adequate, in conceptual and linguistic terms, to describe the situation in languages such as German from a usage-based perspective. Finally, I propose considering the pluricentric model, which is often conceptualized as a rather plurinational model, and the pluriareal model as complementary solutions to describe different sociolinguistic constellations of standard languages.

Keywords: pluriareality, pluricentricity, plurinationality, standardization, Standard German

1. Introduction

In the past quarter of a century, sociolinguists and variation linguists in the German-speaking countries have increasingly raised doubts as to whether a concept of pluricentricity focusing solely on national centers is conceptually and linguistically adequate for all scenarios of standard language variation (e.g. Scheuringer 1996; Pohl 1997; Glauninger 2013; Auer 2013; Elspaß et al. 2017). Conceptually, the overemphasis of (prescriptive) normativity in modeling pluricentric languages has been largely criticized (e.g. Glauninger 2013; Scharloth 2005). Whether or not the notion of "national varieties" is represented in people's minds, however, has received relatively little attention (see, however, Scharloth 2005; Schmidlin 2011; Niehaus, this volume; Ransmayr, this volume). Furthermore, it has been argued that the limitation set by state borders contradicts the center-periphery notion of pluricentricity (Auer 2013, 2021). From a usage-based point of view, recent empirical research has shown that the idea of exclusively national standard varieties can often not be supported by the actual distribution of standard-language variants and varieties, particularly with respect to languages in contiguous areas, such as German (Elspaß & Kleiner 2019). In line with this criticism, the term and model of *"pluriareality"* was proposed as an alternative concept for languages recognized as official languages in two or more countries which form a contiguous area and are characterized as having multiple standard varieties (e.g. Scheuringer 1996 and many others).

The present contribution will start with a brief overview of basic linguistic notions of "standard" (Section 2). Section 3 will discuss the pluricentric model and the pluriareal model from a more general perspective. In Section 4, using the example of German, the two models outlined above will be discussed in light of recent data from three major projects on (1) phonetic, lexical, and grammatical standard variation in German and (2) perceptions of and attitudes towards different varieties of Standard German. In the concluding Section 5, I will discuss the extent to which the concept of pluricentricity in its traditional form may require modification or supplementation by a model of pluriareality.

2. Notions of 'standard language'

Generally speaking, we can distinguish between an idealized-normative and a realistic-descriptive notion of "standard language" (see Maitz & Elspaß 2013: 45–46). The first notion is characterized by the ideal of a homogenous standard language following prescriptive codified norms. These norms — which may or may not be widely used — are legitimized by official or self-declared language authorities. The second notion is usage-based, relying on descriptive norms of usage in texts speakers commonly consider to be "standard language texts," i.e. texts by educated speakers and writers in formal spoken or written contexts and situations (e.g. printed newspaper texts, TV or radio news, written or oral exams). In this case, norms may be codified based on large text corpora or corpora of formal spoken language (cf. Section 4.2). These different notions are supported by different language ideologies. At the heart of idealized-normative notions of standards is the "standard language ideology," i.e. "a bias toward an abstract, idealized homogeneous language, which is imposed and maintained by dominant bloc institutions and which names as its model the written language" (Lippi-Green 2012: 67). From a diachronic perspective, this standard language ideology has resulted in highly teleological narratives of standardization histories, with the idea of a homogeneous standard language existing since the nineteenth century at the latest. As opposed to the homogeneity bias of idealistic-normative concepts, realistic-descriptive notions of standard can be characterized as driven by an "ideology of heterogeneity," even allowing for standardization processes "from below" (Elspaß 2021). At its center is the idea of variable standard languages and co-existing standard varieties since the beginnings of language standardization.

In sociolinguistic research, the realistic-descriptive notion of standard language has been complemented by a perspective on the speakers' concepts of standard(s) and which variants they regard as belonging to this/these standard(s) (e.g. Scharloth 2005; Schmidlin 2011). Haugen (1966: 933) suggests the term "acceptance by the community" as one of four crucial features "in taking the step from 'dialect' to 'language', from vernacular to standard," thus adding an emic aspect to the etic view, which for a long time prevailed in the structuralist research on standardization. This aspect will be taken up in Section 4.1.

3. The pluricentric and the pluriareal models

The seminal works of Stewart (1968), Kloss (1978) and Clyne (1989) on pluricentricity helped to deconstruct earlier concepts of standard languages that were strongly dominated by linguistic ideologies, such as their supposed homogeneity. Linguistically, they highlighted variation within individual "big" standard languages such as English, Spanish or German. Politically, they established a strong link between the concept of pluricentricity and nation-building in their time (Auer 2021: 29–330). As a consequence, the idea of monolithic standard languages was gradually replaced by the notion of pluricentricity. Later, in the context of German, pluriareality was proposed as a complementary model, with both concepts modeling standard languages as a co-existence of standard varieties of a given language. From a sociolinguistic perspective, it is crucial for both models to recognize the co-existence of such varieties on equal terms. As both "*-centric*" and "*-areal*" imply, the distribution of such standard varieties coincides with more or less clearly delimited *geographical* regions, which may also be important cultural and/or economic regions.

What both models disagree on is the interpretation of "*center*," their correspondence with national territories, and the role of codification. According to Clyne, "[t]he term *pluricentric(ity)* indicates that a language has more than one centre, i.e. several centres, each providing a national variety with its own norms" (Clyne 1989: 358; Kloss 1978: 67; Norrby et al. 2020: 201). Since the 1980s, this notion of pluricentricity with a focus on national varieties has been the subject of much discussion and has quickly spread throughout the field of sociolinguistics, subsequently becoming a prevalent topic in language didactics — which, in turn, seems to have helped to reinforce this interpretation. However, this strong version of pluricentricity, which associates standard varieties with *national* varieties, has created new problems from a usage-based perspective of standard. The most obvious problem is that, in this version, political issues and the question of politically promoted (or enregistered) national identities may prevail over linguistic facts (cf. Clyne 1992:3 on Vietnamese).

Thus, critics of this strong version question the unclear status of *centers* in this model (cf. Auer 2021:30–35). In particular, they refer to cases of standard languages in contiguous regions, such as German, Dutch, Korean, or Vietnamese, in which "centers" are more difficult to establish than in languages with dispersed territories — "due to imperialism and/or emigration" — such as English, Chinese, or Portuguese (examples given by Clyne 1992: 2–3). The pluriareal model is to be understood as a response to this criticism. First proposed by Austrian linguists, the model sought to describe the standard language situation in German-speaking countries, with special attention on Austria. I will further describe this situation in Section 4 below, but the remainder of this section will be dedicated to discussing both models from a more general perspective by outlining simplified scenarios of standard variation in up to three different nations (A, B and C).

In the prototype of the "pluricentric = plurinational model" (see Figure 2.1), as outlined by Stewart (1968), Kloss (1987), and Clyne (1989), each of the three nations developed their own distinct standard language variety as a result of, *inter alia*, geographical dispersion and long-term closed (or insurmountable) borders. In this model, varieties *a, b,* and *c* have their individual standard language codices, which constitute prescriptive norms for each entire nation and thus legitimize the national varieties. According to this idealized model, there would be three national standard varieties of that language.

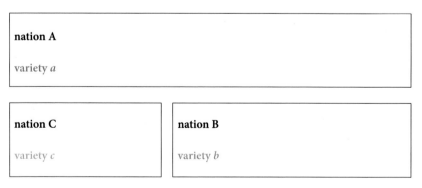

Figure 2.1 Pluricentric = plurinational model

According to Auer (2013), there are two main problems with this model of pluricentricity. Firstly, "the term 'centre' would seem to imply that there is a periphery as well, into which the centre 'radiates,'" but "[t]he issue of radiation is seemingly avoided in the current discussion of pluricentricity; it may therefore be more accurate to simply speak of the (two or more) national standard varieties of a language, instead of a pluricentric language" (Auer 2013: 19–20; cf. also Auer 2021: 32). In this understanding of the "pluricentric = plurinational model", *pluricentricity*, in fact, is a clear misnomer. Secondly, "normativity of the variants of the standard is crucial" so that "pluricentricity is not defined on the level of language use or the language representations of the lay speakers" (Auer 2013: 19).

Both Figure 2.2 and Figure 2.3 account for a more realistic usage-based approach and for the issue of radiation of centers into peripheries. They represent two different aspects of the *pluriareal* model.

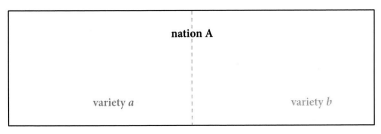

Figure 2.2 Pluriareal model I — one nation with two standard varieties (contiguous language area)

Figure 2.2 sketches a situation in which nation A has developed two standard varieties (*a* and *b*). In this figure, variety *a* dominates in one part of the nation, while variety *b* dominates in a different part. This phenomenon is evident in Norway, which uses two distinct standard varieties (*Nynorsk* and *Bokmål*) in different regions. *Nynorsk* dominates in the west, while *Bokmål* is prevalent in the east and the north of the country (Jahr 2003). There is a clear areal distribution, but no real "centers" and peripheries. Another example is Vietnamese, where, according to Clyne (1992: 3), the long-term division of the country may have led to the development of northern and southern standard varieties of the language.

Figure 2.3 represents the case of standard languages used in three nations in a *contiguous* language area. For historical reasons (e.g. common traditional dialect areas, cultural spaces, shared political territories prior to current border demarcations), there may be situations where more than one center exist per nation, and standard varieties may transcend present-day political borders (here: variety *b* and variety *e*). This indicates that the range of standard varieties is not necessarily tied to specific nations. A prominent example that can be plausibly represented by this model is German, as I will argue in Section 4.

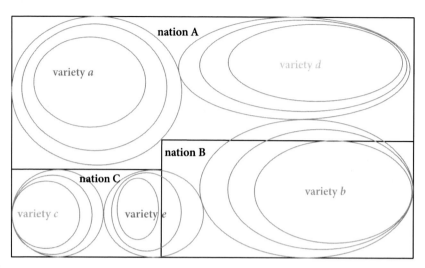

Figure 2.3 Pluriareal model II — three nations with more than three standard varieties (contiguous language area)

Essentially, both models of pluriareality capture situations in which standard varieties are not (necessarily) national varieties. Whereas model II (Figure 2.3) assumes radiating centers, model I (Figure 2.2) does not, (just as the "pluricentric = plurinational model" does not). Models of pluriareality do not rule out codification. However, codices building on pluriareal interpretations of standard language variation are strictly usage-based and descriptive. In the case of Norwegian (pluriareal model I), the codification of one standard variety was based on regional dialects, while the codification of the other was based on the spoken registers of the "educated daily speech" of the upper middle classes (see Jahr 2003: 333–335). In the case of German (pluriareal model II), recent codices are based — strictly corpus-linguistically — on the written language of regional and national newspapers for lexis and grammar, and on the formal spoken registers of educated people for pronunciation.

In sum, the pluriareal model differs from the "pluricentric = plurinational model" in the following key aspects:

1. One nation may have two (or more) standard varieties — just as one nation may have two or more official languages (e.g. Belgium, Switzerland, Canada, or Kosovo).
2. Standard varieties do not necessarily have to be 'national varieties' in the sense of (relatively) homogenous varieties.
3. In contiguous language areas, standard varieties may cross national borders and therefore need not be specific to a single nation.

Based on these aspects, we can modify Clyne's definition of *pluricentric(ity)* and define *pluriareal(ity)* as follows: The term *pluriareal(ity)* indicates that a language has more than one standard variety, each with its own norms of usage. There may be more than one standard variety within a nation and, in contiguous language areas, standard varieties may also transcend national borders.

It should be emphasized that the pluriareal model II presented here has much in common with the notion of "emerging epicentres" (cf. e.g. Hundt 2013) and other "center-periphery" pluricentric concepts in more recent research on English as a pluricentric language. For example, Hänsel & Deuber (2019) report on a perception study of standard accents in five anglophone Caribbean countries. They highlight "the significance of both the national level [...] and of certain varieties that radiate beyond their associated nations (influence from AmE and BrE)" and emphasize the importance of "both regional and subregional aspects" in the research on standard varieties of English (Hänsel & Deuber 2019: 260). Despite these similarities, it makes sense to continue to refer to the *pluriareality* model, as it offers a clear terminological distinction from the widely recognized concept of *pluricentricity* which is still predominantly associated with the "pluricentric = plurinational model".

4. The case of German

In this section, I will use the case of German to investigate whether the "pluricentric = plurinational model" or the pluriareal model II more adequately captures the situation of a language that serves as a standard in multiple contiguous countries. As the title of my paper suggests, I will argue for the latter, building on the two major strands of criticism mentioned earlier, i.e. conceptual and linguistic aspects.

4.1 Conceptual aspects

German is used as an official language by about 87.5 million L1 speakers and about 8.5 million L2 speakers (Ammon 2015: 170) in a contiguous language area in central Europe. This area comprises Germany, the eastern part of Belgium, Luxembourg, Austria, Liechtenstein, the German-speaking part of Switzerland, and South Tyrol in Italy (cf. Figure 2.5 below).

The issue of "pluricentricity vs. pluriareality," especially as it pertains to Standard German in Austria, has been a subject of ongoing debate among (mainly) Austrian linguists. A brief overview of this debate and the discourse on "Standard German varieties in Austria" vs. "Austrian Standard German" is necessary to understand the arguments which I lay out below (also cf. Scherr & Ziegler 2023: 91–92 and Niehaus, this volume).

After the notion of *national variants* (in the sense of "national varieties") was introduced by Austrian-born Soviet-Russian linguist Riesel into the discourse on standard variation in German (see Ammon 1995: 44–45), Australian linguist Clyne (1984: 4–5), who also had Austrian roots, was the first scholar to explicitly advocate adopting the pluricentric model for the language, drawing on the examples of English and Spanish. He opposed the then-prevalent focus on a supposedly homogeneous "Standard German" in (West) Germany, usually labeled *Binnendeutsch* ('internal German'). This monocentric model caused other varieties of Standard German in Austria, Switzerland, Luxembourg, the U.S., Australia etc. to be perceived as deviations from the "ideal" *Binnendeutsch* standard (von Polenz 1999: 419). This concept was deeply rooted in standard language ideology and homogenism, embodying an idealized-normative notion of standard (cf. Section 2). In sociolinguistic terms, the adoption and dissemination of the pluricentricity model was seen as an important step toward the emancipation of various standard varieties of German. This socio-political aspect was embraced by scholars in Austria, in particular, though noticeably less so by those in Switzerland (von Polenz 1999: 435–453). Following Clyne, Austrian linguists like Muhr (e.g. 1995), de Cillia (e.g. 1995) and, recently, Dollinger (2019) have advocated the pluricentric model in the discourse on German as a pluricentric language, focusing on national varieties. They especially elaborate on the differences between "Standard German German" and "Standard Austrian German" (e.g. Dollinger 2019: 39) with the aim of emancipating the latter from the former.

In response, some Austrian scholars have criticized the adoption of the pluricentric model to reflect the linguistic situation in German-speaking countries. They primarily opposed the interpretation of *pluricentric* as "plurinational," referencing actual language use and the sociohistorical background of the standardization of German, which eventually led to *pluriareality* as a proposed alternative term and model (e.g. Wolf 1994; Scheuringer 1996; Pohl 1997; Reiffenstein 2001). The main arguments of the proponents of the pluriareal model echo the criticism of the "pluricentric = plurinational model" discussed in the previous section, namely that the model hardly does justice to standard language varieties in the German-speaking countries, as standard varieties do not conform to homogenous national centers. Furthermore, it was argued that the model tends to neglect the underlying areal divisions in German-speaking regions (Pohl 1997: 69; similarly, Elspaß et al. 2017: 72–74).

The present-day political borders of and between the German-speaking countries and regions are relatively recent. Linguistically, they have been drawn across centuries-old dialect areas. The map by Wiesinger (1983, Figure 2.4) reflects the notion of centers and peripheries in the German-speaking realm on the *dialectal* level. The non-hatched areas represent centers of the main dialect areas, and the hatched areas represent the peripheral areas between centers. It will be discussed below to what extent the standard language centers and peripheries correspond to or differ from the dialectal ones.[1]

Figure 2.4 Areal structure of the German dialects at the beginning of the 20th century (after Wiesinger 1983: after page 830)

A second key issue scholars have addressed regarding the "pluricentric = plurinational model" is the central role of normativity as it pertains to the status

---

1. The dialect map is also shown here to help the reader identify the dialect areas referred to in Section 4.2.

of standard varieties. In the German context, normativity is closely linked to codification and the existence of endonormative codices (cf. Ammon 1995: 80, 96). However, such codices do not exist for all German-speaking countries and regions, or at least not in the same manner. There are two codices covering the lexis of Standard German in Austria, the comprehensive *Österreichisches Wörterbuch* (ÖWB) ('Austrian dictionary', 928 pages) and Ebner (2019, 512 pages), and there is one for Standard German in Switzerland (Bickel & Landolt 2018, 112 pages). Ebner (2019) and Bickel & Landolt (2018), list only (alleged) Austriacisms and (alleged) Helvetisms. There is no such codex for Standard German in Germany, nor are there any nation-specific grammars for German. Muhr (2007) represents the singular attempt to write a pronunciation dictionary of Austrian German (based on data from eight speakers only, cf. Ehrlich 2009: 48–52 for a critical review). There have been no such endeavors to codify the pronunciation of Standard German solely in Germany or solely in Switzerland. This problem becomes even more evident when the "smaller" German-speaking countries and regions are considered. There is one recent (lexical) codex for Luxembourg (Sieburg 2022, 208 pages), but there are no codices for the standard varieties of German spoken in Liechtenstein, East Belgium, or South Tyrol. However, there is no doubt that the varieties written in German-language newspapers and spoken by grammar school students in formal situations in these countries and regions are standard varieties of German.[2]

The aspects discussed here argue against the assumption that the "pluricentric = plurinational model" adequately reflects the standard language situation in the German-speaking countries. The pluriareal model appears more suitable for two reasons.

Firstly, the pluriareal model does not restrict the usage areas of standard varieties to national boundaries, i.e. a division imposed on the basis of purely political criteria, but allows for a strictly data-driven modeling of these domains, including both corpus linguistic and perceptional data. As for corpus linguistic data, we will see in Section 4.2 what a division of the German-speaking language area into various standard varieties might look like based on data from recent projects. Suffice it to say at this point that it will resemble the pluriareal model II in Figure 2.3. In terms of perceptional data, the pluriareal model does not limit the examination of lay linguistic conceptions of standard varieties strictly to comparisons on the national level, but also allows for an exploration of conceptualizations of both intra- and transnational standard variation. (For instance, there has been no perception or accent recognition study on German that has looked at similarities and

---

2. Formal speech by grammar schoolers formed the basis for the inclusion of variants in the AADG, and German-language newspapers for the VG and the VWB.

differences between different regions within German-speaking countries or even with neighboring regions of different countries at the level of standard varieties.) In this context, it is important to note that the linguistic construction of national identities does not have to be tied to the existence of national standard varieties, as is often argued in the discourse on Austrian German, for instance, but can extend to non-standard varieties.[3] Moreover, the pluriareal approach also permits the study of intra- and transnational linguistic identities.

Secondly, building on the first reason, the pluriareal model does not restrict the validation of standard varieties to the existence of national codices (which, in fact, only partially exist for the German-speaking countries). Instead, it takes into account standard variation and the existence of standard varieties in smaller countries and regions as well as within nation states. While the pluriareal model in no way rules out the possibility of codifying standard variation, it requires the codification to reflect a large part of the population's actual standard usage (cf. Elspaß & Dürscheid 2017: 92), rather than focusing on the language use of a select few speakers or writers (who are primarily chosen to represent national differences). Such an approach based on the pluriareal model also avoids the danger of the monocentric standard language ideology simply being replaced by a "pluricentric = plurinational" standard language ideology.

As an alternative to the "pluricentric = plurinational model", linguists have coined the terms *regional pluricentricity* (Reiffenstein 2001: 88) and *regiocentricity* (Niehaus, this volume) to indicate that regions, not only nations, can constitute centers of standard language varieties. At first glance, *regional pluricentricity* or *regiocentricity* might seem to be an ideal compromise term. However, *pluricentricity*, particularly in the context of German, has been conceptually narrowed in the sense of a "plurinational" understanding (Muhr 1995; Dollinger 2019) — and thus used as a misnomer (cf. Section 3). Therefore, it appears appropriate to continue speaking of *pluriareality*, since it has developed as an independent concept explicitly distinct from the "pluricentric = plurinational model". Furthermore, *regio-* and *regional* have invariably been associated with "non-standard" in German linguistics and in the tradition of German lexicography and grammaticography. To avoid terminological confusion and misunderstanding, I would thus advocate continuing to use the term *pluriareality*.

---

3. In fact, Wodak et al. (2009: 193) found that "differences between Austrian German and German German were primarily located at the vernacular or dialectal level".

4.2 Linguistic aspects

Given the arguments in the previous section, it stands to reason that only a precise analysis of language usage and its perception in a particular sociolinguistic situation can adequately model standard language variation. At the height of the debate on the pluricentricity of German in the 1990s, Schrodt (1997: 37) called for more "work on a decisively expanded empirical basis for the codification of national variants and varieties."[4] On the level of language usage, such empirical work has been conducted in the new millennium, most notably in the past decade, within the framework of three major corpus-based projects on areal variation of Standard German:

- *Variantenwörterbuch des Deutschen* (VWB) ('Variational Dictionary of German') for lexis, conducted from 1998 to 2004 (project I) and from 2012 to 2015 (project II, resulting in the second, completely revised edition of the VWB in 2016),
- *Variantengrammatik des Standarddeutschen* (VG), ('Variational Grammar of Standard German') for grammar, conducted between 2011 and 2019,
- *Atlas zur Aussprache des deutschen Gebrauchsstandards* (AADG) ('Atlas on the pronunciation of the German standard of usage'), conducted between 2011 and 2023.

All three empirical projects firstly led to the compilation of balanced corpora of standard language usage in the German-speaking countries, and, secondly, to the development of three new codices of Standard German focusing largely on areal variation. The codices that emerged from the first two projects have the same titles as the underlying projects: one has been published in book format (VWB), and the other in the form of a reference work on the internet (VG). Likewise, the AADG is available on the internet; the AADG itself is not a codex but a linguistic atlas. However, its empirical results have been incorporated into the two most recent editions of the *Duden Pronunciation Dictionary*, a well-established and authoritative codex in the German-speaking countries (e.g. the 8th edition of Duden AW was published in 2023).

---

4. "[...] die Erarbeitung einer entscheidend erweiterten empirischen Grundlage für die Kodifizierung nationaler Varianten und Varietäten" (my translation, S.E.). In striking contrast, Muhr (1997: 40), in the same volume, expressed the wish "that in the future the main focus of (Austrian) variation linguistics should focus on the empirical exploration of the variants of Austrian German and not, as in the past, on the attempt to prove its non-existence" ("daß das Hauptaugenmerk der (österreichischen) Variationslinguistik künftig vor allem der empirischen Erkundung der Varianten des Österreichischen Deutsch gilt und nicht wie bisher dem Versuch, seine Nichtexistenz nachzuweisen", my translation, S.E.).

All three projects are strictly corpus-based and adhere to the concept of "standards of usage" (*Gebrauchsstandards*), i.e. they are based on corpora of texts or data commonly acknowledged as representing standard language. In the area of written language, the corpora comprise texts from regional and national newspapers (ca. 200 for VWB) or only regional newspapers and the regional news sections of supraregionally distributed newspapers (68 for VG), all of which are considered "standard" by their readers, whether in printed or digital form. Regarding pronunciation, "standards of usage" are empirically established forms of language used in formal spoken registers of educated individuals (AADG).[5] In this respect, all three projects assume a much broader notion of standard language than traditional codices of German, which focused mainly on literary language (e.g. the *Duden* Grammar up to its 8th edition from 1998) or the pronunciation of selected, trained speakers, such as actors or newscasters (e.g. the *Duden* Pronunciation Dictionary up to its 6th edition from 2005; Muhr 2007; DAW). In addition to dictionary articles or short commentary texts, the VG and the AADG present their results as maps: the VG as area maps and the AADG as point-symbol maps.

Whereas in the AADG, areas of standard language usage of particular variants emerge from individual maps (Figures 2.6a and 2.6b as examples), the VWB and the VG both divided the German-speaking countries into fifteen areas for practical presentation of the results. These divisions adhere to both political borders and traditional dialect regions, as the areas of standard language usage have proven to reflect the dialect map of the contiguous German-speaking language area to some extent (VWB: lvi; the dialect areas in Figure 2.4). Similarly, the VG adopted the division into fifteen areas as introduced by the VWB (VWB: xliii–xl). Note, however, that the VG analyzed 68 regional newspapers and regional news sections evenly distributed over the contiguous German-speaking area. This allows for data-driven geolinguistic analyses, such as Scherr's & Ziegler's (2023: 97), which do not start from the 15 predefined areas but from 68 newspaper publication locations as data points in space. To sum up, these three projects do not restrict the presentation of their results to national standard variants, but take into account variants from main dialect regions that can encompass various areas in different countries (see isoglosses in black in Figure 2.5).

---

5. The data for the AADG comprise spoken material from different speech styles, ranging from formal contexts (reading out word lists) to informal talk (elicited via map tasks) by 670 speakers with high school educations. Most AADG maps and all data which were considered for the *Duden AW* come from the "reading out word lists" task, cf. http://prowiki.ids-mannheim.de/bin/view/AADG/KorpusTeile (retrieved 31 March 2024) for details.

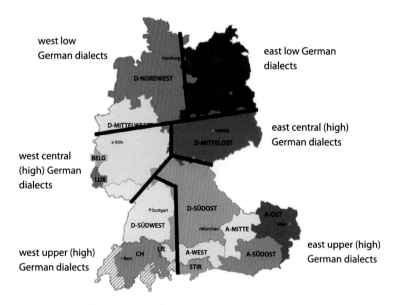

Figure 2.5 Division of German-speaking countries and regions in central Europe into fifteen areas, as used in VG and VWB, and isoglosses of main dialect areas (black lines)

Elspaß & Kleiner (2019) provide the first systematic overview of standard language variation in the German-speaking countries based on the results of the aforementioned three recent projects. In the following section, I will present selected results from this overview, partly using maps for illustrative purposes from the AADG, the VG, and also the AdA (*Atlas zur deutschen Alltagssprache* 'Atlas on Colloquial German') in cases where the areal variation in the standard (according to the VWB) and colloquial German coincide. To save space, I will use the abbreviations for the individual areas from the map in Figure 2.5 (listed here in alphabetical order):

A = Austria
    A-mitte = the central states of Austria, i.e. Upper Austria and Salzburg
    A-ost = the east of Austria, including Vienna, Lower Austria, and the north of Burgenland
    A-südost = the southeast of Austria, including Styria, Carinthia, and the south of Burgenland
    A-west = the western part of Austria, including the state of Vorarlberg and Tyrole
BELG = the German-speaking area in the east of Belgium

CH = Switzerland[6]
D = Germany
> D-mittelwest = the central western area of Germany, including North Rhine-Westphalia, Hessia, and most of Rhineland-Palatinate
> D-mittelost = the central eastern area of Germany, including Thuringia and Saxony
> D-nordwest = the northwest of Germany, including Lower Saxony, Bremen, Hamburg, and Schleswig-Holstein
> D-nordost = the northeast of Germany, including Mecklenburg-Western Pomerania, Brandenburg, Berlin, and Saxony-Anhalt
> D-südwest = the southwest of Germany, including Baden-Württemberg, Saarland, and parts of Rhineland-Palatinate
> D-südost = the southeast of Germany, consisting mainly of Bavaria

LIE = Liechtenstein
LUX = Luxembourg
STIR = South Tyrol

The most notable examples of national lexical variants in the German-speaking countries originate from words for factual concepts or institutions indigenous to specific countries and regions. For example, the names of the parliaments (LUX: *Abgeordnetenkammer*, D: *Bundestag*, LIE, STIR: *Landtag*, A, CH: *Nationalrat*, BELG *Parlament (der Deutschsprachigen Gemeinschaft)*) or the heads of individual states, regions and cantons (area states of D: *Ministerpräsident/in*, city states of D: *Erste/r Bürgermeister/in* [Hamburg], *Regierende/r Bürgermeister/in* [Hamburg], *Präsident/in des Senats* [Bremen], A, STIR: *Landeshauptmann/Landeshauptfrau*, CH-ost/zentral: *Landammann*, CH-nord/west: *Regierungspräsident Nationalrat*; all terms according to VWB). Even within the terminological domain of politics and administration, as the examples show, apart from nation-specific lexical variants, there is also variation within given countries and variants used across national borders. This is also the case with numerous other terms in institutional and administrative contexts, often with respect to the federal or cantonal structure of the education system in these countries. For instance, while an 'announced school test' is called *Klassenarbeit* in most states of Germany, the standard variant in the German state of Bavaria (D-südost) is *Schulaufgabe*. In the Swiss canton of Berne, it is called *Probe*, whereas the other cantons use *Prüfung*. In both Austria and South Tyrol, it is named *Schularbeit*. Another example is the

---

6. Note that the VWB further divides CH into six different areas (VWB: XXV), whereas the VG does not, as Switzerland did not show any further internal variation on the level of grammar.

'bridge day,' a workday sandwiched between a bank holiday and weekend. In most parts of Austria, the standard variant is *Fenstertag*, whereas in Upper Austria and in parts of the state of Salzburg it is *Zwickeltag*.

Apart from these domain-specific lexemes, the distribution of standard language variants only partly adheres to national and other political boundaries. To a more significant extent, as examples from pronunciation, grammar, and lexis will show, it reflects historical territorial boundaries and, particularly regarding pronunciation, traditional dialect areas (cf. Figure 2.6 below).

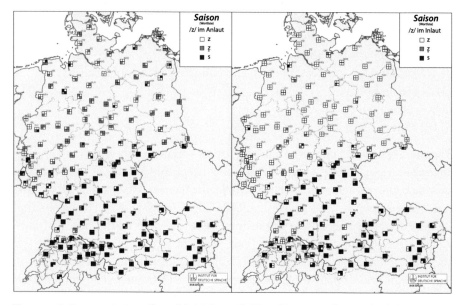

Figure 2.6 Pronunciation of word-initial <s> (left) and intervocalic <s> (right) in *Saison* 'season, period' (from AADG — each small square represents the variant used by one of four informants at the location)[7]

The arguably most distinct contrast in the German-speaking countries is a north-south divide. Consider the following example in the area of pronunciation: In the entire south, the lenis plosives /d/, /b/, /g/, as well as the lenis fricatives /z/, /ʒ/, /dʒ/, are generally voiceless in word-initial and intervocalic positions. Most notably, in the south, there is hardly any voiced /z/ (see Figure 2.6 for the pronun-

---

7. According to AADG (cf. https://prowiki.ids-mannheim.de/bin/view/AADG/SimAnlaut; 31.03.2024), [z̥] stands for an 'intermediate category with either only partial voicing or complete voicelessness, but low duration/intensity or articulation tension' ("Zwischenkategorie [z̥] mit entweder nur partieller Stimmhaftigkeit oder völliger Stimmlosigkeit, aber geringer Dauer/ Intensität bzw. Artikulationsspannung").

ciation of <s> in *Saison* 'season, period'). Another prominent example is the pronunciation of the word-initial <pf> (e.g. *Pfeffer* 'pepper') as a fricative /f/ in the north and as an affricate /pf/ in the south (http://prowiki.ids-mannheim.de/bin/view/AADG/PfimAnlaut). Grammatical north-south divisions become evident, for example, in the use of posture verbs (such as *stehen* 'stand', *liegen* 'lie', *sitzen* 'sit', *hocken* 'squat, sit' etc.) in conjunction with either the auxiliary verb *haben* 'to have' in the north or *sein* 'to be' in the south (cf. Scherr & Ziegler 2023: 95–96). The areas where only voiceless /s/ and the affricate /pf/ are spoken and where the auxiliary *sein* are used in the aforementioned contexts correspond to the Upper German dialect area. Examples regarding lexis include northern *Junge* vs. southern *Bub* 'boy', *Semikolon* vs. *Strichpunkt* 'semicolon', *Gardine* vs. *Vorhang* '(window) curtain', and *Kneifzange* vs. *Beißzange* 'pincher' (all examples from VWB, also mapped in the AdA). These north-south divisions are further evidenced in word formation (e.g. northern *Abzweig* vs. southern *Abzweigung* 'junction', *Sonnenwende* vs. *Sonnwende* 'solstice', and *waagerecht* vs. *waagrecht* 'horizontal'; all examples from VG).

Interestingly, the north-south divide does not correspond to the most prominent dialect isogloss, i.e., the *Benrath* line, which divides the Low German and the High German dialect areas and has never formed a political border (i.e. the isogloss in bold in Figure 2.4). While the north-south divide for the pronunciation examples and the grammatical example coincides with the border between Central and Upper German dialects, the examples from lexis and word formation point to the '*Main* line' ("*Mainlinie*"), a prominent border in the mental map of the German people (also dubbed "*Weißwurstäquator*," literally 'white sausage equator'). It delineates a cultural border between the northern and southern hemispheres of the German-speaking countries and has a rich historical background. The line corresponds to the southern border of the North German Confederation in the 19th century, and thus, in the political discourse of the time, symbolized the limits of the Prussian claim to power. The listed examples of variation in lexis and word formation in the standard correspond to the situation in colloquial German. Dialectometrical studies based on the lexis of *colloquial* German have repeatedly confirmed that the *Main* line is the most central isogloss for the lexical structure of the linguistic landscape in the modern German-speaking countries (cluster analyses: Durrell 1989, Möller 2003; factor analysis: Pickl et al. 2019: 45–47, Figure 2.8 below).

In addition to the north-south divide, a wide range of region-specific features can be identified within the German-speaking countries and in cross-border areas. For instance, the north of Germany (D-nordwest, D-nordost) can be characterized phonetically by a considerable amount of rounding for (near) close front vowels, such as [tyʃ] for *Tisch* 'table' (http://prowiki.ids-mannheim.de/bin/view/AADG/KurzI); lexemes like *fegen* 'to sweep', *Feudel* 'cleaning rag', *plietsch* 'smart'; or word formations such as *Anspitzer* (vs. *Spitzer*) 'pencil sharpener'. The northeast and central east areas of Germany, above all, can be distinguished from the western parts of Germany and, in fact, all other regions in the German-speaking countries by a large group of lexemes such as *Broiler* 'roast chicken', *Eierkuchen* 'pancake', *Pfannkuchen* 'doughnut', *Plaste* 'plastic', *Klammeraffe* 'stapler' (all examples from VWB, also mapped in the AdA). The specific distribution of these and other lexemes across the present-day East German states can be traced back to regional use in these areas, consolidated further after Germany was divided into the separate states (Federal Republic of German and German Democratic Republic).

The central western area of Germany, south of the *Benrath* line and the bordering areas of East Belgium and Luxemburg, coincides with the Ripuarian and Moselle Franconian dialect area (Figure 2.4). As a result, we find evidence of several common standard language variants in this contiguous area. One salient phonetic feature is the devoicing of /r/ to a uvular fricative after short /a/, /ɔ/, and /ʊ/, such as in [haχt], [ʃpɔχt], [kʊχts] for *hart*, 'hard', *Sport* 'sport', *kurz* 'short'. Common lexemes are *Kirmes* '(church) fair', *Kran* '(water) tap, faucet', and *Schuhriemen* 'shoe laces' (VWB). A salient grammatical feature is the advanced grammaticalization of passive constructions with GET-verbs (http://www.atlas-alltagssprache.de/runde-4/f22c-d/). As mentioned above, specific variants are evident where terminology regarding domain-specific concepts is concerned. Thus, *Erkennungstafel* 'number plate', *Klassensaal* 'classroom', and *Leichendienst* 'funeral service' are Luxembourgisms (cf. Sieburg 2018: 133), whereas *Bürgermeisterkollegium* 'municipal council', *Postpunkt* 'post office', or *Heiratsbuch* 'civil status book' are specific to East Belgium (VWB).

Similarly, standard variation in the south of Germany, in Switzerland, Austria, Liechtenstein, and South Tyrol is characterized, on one hand, by variants that can be traced back to the centuries-old common Alemannic dialect area in the southwest (comprising the German state of Baden-Württemberg, the western part of Bavaria, the German-speaking parts of Switzerland, Liechtenstein, and Vorarlberg, the westernmost state of Austria), and the Bavarian dialect area in the southeast (encompassing most parts of Bavaria, most of Austria and South Tyrol). On the other hand, this standard variation is also marked by processes of linguistic divergence and domain-specific terminology.

Standard variants that have emerged from the common Alemannic dialect area are, for example, palatalizations with [ʃ] before /t/ as in *stil(los)* '(without) style', or the pronunciation of long [i:] in the preterite verb forms *ging* 'went', *hing* 'hanged', *fing* 'caught'. Lexemes used throughout this language area include *schaffen* '(to) work', *Kappe* 'woolen hat', or the common word stem *Weck-* 'small bread, bread roll'. Divergence becomes obvious when a diminutive suffix is added to this stem, for example, in southwestern Standard German *Weckle* vs. Swiss

Standard German *Weggli* (or *Weckli*, with alternative spelling). Variants specific to the southwestern variety of Standard German are, for instance, a mid-open articulation for <ä>, such as in *wählen* 'to vote' or *Nägel* 'nails', and lexemes such as *Vesper* 'snack, breakfast break' or *auswellen* 'to roll out (dough etc.)'. According to the available data from VWB, VG and AADG, in Switzerland, Helvetisms (which are also used to a large extent in Liechtenstein) outnumber shared variants in the Alemannic region in the areas of pronunciation, lexis, and grammar, for example, placing stress on the first syllable in loanwords from French, such as *Bálkon, Éngagement, Réstaurant,* or in initialisms, e.g. *SBB* ['ɛsbeːbeː], *DVD* ['deːfaʊ̯deː], *CD* ['tseːdeː] (examples from AADG); lexemes such as *Nüsslisalat* ('lamb's lettuce'), *Velo* ('bicycle') or *tönen* ('to sound (like)') (examples from VWB, also mapped in AdA); word formations such as *Beschrieb* (vs. *Beschreibung*) 'description', *Entscheid* (vs. *Entscheidung*) 'decision' or *Unterbruch* (vs. *Unterbrechung*) 'disruption, break'; and, finally, syntactic variants such as V2 after certain evaluative matrix constructions, as in (1).

(1) a. *Schade, haben wir heute verloren.*
        Pity   have we today lost.
        'It's a pity that we lost today'
    b. *Gut,   gibt es das Wirtschaftsforum*[8]
        Good, there is the Economic Forum.
        'It's good that there is the Economic Forum.'

The similarities of standard language variants in the Bavarian dialect area (cf. *Bairisch* in Figure 2.4) are even more striking than in the Alemannic area. In the following, I will present some characteristic features of the standard language usage in the Bavarian dialect area in Austria. On all descriptive levels, intra-Austrian variation is largely expressed as west-east differences (the examples *Fenstertag* and *Zwickeltag* seen above constitute an exception), especially as they pertain to the contrasts in standard language use between the dialectally Alemannic areas in the westernmost states, Vorarlberg and (partly) Tyrol (A-west), and the dialectally Bavarian areas in the other parts of Austria (A-mitte, A-süd, A-ost) (Elspaß & Kleiner 2019: 171). The latter exhibit many similarities with the standard varieties used in the German state of Bavaria and the autonomous province of Bolzano-South Tyrol in Northern Italy.

The problem with defining specific 'Austriacisms' can be illustrated using the example of the twenty-three culinary expressions listed in the "Protocol No. 10 on the Use of Austrian Expressions of the German Language", an additional doc-

---

8. Examples taken from VG, http://mediawiki.ids-mannheim.de/VarGra/index.php/Verberststellung_in_Subjekt-_und_Objektsätzen (31.03.2024).

ument to Austria's accession treaty before joining the EU in 1995 (De Cillia 1995). All twenty-three lexemes are, of course, listed in the Austrian Dictionary (ÖWB). However, the ÖWB does not systematically differentiate between: (1) lexemes that are specifically used in Austria, (2) lexemes that are also used in Standard German in areas of neighboring countries, and (3) lexemes used only in certain regions of Austria (and thus constitute relative, not absolute variants, cf. Section 3). Out of the twenty-three expressions from the Protocol No. 10, only nine qualify as specific Austriacisms, such as: (1) *Faschiertes* 'ground meat', *Kohlsprossen* 'Brussels sprouts', *Marillen* 'apricots', and *Paradeiser* 'tomatoes'. Fourteen lexemes are not only used in Austria but also in neighboring Bavaria in Germany and/or South Tyrol in Italy, such as *Erdäpfel* 'potatoes', *Topfen* 'white cheese' or *Voge(r)lsalat* 'lamb's lettuce'. Of the variants from group (1) and group (2), *Marillen, Paradeiser, Erdäpfel, Topfen,* and *Voge(r)lsalat* are rarely used in the (Alemannic) west of Austria. In fact, only a minority of speakers, mostly in the east of Austria, seem to use the word *Paradeiser*, as a recent map from AdA suggests (Figure 2.7). The impression from the map on colloquial German is confirmed by figures on standard language texts: A search of the VG corpus revealed a proportion of mentions of *Paradeiser* of less than 19.4% (56 out of 289; compared to 233 for *Tomate*).[9]

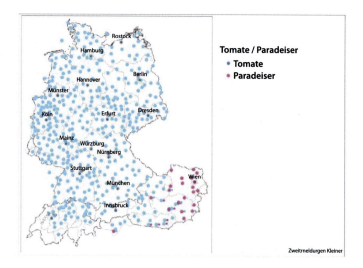

Figure 2.7 Distribution of *Tomate* and *Paradeiser* ('tomato') in German-speaking countries (AdA)

---

9. The percentages for *Paradeiser* in the four Austrian areas are as follows: western Austria 0% (0 out of 34), central Austria 24.4% (32 out of 131), eastern Austria 29.6% (8 out of 19), and southeastern Austria 16.5% (16 out of 97).

In general, the results from this brief overview can be summed up as follows:

1. There is a substantial amount of variation within the German-speaking countries, likely as a result of dialect areas or former political subdivisions within these countries.
2. There are numerous variants used in transborder regions, likely due to the effect of cross-border dialect areas.
3. There are hardly any variants specific to a single nation state within the meaning of "nationally distinctive variants".
4. There exist only few "absolute" variants in a single nation state, but mostly "relative" variants.
5. Most variants that are both exclusive and absolute within the borders of one nation state or any other territory delimited by political boundaries result from terminology in the political or administrative domain. This applies both to the "big" nation states and the two "small" countries, Luxembourg and Liechtenstein, as well as to the federal states within Germany and Austria (*Bundesländer* and *Stadtstaaten*), the cantons in Switzerland, and the two regions in Belgium and Italy, in which German is also recognized as an official language (East Belgium, South Tyrol).

These results clearly illustrate that, from a usage-based perspective, there appear to be more standard varieties in German than just three national varieties. However, it is unclear how many standard varieties actually exist from this perspective. A practicable approach for offering an answer to this question might entail analyzing variants from the areas of pronunciation, lexis, and grammar using dialectometric or geolinguistic methods — similar to what has already been done for data of colloquial German (cf. Figure 2.8). The data analysis would be based on variants from individual location points, a feasible method using data from AADG (194 locations) to analyze phonetic variation and VG (sixty-eight locations) to analyze mainly grammatical, but also lexical variation. Figure 2.8, which is based on data from colloquial German (AdA) (Pickl et al. 2019: 43–50 for details), gives an impression of what a picture of standard variation might look like. It shows the synopsis of the five dominant factors in a factor analysis of 191 — mainly lexical[10] — variables (with approximately seventeen-thousand overall variant tokens) in colloquial German in 934 locations in the German-speaking countries (Pickl et al. 2019: 43–50 for details). This factor solution accounts for 74.2% of the entire variance in the data.

---

10. Lexical variables account for about 56% of the variables in the AdA. About a quarter of all variables are grammatical variables, a tenth are phonological variables and about 9% pragmatic variables.

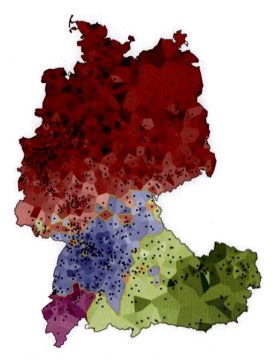

Figure 2.8 Synopsis of five dominant factors in factor analysis for 191 variables in colloquial German (AdA) (Pickl et al. 2019: 47)

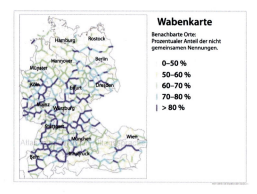

Figure 2.9 'Honeycomb map' on speakers' perceptions of similarities of colloquial German (http://www.atlas-alltagssprache.de/runde-6/f01a/, 31 March, 2024)[11]

---

11. 3,048 informants were given a list of 402 location names, which were evenly distributed over the German-speaking countries, and asked: "In which town (from the list) do people speak similarly to people in your hometown?". On the map, each Voronoi cell represents one

A comparison between the map of the five dominant factors (Figure 2.8) and a "mental map" of cognitive areas of colloquial German language use (Figure 2.9) reveals that there is considerable overlap of (reported) language use and perceived linguistic similarities between different regions (which are indicated by areas with yellow and light green and light blue lines in Figure 2.9). The map clearly shows that, for instance, the everyday language in the north of Germany is perceived as relatively homogeneous over a large area (with a slight indication of differences between west and east), whereas the south of Germany appears much more fragmented. Another large relatively homogenous area can be seen in the Bavarian dialect areas in the southeast, whereas the informants perceived the language use in the Alemannic and Bavarian parts of Austria to be very different. This is marked by the cell in western Austria, which is delimited to the east by a dark blue line.

As already mentioned, dialectometry and geolinguistics provide appropriate methods for an investigation of linguistic variation in the standard based on corpus data. However, this work is still ongoing and forms part of a larger project.[12] The data compiled in Elspaß & Kleiner (2019) from the three recent major projects on standard variation suggest that, at any rate, there are several areas across the German-speaking world with their own varieties of Standard German. Figure 2.10. shows a projection based on these data, based on the pluriareal model II (cf. Figure 2.3 in Section 3).

The map in this projection is pluriareal in nature, as it accounts for the linguistically plausible assumption of, firstly, several standard varieties within a single nation as well as standard varieties transcending national borders, and, secondly, of the center-periphery notion of standard language areas (cf. Section 1). It does not rule out the effect of national borders, but it is not limited to the conceptualization of national varieties. It also accounts for smaller countries and regions

---

location. The thickness of the boundary lines between individual cells indicates the extent to which colloquial German between two neighboring places was marked as not "similar" to the informants' hometown.

12. Scherr & Ziegler (2023) is a first attempt at a data-driven dialectometric analysis of grammatical variation, based on data from the VG and using Cluster Analysis and Factor Analysis. What we learn from this study is that the results appear to depend on the statistical method used. While the cluster analyses consistently result in areas that do not correspond to political borders but either to dialect areas or show unspecific patterns (ibid: 97–99), the factor analysis yields three varying factors that combine (1) Germany, eastern Belgium, and Luxembourg (highest factor loading in Midwest Germany), (2) Austria and South Tyrol (highest factor loading in Southeast Austria), and (3) German-speaking Switzerland and Liechtenstein (highest factor loading in Switzerland; cf. ibid.: 96, Map 6). Scherr & Ziegler conclude that their results "neither support the idea of a uniform German standard language across borders, nor do they underpin the assumption of pluricentric varieties for German" in the sense of plurinational varieties (ibid: 100).

38 Stephan Elspaß

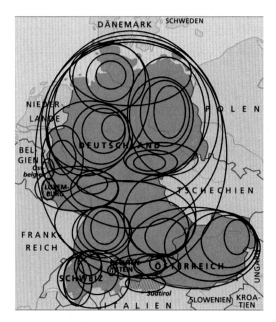

Figure 2.10 Projection of areas of Standard German varieties (based on map from VWB 2016: XLIII)

(which are frequently neglected in the "pluricentric = plurinational model") as possible areas enjoying their own standard varieties. East Belgium, for instance, constitutes a region with an 'acceptance of an independently codifiable East Belgian standard of usage,' suggesting a certain 'affinity with the pluriareal model' (Küpper et al. 2018: 185).[13]

5. Discussion and conclusion

Models are always simplifications of reality. Following Clyne (1992:1), I used the term *model* here — in the sense of a purposeful representation of reality. (I would be reluctant to label pluricentricity or pluriareality as theories, as neither can be regarded as sets of statements or sentences which are falsifiable through experimentation and which offer clear predictions — at least not for historical standard languages.) I have focused here on usage-based modelling, which initially leaves aside aspects such as the indexicalization of standard variants and varieties and

---

13. "die Akzeptanz eines [...] eigenständig kodifizierbaren ostbelgischen Gebrauchsstandards [...] – all dies deutet [...] auf eine Affinität der DG [= Deutschsprachigen Gemeinschaft Ostbelgiens] als Forschungsgegenstand zum Pluriarealitätsmodell hin" (my translation, S.E.).

the resulting hierarchization of standard variants and varieties in the minds of speakers (cf. Auer's 2021 critical assessment, and cf. Niehaus in this volume for an integrative model). The question posed in this paper was whether the "pluricentric = plurinational model" or the "pluriareal model" better represent the variation observed in the use of standard languages in contiguous areas such as Germany. The results can be summarized as follows:

1. Historically (in the 1980s) and politically, modeling German as a pluricentric language was a necessary step to overcome the monocentric ideology which was still prevalent at the time.
2. For conceptual and linguistic reasons, the pluriareal model appears to represent the present-day situation in the German-speaking realm more adequately than the pluricentric model, as the latter has been defined, or, more accurately, reduced to a normative "pluricentric = plurinational model" in the discourse on pluricentricity in recent decades. It is worth noting again that the pluriareal model presented here (cf. Figure 3.1) has great similarities with the notion of "emerging epicenters" and other "center-periphery pluricentricity" concepts which are discussed in the more recent studies on World Englishes. For reasons of terminological precision, however, I have argued in favor of the term "pluriareality".
3. Conceptually, the pluriareal model does not restrict the existence of standard language varieties to political-national boundaries and the existence of national norm codices, as propagated in the "pluricentric = plurinational model". In this respect, the pluriareal model is more open to the primarily usage-based conceptualization of standard varieties, in which norms of usage form the basis of new codices. Such codices (e.g. Duden AW, VWB, and VG for German) can account for both standard varieties that are valid across nations (particularly in contiguous areas) and standard varieties that are only valid for parts of nations. Moreover, a strict plurinational view regarding standard variation does not correspond to the perceptions of users, as studies have found a strong asymmetry in views when only comparing national varieties (e.g. Scharloth 2005 for German). A *"pluricentric linguistic justice* between varieties of pluricentric languages" (Norrby et al. 2020:209, quoting Oakes & Peled 2018) would be highly welcome, but should not be restricted to national varieties of standard languages.
4. From a linguistic perspective, recent data of standard language usage lend support to the idea that present-day German is not a pluricentric language consisting of clear-cut "national varieties", but that German is a pluriareal language with several standard varieties, including standard varieties within and (partially) across the "big" countries of Germany, Austria and Switzerland

(i.e. in its German-speaking parts), the "small" countries of Luxemburg and Liechtenstein, and in the regions where German is recognized as an official language, i.e. East Belgium and South Tyrol in northern Italy. So far, corpus-linguistic projects on the lexis and grammar of German have focused on the analysis of large newspaper corpora; future studies should consider others, including more spoken language corpora. Perceptual linguistic studies, which have so far focused on the differences between the three major German-speaking countries, should look even more closely at the variation within the countries or across national borders.

Thus, from a usage-based perspective, the pluriareal model appears to better reflect the sociolinguistic situation in Germany. However, this in no way excludes the validity of the "pluricentric = plurinational model" in its characterization of other standard languages, e.g. Portuguese. In fact, both models are largely justifiable depending on the given sociolinguistic circumstances in different standard languages. It appears that the pluriareal model can characterize standard languages in mainly contiguous areas more adequately, whereas the "pluricentric = plurinational model" seems to be more applicable to standard languages with dispersed territories. Thus, both models are relatively complementary to one another. (But cf. Niehaus, this volume, for an approach to reconcile the pluricentric and the pluriareal model, which utilizes the concept of enregisterment.) Moreover, a mixed plurinational-pluriareal model is conceivable for languages which have developed standard varieties both in the contiguous areas of their origins and overseas, e.g. in former colonial territories. It may very well be that in such cases, as Avanzi (2017: 157) points out for French, 'there are as many norms as there are regions — or dominant uses.'[14]

References

AADG = Kleiner, Stefan & Ralf Knöbl. 2011–2023. *Atlas zur Aussprache des deutschen Gebrauchsstandards (AADG)*, http://prowiki.ids-mannheim.de/bin/view/AADG/. (31 March, 2024.)

AdA = Elspaß, Stephan & Robert Möller. 2003ff. *Atlas zur deutschen Alltagssprache*. http://www.atlas-alltagssprache.de. (31 March, 2024.)

Ammon, Ulrich. 1995. *Die deutsche Sprache in Deutschland, Österreich und der Schweiz. Das Problem der nationalen Varietäten*. Berlin, New York: De Gruyter.

---

14. "il existe autant de normes qu'il existe de régions ... ou d'usage dominants!" (My translation, S.E.)

Ammon, Ulrich. 2015. *Die Stellung der deutschen Sprache in der Welt*. Berlin, München, Boston: De Gruyter.

Auer, Peter. 2013. Enregistering pluricentric German. In Augusto Soares da Silva (ed.), *Pluricentricity. Language variation and sociocognitive dimensions* (Applications of Cognitive Linguistics 24). Berlin, Boston: De Gruyter-Mouton, 19–48.

Auer, Peter. 2021. Reflections on linguistic pluricentricity. In Camilla Wide, Catrin Norrby & Leigh Oakes (eds.), *Sociolinguistica. European Journal of Sociolinguistics* 35, Special issue: *New perspectives on pluricentricity*. Berlin, Boston: De Gruyter, 29–47.

Avanzi, Mathieu. 2017. *Atlas du Français de nos régions*. Malakoff: Armand Colin.

Bickel, Hans & Christoph Landolt (Bearb.). 2018. *Schweizerhochdeutsch. Wörterbuch der Standardsprache in der deutschen Schweiz*. 2nd. rev. ed. Berlin: Dudenverlag.

Clyne, Michael. 1984. *Language and society in the German-speaking countries*. Cambridge: Cambridge University Press.

Clyne, Michael. 1989. Pluricentricity: National Variety. In Ulrich Ammon (ed.), *Status and function of languages and language varieties*. Berlin, New York: De Gruyter, 357–371.

Clyne, Michael (ed.). 1992. *Pluricentric languages. Differing norms in different nations* (Contributions to the Sociology of Language 62). Berlin, New York: Mouton de Gruyter.

de Cillia, Rudolf. 1995. Erdäpfelsalat bleibt Erdäpfelsalat. Österreichisches Deutsch und EU-Beitritt. In Rudolf Muhr, Richard Schrodt & Peter Wiesinger (eds.), *Österreichisches Deutsch. Linguistische, sozialpsychologische und sprachpolitische Aspekte einer nationalen Variante des Deutschen*. Wien: Hölder-Pichler-Tempsky, 121–131.

DAW = Krech, Eva-Maria, Eberhard Stock, Ursula Hirschfeld & Lutz Christian Anders. 2010. *Deutsches Aussprachewörterbuch*. Berlin, New York: De Gruyter.

Dollinger, Stefan. 2019. *The Pluricentricity Debate. On Austrian German and other Germanic Standard Varieties* (Routledge Focus). New York, London: Routledge.

Duden AW = Kleiner, Stefan & Ralf Knöbl, & Duden (eds.). 2023. *Duden. Das Aussprachewörterbuch*, 8th edn. Berlin: Dudenverlag.

Durrell, Martin. 1989. Die „Mainlinie" als sprachliche Grenze. In Wolfgang Putschke, Werner Veith & Peter Wiesinger (eds.), *Dialektgeographie und Dialektologie*. Marburg: Elwert, 89–109.

Ebner, Jakob. 2019. *Duden. Österreichisches Wörterbuch. Wörterbuch der Gegenwartssprache in Österreich*. 5th. rev. ed. Berlin: Dudenverlag.

Ehrlich, Karoline. 2009. Die Aussprache des österreichischen Standarddeutsch: Umfassende Sprech- und Sprachstandserhebung der österreichischen Orthoepie. Vienna, AT: University of Vienna PhD thesis. http://othes.univie.ac.at/6128/1/2009-07-14_9950303.pdf. (31 March, 2024.)

Elspaß, Stephan & Stefan Kleiner. 2019. Forschungsergebnisse zur arealen Variation im Standarddeutschen. In Joachim Herrgen & Jürgen Erich Schmidt (eds.), *Language and Space. An International Handbook of Linguistic Variation. Vol. 4: German*. Berlin, Boston: De Gruyter (Handbücher zur Sprach- und Kommunikationswissenschaft 30.4), 159–184.

Elspaß, Stephan. 2021. Language Standardization in a View 'from Below'. In Wendy Ayres-Bennett & John Bellamy (eds.), *The Cambridge Handbook of Language Standardization*. Cambridge: Cambridge University Press, 93–114.

Elspaß, Stephan & Christa Dürscheid. 2017. Areale Variation in den Gebrauchsstandards des Deutschen. In Marek Konopka & Angelika Wöllstein (eds.), *Grammatische Variation. Empirische Zugänge und theoretische Modellierung*. Berlin, Boston: De Gruyter Mouton (IDS-Jahrbuch 2016), 85–104.

Elspaß, Stephan, Christa Dürscheid & Arne Ziegler. 2017. Zur grammatischen Pluriarealität der deutschen Gebrauchsstandards – oder: Über die Grenzen des Plurizentrizitätsbegriffs. *Zeitschrift für deutsche Philologie* 136. 69–91.

Glauninger, Manfred Michael. 2013. Deutsch im 21. Jahrhundert: "pluri-", "supra-" oder "postnational"? In Doris Sava & Hermann Scheuringer (eds.), *Dienst am Wort. Festschrift für Ioan Lăzărescu zum 60. Geburtstag*. Passau: Stutz (Forschungen zur deutschen Sprache in Mittel-, Ost- und Südosteuropa 3), 123–132.

Hänsel, Eva Canan & Dagmar Deuber. 2019. *The interplay of the national, regional, and global in standards of English: A recognition survey of newscaster accents in the Caribbean. English World-Wide* 40(3). 241–268.

Haugen, Einar. 1966. Dialect, Language, Nation. *American Anthropologist* 68(4). 922–935.

Hundt, Marianne. 2013. The diversification of English: Old, new and emerging epicentres. In Daniel Schreier & Marianne Hundt (eds.), *English as a contact language*. Cambridge: Cambridge University Press, 182–203.

Jahr, Ernst Håkon. 2003. Norwegian. In Ana Deumert & Wim Vandenbussche (eds.), *Germanic Standardizations. Past to Present*. Amsterdam, Philadelphia: John Benjamins, 331–353.

Kloss, Heinz. 1978. *Die Entwicklung neuer germanischer Kultursprachen seit 1800*, 2nd edn. Düsseldorf: Schwann.

Küpper, Achim, Torsten Leuschner & Björn Rothstein. 2018. Die deutschsprachige Gemeinschaft Belgiens als emergentes Halbzentrum. Sprach- und bildungspolitischer Kontext — (Sub-) Standard — Sprachlandschaft. *Zeitschrift für deutsche Philologie* 136. 169–192.

Lippi-Green, Rosina. 2012. *English with an Accent. Language, ideology, and discrimination in the United States*, 2nd edn. London, New York: Routledge.

Maitz, Péter & Stephan Elspaß. 2013. Zur Ideologie des ‚Gesprochenen Standarddeutsch'. In Jörg Hagemann, Wolf Peter Klein & Sven Staffeldt (eds.), *Pragmatischer Standard*. Tübingen: Stauffenburg (Stauffenburg Linguistik 73), 35–48.

Möller, Robert. 2003. Zur diatopischen Gliederung des alltagssprachlichen Wortgebrauchs. Eine dialektometrische Auswertung von Jürgen Eichhoff: Wortatlas der deutschen Umgangssprachen (Bd. 1–4; 1977, 1978, 1993, 2000). *Zeitschrift für Dialektologie und Linguistik* 50(3). 259–277.

Muhr, Rudolf. 1995. Zur Terminologie und Methode der Beschreibung plurizentrischer Sprachen und deren Varietäten am Beispiel des Deutschen. In Rudolf Muhr & Richard Schrodt (eds.), *Österreichisches Deutsch und andere nationale Varietäten plurizentrischer Sprachen in Europa. Empirische Analysen*. Wien: Hölder-Pichler-Tempsky, 40–67.

Muhr, Rudolf. 1997. Zur Terminologie und Methode der Beschreibung plurizentrischer Sprachen und deren Varietäten am Beispiel des Deutschen. In Rudolf Muhr & Richard Schrodt (eds.), *Österreichisches Deutsch und andere nationale Varietäten plurizentrischer Sprachen in Europa. Empirische Analysen*. Wien: Hölder-Pichler-Tempsky, 40–66.

Muhr, Rudolf. 2007. *Österreichisches Aussprachewörterbuch. Österreichische Aussprachedatenbank*. Frankfurt et al.: Peter Lang.

Norrby, Catrin, Jan Lindström, Jenny Nilsson & Camilla Wide. 2020. Pluricentric languages. In Jan-Ola Östman & Jef Verschueren (eds.), *Handbook of Pragmatics. 23rd Annual Installment*, 201–220.

Oakes, Leigh & Yael Peled. 2018. *Normative Language Policy. Ethics, Politics, Principles*. Cambridge: Cambridge University Press.

ÖWB = Christiane M. Pabst, Herbert Fussy & Ulrike Steiner. 2016. *Österreichisches Wörterbuch*. 43th ed., Wien: öbv.

Pickl, Simon, Simon Pröll, Stephan Elspaß & Robert Möller. 2019. Räumliche Strukturen alltagssprachlicher Variation in Österreich anhand von Daten des „Atlas zur deutschen Alltagssprache (AdA)". In Lars Bülow, Ann Kathrin Fischer & Kristina Herbert (eds.), *Dimensions of Linguistic Space: Variation – Multilingualism – Conceptualisations*. (Schriften zur deutschen Sprache in Österreich 45). Berlin, Bern, Bruxelles, New York, Oxford, Warszawa, Wien: Lang, 39–60.

Pohl, Heinz Dieter. 1997. Gedanken zum Österreichischen Deutsch (als Teil der „pluriarealen" deutschen Sprache). In Rudolf Muhr & Richard Schrodt (eds.), *Österreichisches Deutsch und andere nationale Varietäten plurizentrischer Sprachen in Europa. Empirische Analysen*. Wien: Hölder-Pichler-Tempsky, 67–87.

von Polenz, Peter. 1999. *Deutsche Sprachgeschichte vom Spätmittelalter bis zur Gegenwart*. Vol. III: *19. und 20. Jahrhundert*. Berlin, New York: De Gruyter.

Reiffenstein, Ingo. 2001. Das Problem der nationalen Varietäten. […] In *Zeitschrift für deutsche Philologie* 120, 78–89.

Scharloth, Joachim. 2005. Asymmetrische Plurizentrizität und Sprachbewusstsein. Einstellungen der Deutschschweizer zum Standarddeutschen. *Zeitschrift für Germanistische Linguistik* 33(2). 236–267.

Scherr, Elisabeth & Arne Ziegler. 2023. A question of dominance: Statistically approaching grammatical variation in German standard language across borders. *Journal of Linguistic Geography* 11(2). 91–103.

Scheuringer, Hermann. 1996. Das Deutsche als pluriareale Sprache. Ein Beitrag gegen staatlich begrenzte Horizonte in der Diskussion um die deutsche Sprache in Österreich. *Die Unterrichtspraxis / Teaching German* 29(2). 147–153.

Schmidlin, Regula. 2011. *Die Vielfalt des Deutschen: Standard und Variation. Gebrauch, Einschätzung und Kodifizierung einer plurizentrischen Sprache*. Berlin, New York: De Gruyter.

Schrodt, Richard. 1997. Nationale Varianten, areale Unterschiede und der „Substandard": An den Quellen des Österreichischen Deutsch. In Rudolf Muhr & Richard Schrodt (eds.), *Österreichisches Deutsch und andere nationale Varietäten plurizentrischer Sprachen in Europa. Empirische Analysen*. Wien: Hölder-Pichler-Tempsky, 12–39.

Sieburg, Heinz. 2018. ,Luxemburger Standarddeutsch'? Hintergründe und Perspektiven. *Zeitschrift für deutsche Philologie* 136. 125–143.

Sieburg, Heinz. 2022. *Luxemburger Standarddeutsch. Wörterbuch der deutschen Gegenwartssprache in Luxemburg*. Berlin: Dudenverlag.

Stewart, William. 1968. A sociolinguistic typology for describing national multilingualism. In Joshua A. Fishman (ed.), *Readings in the Sociology of Language*, 530–545. The Hague: Mouton.

VG = *Variantengrammatik des Standarddeutschen*. 2018. An open access online reference work compiled by a team under the leadership of Christa Dürscheid, Stephan Elspaß & Arne Ziegler, http://mediawiki.ids-mannheim.de/VarGra. (31 March, 2024.)

VWB = Ammon, Ulrich, Hans Bickel, & Alexandra N. Lenz. 2016. *Variantenwörterbuch des Deutschen. Die Standardsprache in Österreich, der Schweiz, Deutschland, Liechtenstein, Luxemburg, Ostbelgien und Südtirol sowie Rumänien, Namibia und Mennonitensiedlungen*. 2nd edn. Berlin, Boston: De Gruyter.

Wiesinger, Peter. 1983. Die Einteilung der deutschen Dialekte. In Werner Besch, Ulrich Knoop, Wolfgang Putschke & Herbert Ernst Wiegand (eds), *Dialektologie. Ein Handbuch zur deutschen und allgemeinen Dialektforschung*, vol. 2, Berlin, New York: de Gruyter (Handbücher zur Sprach- und Kommunikationswissenschaft 1.2), 807–900.

Wodak, Ruth, Rudolf de Cillia, Martin Reisigl & Karin Liebhart. 2009. *The Discursive Construction of National Identity*. 2nd edn. Edinburgh: Edinburgh University Press.

Wolf, Norbert Richard. 1994. Österreichisches zum österreichischen Deutsch. Aus Anlaß des Erscheinens von: Wolfgang Pollak: Was halten die Österreicher von ihrem Deutsch? Eine sprachpolitische und soziosemiotische Analyse der sprachlichen Identität der Österreicher. *Zeitschrift für Dialektologie und Linguistik*, vol. 61, 66–76.

CHAPTER 3

Conceptualization of German from an Austrian perspective
Empirical evidence from Austrian schools

Jutta Ransmayr
University of Vienna, Austria

This contribution presents insights from a nation-wide Austrian survey on how Austrian school teachers and students conceptualize German. The results indicate that German is conceptualized in a pluricentric manner by most teachers and students in Austrian schools, with the notion of Austrian Standard German as a distinct standard variety of the German language, particularly among Austrian language norm authorities. In light of this, the differences and commonalities between the pluricentricity and pluriareality models are discussed, and a method for integrating both is presented, illustrating what each of the models imply, how they complement each other, and how terminological issues could be solved.

Keywords: pluricentricity model, pluriareality model, Austrian Standard German, German, language attitudes, conceptualization, national identity, survey

1. Introduction

German is considered to be one of the languages richest in variation among European languages (Barbour & Stevenson 1998), with its variation comprising both standard and non-standard varieties. At the level of the standard, we find systematic variation across all German-speaking countries (and regions where German is an official language). Though such geographical variation is mostly state-bound, it is also region-based and can transcend national borders (Ammon et al. 2016: XLI–XLII; Schmidlin 2017: 45).

For more than three decades, linguists have attempted to describe variation in German using theoretical concepts and models. Today, the two most frequently used models regarding German standards are the pluricentric model (e.g. Ammon 1995, 2005; Ammon et al. 2004, 2016; Clyne 1992, 1995, 2005; Kellermeier-Rehbein

2014; Muhr 2005, 2007; Schmidlin 2011) and the pluriareal model (e.g. Wolf 1994; Scheuringer 1996; Dürscheid et al. 2015).

Both approaches emphasize standard variation in German, but, while pluricentricity considers aspects such as normativity, prestige and status, dominance and non-dominance, linguistic identity and linguistic insecurity, and national context (Schmidlin et al. 2017: 16), pluriareality focuses on dialectal boundaries within and across German-speaking countries *("durch dialektale Großräume bestimmte Areale"*; Pohl 1997: 69). Both approaches attempt to describe certain parts of linguistic reality: the pluricentric approach considers more dimensions than just descriptive geographical ones, such as attitudes towards national standard varieties (in connection with German e.g. Ransmayr 2006; Pfrehm 2011; Schmidlin 2011), the connection between (national) identity and language, and the difference in status of trans-border variants in the respective countries, amongst others (Ammon 1995; Ammon et al. 2004, 2016; Clyne 1992; Pfrehm 2011; Schmidlin 2011; Auer 2013).

Underpinning the rationale for these scientific linguistic approaches are implicit normative language conceptualizations among language experts and laypersons (de Cillia & Ransmayr 2019; Beuge 2019; Ransmayr 2006; Pfrehm 2011). In this regard, the educational domain deserves particular attention since language attitudes are often shaped there by language experts (such as language teachers), who can influence the linguistic identity of speakers (Wodak et al. 1998, 2009; de Cillia & Wodak 2006, 2009).

In this contribution, findings from a research project on the conceptualization of German among a large sample of Austrian speakers, consisting of German teachers and upper secondary school students, will be presented. The project results show that the vast majority of Austrian teachers and students perceive German mainly as a pluricentric language, but that regional (= pluriareal) variation phenomena can also be easily integrated into the pluricentric model of description. The results demonstrate that the pluricentric and the pluriareal approaches do not inherently contradict each other. In fact, I will show that pluricentricity and pluriareality share and even complement each other in several respects.

2. Conceptualization of German: Pluri-(...) – ?

Despite standardization and codification in official dictionaries, German is subject to a high degree of variation at both the non-standard and standard levels. This variation is systematically influenced by factors such as region, nation, or state borders (*"Region und Nation als varietätsprägende Kräfte"*) (Ammon 1995: 505f.). So, how have linguists tried to grasp this abundance of variation in the German-speaking regions and countries? In addition to the theory of pluricentric languages, which is internationally recognized and used to describe and conceptualize languages and their variation at the standard level[1] (e.g. Clyne 1992; Muhr & Marley 2014; Muhr & Meisnitzer 2018; Soares de Silva 2013; Auer 2013), another approach has been used by linguists in German-speaking countries: pluriareality (e.g. Dürscheid et al. 2015; Elspaß & Niehaus 2014).

With its origins in the 1990s and mainly found in German-speaking linguistics, **pluriareality** seems to oppose key points of pluricentricity. While the acknowledgement of national varieties (Austrian Standard German, German Standard German, Swiss Standard German) is a core component of pluricentricity, pluriareality argues against this conceptualization (Scheuringer 1996; Wolf 1994; Putz 2002; Glauninger 2007; Dürscheid et al. 2015; T. Seifter & I. Seifter 2015; Herrgen 2015; Pohl 1997). Pluriareality focuses on regional ("*areale*") language variation based on smaller areas and dialectal regions rather than national states, and argues that linguistic variation does not correspond with political borders. Supra-regional and state-bound features are considered marginal. Concerning the influence of national borders on standard varieties, however, Ebner (2014: 8) states that political borders and national media do substantially influence respective national standard varieties. The political factors "state-hood" or "nation-hood", which can be reflected in a person's linguistic identity (Wodak et al. 1998; de Cillia et al. 2020), are not included in pluriareal descriptions of language variety, nor is the dimension of linguistic normativity in connection with school and education.

In the pluriareal model, we do not find distinctive terminology or axioms. Its foundations emerge from the publications on pluriareality versus pluricentricity in two phases: the 1990s and the years from 2010 onwards (Muhr 2020: 12). The concept focuses on some central assumptions. The first group of linguists who proposed the pluriareal model in the 1990s argued — and this line of argumentation is found in most pluriareal publications of the period — that there are many lexical similarities between Austria and Southern Germany, as well as substantial regional variation within Austria, leading to the conclusion that the state-based, pluricentric description of variation is inadequate (Wolf 1994: 72) and that "Austrian German" as such should not be automatically assumed (Wolf 1994: 75). Additionally, the publication of the Austrian Dictionary (*Österreichisches Wörterbuch*) in 1951 has been singled out as an act of restorative cultural policy following the Second World War, one guided by a "separatist ideology" (Wolf 1994: 67). Other linguists in this earlier pluriareal phase argue that Austrians should acknowledge the fact that they too can be considered to be "Germans" ("*Bürger deutscher Kultur und in diesem Sinne Deutsche*"), both in linguistic and cultural terms (Scheuringer 1992: 171).

---

1. Since 2011, there has been an international working group on pluricentric languages worldwide.

In a later phase of pluriareal publications, the term "*Gebrauchsstandards*" (standards of use) was introduced as an alternative conception of describing standards, taking into account language as it is used on a daily basis (Elspaß 2005: 6ff.). Central points made in earlier publications are re-emphasized using the terms 'absolute and relative variants' ("*absolute und relative Varianten*") (Dürscheid/Elspaß/Ziegler 2015) since many variants are not found exclusively in one state but frequently occur in parts of another as well. However, this idea is not a new element in theoretical frameworks, since pluricentricity has described the same phenomenon in the 1990s using the terms "*spezifische*" or "*unspezifische*" variant.

The concept of **pluricentricity** itself dates back nearly 50 years:[2] Kloss (1978: 66–67) initially applied the term "pluricentric language" to languages with several interacting centers, each providing a national variety with its own (codified) norms to varying degrees (Clyne 1992: 1). In particular, both Clyne and Ammon applied the concept to German in the 1990s, with the latter refining it by adding descriptive terms and axioms (Ammon 1995) and the former highlighting the function of national standard varieties as symbolic markers of independent identity (Clyne 1992: 137). Today, even with a reduced importance of borders in Europe (Spolsky 2009: 257), pluricentricity continues to matter: the connection between nation, language and identity continues to be relevant (de Cillia et al. 2020; Schneider 2003).

One of the major tenets of the concept is that it describes a standard language which has official status in more than one national center. In Ammon's terminology, Germany, Austria and Switzerland are "full centers" of German (see Ammon 1995: 61 ff. and in particular 101ff. for a complete overview of the terminology used to describe pluricentric variation such as *Variante/Varietät, spezifisch/unspezifisch; zentrumsinterne Variable/zentrumsinterne invariante nationale Variablen; full center/half center* etc.). As such, Standard German consists of three equivalent, state-bound varieties according to the concept of pluricentric languages: Austrian Standard German, German Standard German, and Swiss Standard German (Clyne 1995, 2005; Ammon 1995, 2005; Ammon et al. 2004; Eichinger 2006; Kellermeier-Rehbein 2014; Ammon et al. 2016; Ebner 2019; Dollinger 2019). Pluricentricity is particularly useful in normatively oriented contexts such as administration, schooling, and education, where the framework and relevant documents are defined by political entities such as the state or federal country (e.g. curricula for schools and universities and/or teaching materials).

Like a scientific theory, pluricentricity provides terminology and a system of statements for the description, explanation, and prediction of a section of (socio-linguistic) reality. It contains propositions with explanatory and predictive power

---

2. Ammon provides a detailed outline of the history of the term (1995: 42ff. and 1998: 331ff.).

(they work equally well for other pluricentric languages than German), such as these general ones sketched by Clyne:

> The national varieties of pluricentric languages do not necessarily enjoy equal status either internationally or in the individual countries, i.e. pluricentricity may be symmetrical, but is usually asymmetrical. [...] The national varieties of the more dominant nations [...] have been afforded a higher status than non-dominant varieties. [...] The status of national varieties is determined by the relative population size of the nations, their economic and political power, [and] historical factors [...]. (Clyne 1995: 21)[3]

Many of these propositions, especially concerning asymmetry in various aspects such as prestige and status, correctness and normativity, degree of respective knowledge, and linguistic insecurity and dominance, have been examined and confirmed in a substantial number of studies (Markhardt 2005; Scharloth 2005; Ransmayr 2006; Heinrich 2010; Pfrehm 2011; Schmidlin 2011; Peter 2015; Davies 2017; Hofer 2017, 2020; de Cillia & Ransmayr 2019; Leonardi 2021).

However, despite the different notions and maybe even because of the different approaches and intentions involved, pluricentricity and pluriareality do not stand in opposition to each other in all points. In fact, they could be seen as partly compatible, as stated by Ammon in 1998: A "nuanced description based on varying perspectives (*nach Blickwinkeln differenzierte Charakterisierung des Deutschen*)" is possible (Ammon 1998: 320).

3. Conceptualization of German among Austrian school teachers and students – results from an Austria-wide survey

The Austrian Science Fund (FWF)-funded research project "Austrian German as a language of instruction and education" investigated the role of Austrian German and other varieties of German in the context of German school teaching at Austrian schools. This was achieved by (1) analyzing relevant instructional documents such as teaching materials, school curricula, and teacher training curricula, and (2) collecting quantitative/qualitative data via oral and written surveys, panel discussions, and observations. The method and project design are outlined in Section 3.1 below.

---

3. For a complete overview of central axioms and characteristic features of dominant and non-dominant varieties and the respective asymmetries between them see Clyne (1995: 22ff, 2005: 297), and Ammon (1995: 484ff).

3.1 Project design

The project set out to achieve methodological triangulation by creating different data sets in separate project modules. In a first module, documents relevant for school teaching were analyzed regarding the representation of linguistic variation using Mayring's content analysis, following a classification system designed for this step of analysis. This included: school curricula for German from primary to upper secondary levels, teacher training curricula, and the most commonly used German school books in primary and secondary schools. In a second project module, quantitative and qualitative research instruments were used, consisting of an Austrian-wide survey examining the language attitudes and conceptualizations of German among German teachers (across all school types and all federal states of Austria; $n=165$, 30%: 22–40 years old, 70%: 41–63 years old; 79.3% female, 20.7% male) and upper secondary school students ($n=1253$; 13–21 years old). Furthermore, interviews with German teachers ($n=21$) were conducted, as well as two group discussions with teachers and upper secondary school students for the communicative validation of the survey results. Additionally, seven participatory classroom observations in upper secondary school classes were carried out. The survey data were analyzed statistically (using SPSS), while the interviews and group discussions were recorded, transcribed (following HIAT[4] transcription guidelines), and analyzed using content and discourse analysis.[5]

As for the underlying theoretical approach of the project, the pluricentric concept formed the foundation, as it is an adequate approach not only aiming to describe standard varieties, but also the connection between language and identity, and linguistic norms and language attitudes among speakers of dominant and non-dominant standard varieties. Moreover, the subject of investigation was based in the educational context and in a normative realm. Schools and education – from teacher training to teaching materials or curricula for schools and universities – are state-organized and state-approved in Austria. The theory of pluricentric languages acknowledges and incorporates, as one of its integral parts, the fact that the political dimension may influence language use in a state to some degree, especially in normative contexts (Ebner 2014; Ammon et al. 2016).

All results presented in the following chapter are taken from the surveys among teachers, upper secondary school students, and the panel discussions.[6]

---

4. HIAT = "Halbinterpretative Arbeitstranskriptionen": https://exmaralda.org/de/hiat/ (31.8.2021)
5. Wiener Kritische Diskursanalyse; see Reisigl 2007.
6. See de Cillia & Ransmayr (2019) for full survey results, research questions, and hypotheses.

3.2 How do teachers and students conceptualize German?

Teachers of all academic levels (from primary school to upper secondary school) and students (upper secondary school) were given questionnaires. The teachers' questionnaire consisted of 65 open and closed-format questions surrounding issues such as language attitudes, knowledge about (standard) language variation, their conceptualizations of German (specifically as used in Austria), and didactic as well as normative aspects. The students' questionnaires contained 47 questions in both open and closed formats, largely mirroring the teachers' questionnaires but excluding German didactic aspects. The survey results were analyzed with respect to various meta-data (i.e. age, region, gender, language background, school type, etc.). While we cannot present all results here due to the limited scope of this chapter, some pertinent findings are highlighted.

The survey's first open-format question addressed the issue of naming the language or variety spoken by the majority of the population in Austria.[7] The responses were categorized into four main groups: "German", "Austrian German", "Austrian", and "dialects", and subgroups of mixed answers (e.g. "German and Upper Austrian dialect"). As shown in Figure 3.1, both teachers and students mentioned "German" (*Deutsch*) the most (approximately 50%), followed by "Austrian German" (*Österreichisches Deutsch*), which was mentioned by a fifth of teachers and 11% of students. Apart from "dialect", most other answers were mixed. Interestingly, only very few students and teachers (9.9% / 5.9%) mentioned "Austrian" (*Österreichisch*) outright, which is surprising since the term "*Österreichisch*" is frequently used in the media when discussing the topic of "language" with Austrian identity-related specifications, or in topic-related discourse on social media platforms such as YouTube.[8] Cumulatively, though, many of the teachers' and students' answers contained explicit Austria-related mentions in addition to German (e.g. "Austrian German", "Austrian", "Austrian dialect", "German with Austrian accent"). So, while "Austrian" itself might not be exclusively chosen as a variety label, there does indeed seem to be a widespread Austrian-related element in the respondents' conceptualizations of the German in Austria.

Regarding the extra-linguistic variable of the respondents' region, no significant differences (as shown by Chi²-tests) were found among the teachers. However, within the group of students, there were significant differences in this question depending on the region in which they attended school ($\chi^2(16) = 25.379$,

---

7. *Wie würden Sie die Sprache, die die Mehrheit der Österreicher/innen als Muttersprche spricht, nennen?*

8. „Ist Österreichisch eine eigene Sprache?" DerStandard 11.5.2021; „Österreichisch für Anfänger" YouTube 17.4.2015; Sprachkurs Österreichisch" YouTube 30.4.2020.

$p = .082$). Sixty percent of students from the eastern regions of Austria (Vienna, Niederösterreich, and Burgenland) identified "German" as the language spoken by the majority of Austrians. Tyrolean students, on the other hand, mentioned "German" less frequently (41.2%), and in Vorarlberg "German" was only mentioned by 36%. There were also significant differences depending on the language background of the pupils: students with an L1 other than German stated "German" most frequently (62%), while those with German as their L1 mentioned it less frequently (47.2%), and were more likely to mention dialect (13.6%) than students with a non-German L1 (5.5%) ($\chi^2(14) = 35.344$, $p = .001$).

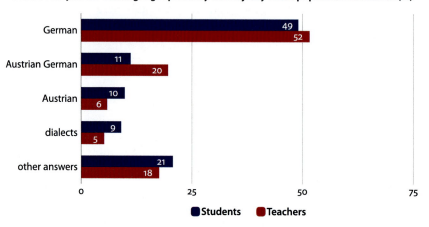

Figure 3.1 Terms used to name the majority language in Austria (%)

Since some of the relevant literature has suggested that varieties other than the standard play an important role in the everyday life of Austrians, including school (see Ender & Kaiser 2009; Rastner 1997; Neuland 2006; Steiner 2008), another question asked what participants understood by the term "Austrian German" (*österreichisches Deutsch*), and whether they associated it with standard language, colloquial language, and/or traditional rural dialectal varieties.[9] Results revealed that teachers generally categorize all varieties, from the standard to other dialects spoken in Austria, under the term "Austrian German" because they mentioned all varieties in their answers (see Figure 3.2). Since multiple answers were possible, there were also some combinations of answers. These made it evident that teachers associated not only the standard language as used in Austrian television and radio news

---

9. *Was ist Ihrer Meinung nach österreichisches Deutsch?* (1) *das, was man in österreichischen TV- und Radionachrichten spricht;* (2) *das, was man in Österreich im Alltag spricht (Umgangssprache);* (3) *die verschiedenen Dialekte in Österreich;* (4) *Sonstiges*

broadcasting with "Austrian German" (approximately 50%), but also colloquial language (*Umgangssprache*) (70%), and — with slightly less frequency than news broadcasting language — traditional rural dialects. The majority of the students associated "Austrian German" with colloquial language, but — in contrast to teachers — more frequently with traditional dialects: more than two-thirds of pupils chose colloquial language, while 70% mentioned dialects. The standard variety of TV and radio news was only named by one fifth of the students. Consequently, the survey results were discussed in two panel groups (one teacher group and one student group) with some focus on the survey respondents' association of colloquial Austrian German (*Umgangssprache*) with "Austrian German". Both discussions supported the quantitative result that all varieties found in Austria are subsumed under the "Austrian German" label by the respondents, as one teacher (F7) notes:

> Well, all of it is Austrian German. Every variety, isn't it? Whether it is — I don't know — well, deepest colloquial language or, more or less (oriented), deepest dialect, or more formal colloquial language, like, yes, frequently [used] in everyday life or in the media with the typical accents and the typical Austrian words. There are simply various nuances. (translation JR)[10]

The group discussions also showed that it can be difficult for speakers (especially students, but also teachers) to use the terms necessary to conceptualize the variation of German in Austria and the dialect-standard continuum, as illustrated by the following statement in the students' group discussion: "Yes, it is somehow difficult to draw a line and say that this is High German and that is colloquial language, because it always moves in between somehow, I think."[11] (F2) (translation JR).

The question of whether teachers and students conceptualized German generally in a monocentric, pluriareal, or pluricentric way was of particular interest. Therefore, a number of questions specifically addressing the topic of conceptualization of the German language from various angles were included in the questionnaire at different points, with some serving as control items to gauge the degree of influence the social desirability bias may have played in the data, if possible.

---

10. „Najo, es ist alles österreichisches Deutsch. Jede Variante, na? Ob jetzt in einem, was i net, a/ aso tiefste Umgangssprache mehr oder weniger (orientiert), tiefster Dialekt, oder geHOBene Umgangssprache, w:ie, w:/ jo, im Alltag häufig oder auch in den, (in den) Medien mit den typisch/ mit der typischen Betonung und den typisch österreichischen Wörtern. (Gibts) anfoch verschiedene Abstufungen."

11. „Ja es is irgendwie schwer da eine Linie zu ziehen und zu sagen, das is jetzt Hochdeutsch und das is Umgangssprache, weil es bewegt sich immer irgendwie dazwischen, finde ich."

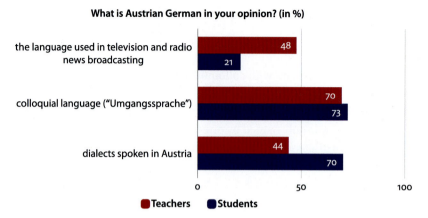

Figure 3.2 Conceptions of Austrian German among teachers and students (%)

Some of these questions approached the issue of conceptualization quite openly, such as the following: When participants were asked whether they viewed German as "a uniform language with one standard" or "a language with differences in the standard between the German-speaking countries",[12] a clear majority, both among teachers and students, decided for the latter answer: 90% of teachers and 79% of students chose the answer "language with differences in the standard between the individual countries" (see Figure 3.3).

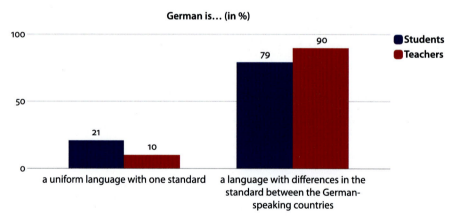

Figure 3.3 Conceptualization of German — one or more standards? (%)

---

12. *Deutsch ist... (1) eine einheitliche Sprache mit einer einzigen standardsprachlichen Form; (2) eine Sprache mit Unterschieden in der Standardsprache zwischen den einzelnen Ländern*

A follow-up item in the questionnaire examined the participants' attitudes towards the existence of an Austrian standard variety. We asked if they thought that such a thing as "Austrian Standard German" (*österreichisches Standarddeutsch*) existed at all.[13] When formulating this question, particular care was taken to use as neutral terms as possible. In lay discourse, "*Hochdeutsch*" (High German) is predominantly used to refer to the standard language associated with German German. If we had used *Hochdeutsch* in combination with Austria, a slight contradiction might have been induced, since Austrians tend to associate *Hochdeutsch* with a rather distanced variety and/or with German spoken in Northern Germany (Dollinger 2019:79–80), but not necessarily with the most formal Austrian register. School curricula and most schoolbooks today refrain from using *Hochdeutsch* and use *Standarddeutsch* instead. Therefore, *Standarddeutsch* was used in the questionnaire (with *Hochdeutsch* added only in brackets).

Results indicate that the majority of teachers (80%) and students (59%) think that Austrian Standard German exists (see Figure 3.4). This can be taken as another indication of a pluricentric conceptualization among Austrian teachers and students. When asked explicitly, barely 15% of teachers and at most 8% of the students were familiar with the term "pluricentricity".

Significant differences (as revealed via Chi²-tests) within the group of teachers were found depending on the respective institution of teacher education (pedagogical college vs. university) ($\chi^2(11) = 6.793$, $p = .009$). Teachers with a university education stated almost unanimously (95.4%) that German is a language with differences in the standard language between the individual countries. This opinion was also strongly held among teachers who had completed their training at a pedagogical college, but not quite as strongly at 82.9%.

Among students, significant differences were found depending on the region of the respective school location, $\chi^2(8) = 48.153$, $p < .001$, and the number of languages the students had learned at school, with students with more languages generally tending to answer "yes" more frequently to the question of whether they thought Austrian Standard German existed, $\chi^2(4) = 13.278$, $p = .01$. Students from central Austria (81.8%) and south-eastern Austria (81.6%) most frequently chose the answer that German is a language with differences in the standard language between the individual countries. The relatively highest level of agreement with the alternative answer (German as uniform language with just one standard) was found among students in Vorarlberg (33%), $\chi^2(4) = 10.23$, $p = .037$.

---

13. *Glauben Sie, dass es ein österreichisches Standarddeutsch (Hochdeutsch) gibt?*

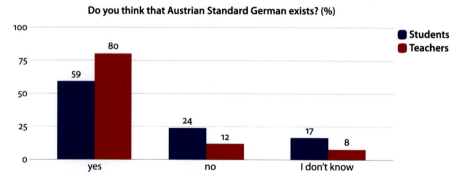

Figure 3.4 Existence of Austrian Standard German according to teachers and students (%)

When questioned regarding the perceived differences between Austrian German and German German[14] in formal, oral contexts,[15] approximately two thirds of both teachers and students stated that spoken formal Austrian and German German differed "very strongly" or "strongly". About a third in both groups stated that they differed "a little." Hardly anyone thought that there were no differences (see Figure 3.5).

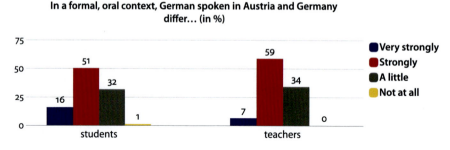

Figure 3.5 Views on degree to which German spoken in Austria and Germany differ

Both groups of respondents agreed nearly unanimously (teachers: 100%; students: 98%) that there are linguistic differences between Austria and Germany. When asked to specify on which levels such differences were perceived, teachers and students mostly agreed concerning differences on the level of pronunciation ("*Aussprache*") (97% and 93%, respectively), $\chi^2(1) = 3.641, p = .056$. However, regarding other levels of the linguistic system such as lexis ("*Wortschatz*"; $\chi^2(1) = 29.407$,

---

14. Swiss German was also included in the survey. For results see de Cillia & Ransmayr (2019).
15. *Das in Österreich gesprochene Deutsch unterscheidet sich von dem in Deutschland gesprochenen Deutsch in einer mündlichen, formellen Situation* ... (1) *sehr stark*; (2) *stark*; (3) *wenig*; (4) *gar nicht*.

Chapter 3. Conceptualization of German from an Austrian perspective 57

$p < .001$, grammar ("*Grammatik*"; $\chi^2(1) = 55.210$, $p < .001$, and pragmatics ("*Kommunikationsverhalten in Gesprächen*"; $\chi^2(1) = 4.753$, $p = .029$, the responses from teachers indicated that they perceived significantly more differences than students (see Figure 3.6). This difference could be attributed to their longer life experience, resulting in more language exposure and experience with varieties.[16] Ninety percent of the teachers stated that there are differences between Austria and Germany in vocabulary. Concerning grammar and pragmatics, 59% and 56% of teachers, respectively, reported noticing differences. Students, still in the process of developing language awareness, seemed less sure whether there were differences on a grammatical and pragmatic level, but most of them were clearly aware of lexical differences as well: 69% of the students stated that they perceived differences between Austria and Germany at the level of vocabulary, 30% at the level of grammar, and 46% at the level of pragmatics.

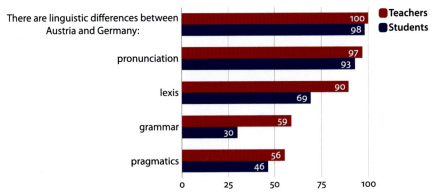

Figure 3.6 Views on language-related differences between Austria and Germany

Two other questions focused on inner-Austrian linguistic variation and cross-border language variation – both are often mentioned as counterarguments against the pluricentricity of German and the existence of national varieties (see Section 2). Participants were asked if they agreed or disagreed with the following statements: (1) "Austria and southern Germany have language-wise more in common than northern and southern Germany,"[17] and (2) "There is too much regional language variation in Austria (e.g. between the West and the East of Austria) for

---

16. Teacher training at university seems to have had no considerable impact on this question: More than 70% of the teachers stated that linguistic variation had not been or was insufficiently addressed during their teacher training (de Cillia & Ransmayr 2019: 103).
17. *Österreich und Deutschland haben sprachlich mehr gemeinsam als Nord- und Süddeutschland.*

Austrian Standard German to exist."[18] Results showed that 45% of students were not aware of the fact that there are linguistic similarities between Austria and southern Germany (see Figure 3.7). On the other hand, these questions exploring their conceptualization of inner-Austrian and cross-border language variation showed that teachers actually integrate both phenomena into their concepts of German: more than three quarters of teachers acknowledged linguistic similarities between the South of Germany and Austria. At the same time, the majority (82%) dismissed the frequently cited pluriareal point – inner-Austrian regional language variation – as a case against the existence of Austrian Standard German. Students' views on the latter were slightly less clear: 57% of students, compared to 82% of teachers, disagreed with the statement that there was "too much regional language variation in Austria for Austrian Standard German to exist". 43% of students and only 18% of teachers agreed with this (see Figure 3.7).

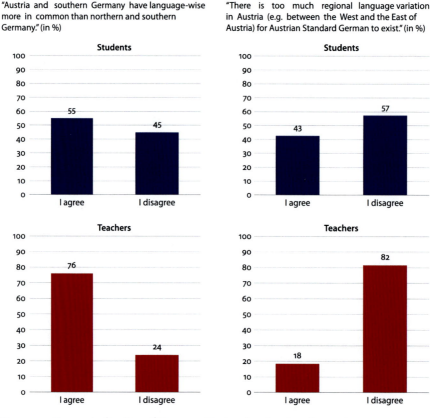

Figure 3.7 Conceptualization of German: Regional and national aspects

---

18. *Innerhalb Österreichs gibt es zu große regionale sprachliche Unterschiede (z.B. zwischen Ost- und Westösterreich), als dass es ein eigenes österreichisches Standarddeutsch geben kann.*

Concerning the question of "too much regional language variation in Austria for Austrian standard German to exist," we found significant differences among the teachers depending on the institution where they completed their teacher training ($\chi^2(1) = 7.301$, $p = .007$) and the school type at which they taught ($\chi^2(2) = 8.99$, $p = .011$: the highest rates in support of the statement that there was "too much regional variation for Austrian standard German to exist" were found among primary school teachers (30%). Significantly less agreement came from the other groups of teachers (between 10 and 19%). Only 10% of teachers who had completed a university degree agreed. The figure among graduates of a pedagogical college was 26.7%.

4. Discussion and conclusion

In this contribution, an Austrian perspective on variation within Standard German was explored, showcasing the views of Austrian school teachers and students along with their conceptualizations of the German language and Austrian German. Apart from depicting these conceptualizations, another aim was to present evidence suggesting the usefulness of considering some pluriareal aspects as an integral part of pluricentricity, and to discuss the possibilities and limitations of both approaches.

Overall, the results revealed predominantly pluricentric conceptualizations among Austrian teachers and, to a slightly lesser extent, among school students in Austria — despite the fact that curricula have not addressed questions of conceptualizations and have not explicitly introduced pluricentricity as a notion to be taught.[19] Although students demonstrated slightly less awareness of linguistic differences and similarities concerning features of German in Austria and Germany compared to teachers, they also predominantly viewed German implicitly as a pluricentric language and assumed the existence of Austrian Standard German (*österreichisches Standarddeutsch*). Additionally, the results suggested that students are likely still in the process of learning about linguistic issues and developing language reflection skills at school, while simultaneously gaining language experience outside of it.

The teachers demonstrated a strong conviction regarding the existence of Austrian Standard German and held a predominantly pluricentric conceptualization, which nonetheless contained elements of a pluriareal view. The glimpses into the project results illustrate that pluricentricity was implicitly present among

---

19. In the new Austrian curricula for German for lower secondary level (legally binding since in January 2024), pluricentricity has explicitly been mentioned.

the Austrian respondents, despite their unfamiliarity with the terms "pluricentric" or "pluriareal." Additionally, the data revealed some pluriareal aspects in the respondents' conceptualizations: the Austrian participants were aware of variation on a state-focused, national level; at a smaller-scale, regional level; and also of transborder similarities with Southern German regions. This confirms that regional, inner-state variation, cross-border variation, and national standard variation do not contradict each other — neither at the level of folk-linguistic perceptions as the students' views suggested, nor in terms of the perceptions of language experts (teachers). These perceptions can be integrated into a descriptive concept containing variation at a state-bound, national level *and* variation perceived on an intrastate level. This supports the depiction in the relevant literature: Cross-border variation phenomena have been described in the pluricentric model as "unspecific variants" (Ammon et al. 2016: XLII), while those primarily restricted to one state are classified as "specific variants" — or, if two pluriareal terms are applied with the same meaning, "relative" or "absolute variants". The existence of language variation within the individual national states has been described as the "second level of pluricentricity" or "regional pluricentricity" (Reiffenstein 2001: 88), which corresponds with the term "pluriareality".

The data provided in this research project are limited to Austria and its educational perspective, thus excluding attitudes among language teachers and students in Switzerland or Germany. For a complete picture, further research and data collection will be necessary to understand attitudes and perceptions from other contexts.

Despite these limitations, the findings of this research project suggest that (1) Austrian speakers conceptualize German as a language with both national standard varieties *and* regional variation, and that (2) pluricentricity is a concept which can incorporate pluriareal aspects. Therefore, it is reasonable to view pluriareality as (partly) overlapping with pluricentricity, as it mainly addresses geographical and areal variation within German-speaking countries and regions, and is able to complement — especially with regard to some of the publications of the later pluriareal phase as described earlier on — pluricentricity, rather than contradict it.

Describing geographical, areal variation is the first step in this process, and, as such, a fundamental one. Pluricentricity explores the connection between languages and (national) identities and takes a multidimensional approach to describe standard varieties as a part of socio-linguistic reality. This approach enables researchers to make predictions about language variation and attitudes of speakers, incorporating explanatory assertions (Schurz 2014: 26–27). The focus is therefore on questions like: (i) Who uses which variants in which context and with whom? (ii) What status do they have in which regions or countries? (iii)

How do speakers feel about them and why? (iv) How do speakers feel about varieties? (v) Are there certain (official, national, political) normative preconditions and explicit/implicit influences?

The pluri-debate often centers on the extent to which dimensions like "state-bound influence on a standard variety" and "(national or regional) identity" are necessary for a systematic and adequate description of standard varieties, as well as the question of whether or not national standard varieties exist in the German-speaking countries. In addition, some discussions suggest that political or ideological motivations may influence research supporting the pluricentric theory. However, it can be argued that neither model can be completely apolitical or applied without a political angle. As far as standard varieties are concerned, there is always a political dimension involved because standard varieties are closely associated with normative expectations (Ammon 2005: 32), are often nationally defined by their users, and play a crucial role especially in national education, media, administration, and the law.

As a concluding suggestion which may help to move away from contentions in these concepts, it might be useful to adopt internationally and consistently recognized terminology. Thus, using the term "pluricentric" for state-focused or national standard variation, and "regional pluricentricity" for "pluriareality" for regional variation as the two are practically synonymous in meaning and the former is better known internationally.

Funding

FWF-funded research project "Austrian German as a language of instruction and education" (2012–2015, University of Vienna; de Cillia & Ransmayr 2019). FWF-Projekt Nr. P23913-G18

References

Ammon, Ulrich. 1995. *Die deutsche Sprache in Deutschland, Österreich und der Schweiz: Das Problem der nationalen Varietäten*. Berlin u.a.: De Gruyter.

Ammon, Ulrich. 1998. Plurinationalität oder Pluriarealität? Begriffliche und terminologische Präzisierungsvorschläge zur Plurizentrizität des Deutschen — mit einem Ausblick auf ein Wörterbuchprojekt. In Peter Ernst & Franz Patocka (eds.), *Deutsche Sprache in Raum und Zeit: Festschrift für Peter Wiesinger zum 60. Geburtstag*, 313–323. Wien: Edition Praesens.

Ammon, Ulrich, Hans Bickel & Alexandra Lenz. 2004. *Variantenwörterbuch des Deutschen*. Berlin/New York: De Gruyter.

Ammon, Ulrich. 2005. Standard und Variation. Norm: Autorität, Legitimation. In Ludwig Eichinger & Werner Kallmeyer (eds.), *Standardvariation Wie viel Variation verträgt die deutsche Sprache? Jahrbuch des IDS 2004*, 28–40. Berlin/New York: De Gruyter.

Ammon, Ulrich, Hans Bickel & Alexandra Lenz. 2016. *Variantenwörterbuch des Deutschen: (2., völlig neu bearbeitete und erweiterte Auflage)?. Die Standardsprache in Österreich, der Schweiz, Deutschland, Liechtenstein, Luxemburg, Ostbelgien und Südtirol sowie Rumänien, Namibia und Mennonitensiedlungen*. Berlin, Boston: De Gruyter.

Auer, Peter. 2013. Enregistering pluricentric German. In Augusto Soares Da Silva (ed.), *Pluricentricity: Language Variation and Sociocognitive Dimensions*, 17–43. Berlin, Boston: De Gruyter.

Barbour, Stephen & Patrick Stevenson. 1998. *Variation im Deutschen: Soziolinguistische Perspektiven*. Berlin, New York: De Gruyter.

Beuge, Patrick. 2019. *Was ist gutes Deutsch? Eine qualitative Analyse laienlinguistischen Sprachnormwissens*. Berlin, Boston: De Gruyter.

Clyne, Michael G. (ed.). 1992. *Pluricentric Languages*. Berlin: De Gruyter.

Clyne, Michael G. 1995. *The German language in a changing Europe*. Cambridge: Cambridge University Press.

Clyne, Michael G. 2005. Pluricentric Language/Plurizentrische Sprache. In Ulrich Ammon, Norbert Dittmar, Klaus Mattheier & Peter Trudgill (eds.), *Sociolinguistics/Soziolinguistik: An International Handbook of the Science of Language and Society/Ein internationales Handbuch zur Wissenschaft von Sprache und Gesellschaft, 1. Teilband*, 296–300. Berlin, Boston: De Gruyter.

Davies, Winifred V. 2017. Gymnasiallehrkräfte in Nordrhein-Westfalen als SprachnormvermittlerInnen und Sprachnormautoritäten. In Davies, Winifred et al. (eds.), *Standardsprache zwischen Norm und Praxis:Theoretische Betrachtungen, empirische Studien und sprachdidaktische Ausblicke*, 123–146. Tübingen: Narr Francke Attempto.

de Cillia, Rudolf & Ruth Wodak. 2006. *Ist Österreich ein „deutsches" Land? Sprachenpolitik und Identität in der Zweiten Republik*. Innsbruck: Studien Verlag.

de Cillia, Rudolf & Ruth Wodak. 2009. *Gedenken im 'Gedankenjahr': Zur diskursiven Konstruktion österreichischer Identitäten im Jubiläumsjahr 2005*. Wien, Innsbruck: Studien Verlag.

de Cillia, Rudolf & Jutta Ransmayr. 2019. *Österreichisches Deutsch macht Schule: Bildung und Deutschunterricht im Spannungsfeld von sprachlicher Variation und Norm*. Wien: Böhlau.

de Cillia, Rudolf, Ruth Wodak, Markus Rheindorf & Sabine Lehner. 2020. *Österreichische Identitäten im Wandel*. Wiesbaden: Springer Fachmedien Wiesbaden.

Dollinger, Stefan. 2019. *The pluricentricity debate: On Austrian German and other Germanic standard varieties*. New York/London: Routledge.

Dürscheid, Christa, Stephan Elspaß & Arne Ziegler. 2015. Variantengrammatik des Standarddeutschen. Konzeption, methodische Fragen, Fallanalysen. In Alexandra Lenz & Manfred Glauninger (eds.), *Standarddeutsch im 21. Jahrhundert: Theoretische und empirische Ansätze mit einem Fokus auf Österreich*, 207–235. Wien: Vienna University Press.

Ebner, Jakob. 2014. Österreichisches Deutsch. Ein Klärungsversuch. In Bundesministerium für Bildung (ed.), *Österreichisches Deutsch als Unterrichts – und Bildungssprache*, 7–9. Wien.

Ebner, Jakob. 2019. *Duden. Österreichisches Deutsch. Wörterbuch der Gegenwartssprache in Österreich. 5. völlig überarbeitete und erweiterte Auflage*. Berlin: Dudenverlag.

Eichinger, Ludwig M. 2006. Das Deutsche als plurizentrische Sprache betrachtet. In *Dokumentation der EFNIL Jahrestagung Madrid 2006*. https://ids-pub.bsz-bw.de /frontdoor/deliver/index/docId/1894/file/Eichinger_Das_Deutsche_als_plurizentrische _Sprache_betrachtet_2007.pdf

Elspaß, Stephan. 2005. Standardisierung des Deutschen. Ansichten aus der neueren Sprachgeschichte ‚von unten'. In Eichinger, Ludwig M. & Werner Kallmeyer (eds.), *Standardvariation: Wie viel Variation verträgt die deutsche Sprache?*, 63–99. Berlin/New York: de Gruyter.

Elspaß, Stephan & Konstantin Niehaus. 2014. The standardization of a modern pluriareal language. Concepts and corpus designs for German and beyond. *Orð og tunga* 16. 47–67.

Ender, Andrea & Irmtraud Kaiser. 2009. Zum Stellenwert von Dialekt und Standard im österreichischen und Schweizer Alltag. *Zeitschrift für germanistische Linguistik (ZGL)* 37(2). 266–295.

Glauninger, Manfred M. 2007. Deutsch im 21. Jahrhundert: „pluri"-, „supra" – oder „postnational"? *Vortrag am II. Kongress des Mitteleuropäischen Germanistenverbandes (MGV), Olmütz, 13. – 16. September 2007*. https://homepage.univie.ac.at/manfred .Glauninger/Vorlesung/Glauninger%20Olm%FCtz.pdf. (5 July, 2021.)

Heinrich, Ilona E. 2010. *Österreichisches Deutsch in Lehrbüchern der Sekundarstufe I für Deutsch als Muttersprache*. Dipl. Univ. Wien.

Herrgen, Joachim. 2015. Entnationalisierung des Standards. Eine perzeptionslinguistische Untersuchung zur deutschen Standardsprache in Deutschland, Österreich und der Schweiz. In Alexandra Lenz & Manfred Glauninger (eds.), *Standarddeutsch im 21. Jahrhundert: Theoretische und Empirische Ansätze mit einem Fokus auf Österreich*, 139–164. Wuppertal: V&R unipress.

HIAT. (31.8.2021). EXMARaLDA. https://exmaralda.org/de/hiat/

Hofer, Silvia. 2017. Das Korrekturverhalten von Südtiroler Deutschlehrpersonen und ihre Rolle als Normautoritäten im sozialen Kräftefeld der deutschen Standardsprache in Südtirol. In Österreichischer Verband für Deutsch als Fremdsprache/Zweitsprache (ÖDaF-Mitteilungen) (ed.), *"Man lernt nicht mit dem Kopf allein". Zur Rolle von Emotionen im DaF/DaZ-Unterricht*, 79–95. Göttingen: V&R unipress.

Hofer, Silvia. 2020. *Deutsch ist nicht gleich Deutsch: Zum Umgang mit der plurizentrischen Sprache Deutsch und standardsprachlicher Variation an Südtiroler Oberschulen*. Universität Wien: Ph.D. dissertation.

Kellermeier-Rehbein, Birte. 2014. *Plurizentrik. Eine Einführung in die nationalen Varietäten des Deutschen*. Berlin: Erich Schmidt.

Kloss, Heinz. 1978. *Die Entwicklung neuer germanischer Kultursprachen seit 1800*, 2nd edn. Düsseldorf: Schwann.

Leonardi, Mara M. 2021. Attitudes of South Tyrolean University Students towards German Varieties. *Languages*, vol. 6, 137.

Markhardt, Heidemarie. 2005. *Das Österreichische Deutsch im Rahmen der EU*. Frankfurt/Main: Peter Lang.

Muhr, Rudolf (ed.). 2005. *Standardvariationen und Sprachideologien in verschiedenen Sprachkulturen der Welt. Standard Variations and Language Ideologies in Different Language Cultures around the World*. Frankfurt/Main: Peter Lang.

Muhr, Rudolf. 2007. *Österreichisches Aussprachewörterbuch – Österreichische Aussprachedatenbank*. Frankfurt/Main: Peter Lang. www.adaba.at

Muhr, Rudolf & Dawn Marley (eds.). 2014. *Pluricentric languages: New perspectives in theory and description*. Frankfurt/Main: Peter Lang.

Muhr, Rudolf & Benjamin Meisnitzer (eds). 2018. *Languages and Non-Dominant Varieties Worldwide. New Pluricentric Languages – Old Problems*. Frankfurt/Main: Peter Lang.

Muhr, Rudolf. 2020. Pluriarealität in der Soziolinguistik: Ein umfassender Überblick über die Schlüsselbegriffe des Konzepts und eine Kritik der verwendeten linguistischen Daten. In Rudolf Muhr & Juan Thomas (eds.), *Pluricentric Theory beyond Dominance and Non-dominance*, 9–83. Graz/Berlin: PCL-PRESS.

Neuland, Eva (ed.). 2006. *Variation im heutigen Deutsch: Perspektiven für den Sprachunterricht*. Frankfurt/Main: Peter Lang.

Peter, Klaus. 2015. Sprachliche Normvorstellungen in Österreich, Deutschland und der Schweiz. In Lenz, Alexandra N. et al. (Hrsg.), *Dimensionen des Deutschen in Österreich. Variation und Varietäten im sozialen Kontext*, Frankfurt am Main u.a.: Peter Lang, 123–147.

Pfrehm, James W. 2011. The Pluricentricity of German: Perceptions of the Standardness of Austrian and German Lexical Items. *Journal of Germanic Linguistics* 23.1, 37–64. Cambridge: Cambridge University Press.

Pohl, Heinz Dieter. 1997. Gedanken zum Österreichischen Deutsch (als Teil der "pluriarealen" deutschen Sprache). In Rudolf Muhr & Richard Schrodt (eds.), *Österreichisches Deutsch und andere nationale Varietäten plurizentrischer Sprachen in Europa*, 67–88. Wien: HPT.

Putz, Martin. 2002. „Österreichisches Deutsch" als Fremdsprache? Kritische Überlegungen. *German as a Foreign Langauge (GFL Journal), vol. 3*, http://www.gfl-journal.de/3-2002/putz.html. (5 July, 2021.)

Ransmayr, Jutta. 2006. *Der Status des österreichischen Deutsch an nichtdeutschsprachigen Universitäten: Eine empirische Untersuchung*. Frankfurt/Main: Peter Lang.

Rastner, Eva Maria. 1997. Sprachvarietäten im Unterricht. Eine Umfrage unter Österreichs LehrerInnen zu Standardsprache – Umgangssprache – Dialekt. *Informationen zur Deutschdidaktik (ide)*, vol. 3, 80–93.

Reiffenstein, Ingo. 2001. Das Problem der nationalen Varietäten. Rezensionsaufsatz zu Ulrich Ammon: Die deutsche Sprache in Deutschland, Österreich und der Schweiz. Das Problem der nationalen Varietäten. *Zeitschrift für deutsche Philologie* 120(1). 78–8.

Reisigl, Martin. 2007. Projektbericht: Der Wiener Ansatz der Kritischen Diskursanalyse. *Forum Qualitative Social Research (FQS)* 8(2).

Scharloth, Joachim. 2005. Zwischen Fremdsprache und nationaler Varietät. Untersuchungen zum Plurizentrizitätsbewusstsein der Deutschschweizer. In Rudolf Muhr, (ed.), *Standardvariationen und Sprachideologien in verschiedenen Sprachkulturen der Welt. Standard Variations and Language Ideologies in Different Language Cultures around the World*. Frankfurt am Main: Peter Lang, 21–44.

Scheuringer, Hermann. 1992. Deutsches Volk und deutsche Sprache. Zum Verhältnis von Deutsch-Sprechen und Deutsch-Sein in der Schweiz und in Österreich nach 1945. In *Österreich in Geschichte und Literatur 36*, 162–173. Wien/Graz: Braumüller.

Scheuringer, Hermann. 1996. Das Deutsche als pluriareale Sprache: Ein Beitrag gegen staatlich begrenzte Horizonte in der Diskussion um die deutsche Sprache in Österreich. *Die Unterrichtspraxis/Teaching German* 2(29). 147–153.

Schmidlin, Regula. 2011. *Die Vielfalt des Deutschen: Standard und Variation: Gebrauch, Einschätzung und Kodifizierung einer plurizentrischen Sprache*. Berlin, Boston: De Gruyter.

Schmidlin, Regula. 2017. Normwidrigkeit oder Variationsspielraum? Die Varianten des Standarddeutschen als sprachliche Zweifelsfälle. In Winifred V. Davies, Annelies Häcki Buhofer, Regula Schmidlin, Melanie Wagner & Eva Wyss, (eds.), *Standardsprache. zwischen Norm und Praxis. Theoretische Betrachtungen, empirische Studien und sprachdidaktische Ausblicke*, 41–60. Tübingen: Narr.

Schmidlin, Regula, Eva L. Wyss, Winifred V. Davies. 2017. Plurizentrik revisited – aktuelle Perspektiven auf die Variation der deutschen Standardsprache. In Winifred V. Davies., Annelies Häcki Buhofer, Regula Schmidlin, Melanie Wagner & Eva Wyss, (eds.), *Standardsprache zwischen Norm und Praxis: Theoretische Betrachtungen, empirische Studien und sprachdidaktische Ausblicke*, 8–20. Tübingen: Narr.

Schneider, Edgar W. 2003. The dynamics of New Englishes: From identity construction to dialect birth. *Language* 79(2). 233–281.

Schurz, Gerhard. 2014. *Philosophy of Science*. New York: Routledge.

Seifter, Thorsten & Ingolf Seifter. 2015. Warum die Frage, ob sich „pfiati vertschüsst", keine linguistische ist. Zur Fundamentalkritik am „Österreichischen Deutsch". In Heinz-Helmut (eds.), *Beiträge zur Fremdsprachenvermittlung*, 65–90. Landau: Verlag Empirische Pädagogik.

Soares da Silva, Augusto. 2013. *Pluricentricity: Language Variation and Sociocognitive Dimensions*. Berlin, Boston: De Gruyter.

Spolsky, Bernard. 2009. *Language Management*. Cambridge: Cambridge University Press.

Steiner, Astrid. 2008. *Unterrichtskommunikation. Eine linguistische Untersuchung der Gesprächsorganisation und des Dialektgebrauchs in Gymnasien der Deutschschweiz*. Tübingen: Gunter Narr.

Wodak, Ruth, Rudolf de Cillia, Martin Reisigl & Karin Liebhart. 1998. *Zur diskursiven Konstruktion nationaler Identität*. Frankfurt/M.: Suhrkamp.

Wodak, Ruth, Rudolf de Cillia, Martin Reisigl & Karin Liebhart. 2009. *The Discursive Construction of National Identity*, Edinburgh: Edinburgh University Press.

Wolf, Norbert R. 1994. Österreichisches zum Österreichischen Deutsch. *Zeitschrift für Dialektologie und Linguistik (ZDL)*, vol. 61, 66–76.

CHAPTER 4

Regiocentric use and national indexicality
Enregisterment as a theoretical integration for standard German

Konstantin Niehaus
University of Salzburg, Austria

Contemporary German linguistics uses either pluricentric or pluriareal models to investigate geographic variation in standard German. In this article, I argue for an integration of both concepts by including language ideologies and *enregisterment* (Agha 2007) more rigorously. First, I will elaborate on the idea of "core" areas in standard language use and ideologies where specific standard variants are most frequent or are promoted in discourse by ideology brokers. Speakers' ideologies allow for salient geographic variants to index social meaning (e.g. national stereotypes) and constitute a linguistic *register* of identity. The interaction of use and indexicality is mediated by attitudes. I propose to integrate standard use, attitudes, and indexicality in a single preliminary framework which could also be useful for other languages with several standards.

Keywords: standard German, enregisterment, language and identity, language ideologies, standardization

1. Motivation: The 'pluri'-debate

One of the most prominent debates in German linguistics is the question of whether German is a *pluricentric* or *pluriareal* language (cf. Langer 2021a: 1–2). Both models seek to describe the variation of standard German across geographic space. The main issue is to what degree national borders should be considered and how (socio-)linguistic norms should be defined (cf. Auer 2021: 29). The contemporary discussion among scholars in this "pluri"-debate is not as heated as it was in the past. Still, there is need for reconciliation. A short history of the two concepts will demonstrate this.

One can characterize four stages of academic research and discourse on pluricentric or pluriareal German:[1]

1. *Pluricentricity* as a countermovement in the 1980s and early 1990s: The dominant notion of standard German in post-war German linguistics was *Binnendeutsch* (Moser 1959): It depicted the northern standard German of the Federal Republic of Germany as *Hauptvariante* 'main variant' and *de facto* sole center. Other geographic variants were regarded as *Nebenvarianten* 'minor variants' of so-called *Außengebiete* 'outer territories'. The work of Clyne (e.g. 1982, 1995) and Ammon (1995) — to name but a few — established *pluricentricity* in German linguistics, i.e. the idea that emancipated national varieties exist rather than a quasi-monolithic standard.

2. The dispute over pluricentricity and pluriareality in the 1990s: While most researchers agreed that *Binnendeutsch* was a biased and outdated model, some also questioned the pluricentric conceptualization predominantly based on attitudes toward national variation and national norms of codification. In the eyes of these critics, pluricentricity adhered to a covert or inadvertent nationalism which did not hold up to empirical evidence on *Gebrauchsstandards* 'standards of usage' (e.g. Wolf 1994 for Austria, Koller 1999 for Switzerland).[2] *Pluriareality* was proposed as an alternative: The basic thought was that, aside from a few nation-specific variants, standard usage primarily reflected historically grown cultural spaces, especially dialect areas. It followed, then, that regional standards should be prioritized in any model of standard German. The concept also stressed that multiple standard variants were in use in each geographic space instead of uniform national variants.

3. The first empirical phase, ca. 2001–2011: The theoretical disagreements of the 1990s saw the need for more empirical input, which sparked large research projects. This third phase ultimately provided broad empirical insights on standard language use and, to a lesser extent, perceptions of and attitudes toward, geographic standard German. Most noteworthy was the introduction of a usage-based dictionary of geographic variation in standard German, the *Variantenwörterbuch des Deutschen* (Ammon et al. 2004). Based on the pluricentric model, it nonetheless concedes to some pluriareal assumptions, such as an intra-national differentiation of usage. The stage closes with Schmidlin's extensive analysis of language use, perception, and attitudes (Schmidlin 2011) and Kellermeier-Rehbein's (2014) textbook on pluricentricity.

---

1. I refer to "standard German" when I speak of "pluricentric/pluriareal German".
2. In this article, "Switzerland" and "Swiss" refer to German-speaking Switzerland only.

4. The second empirical phase, ca. since 2011: Comprehensive corpus-linguistic research projects on pronunciation and grammar embraced the pluriareal model and its principles, culminating in the online dictionaries *Atlas zur Aussprache des deutschen Gebrauchsstandards* (Kleiner 2011–present) and the *Variantengrammatik des Standarddeutschen* (2018) which provide the reader with more precise descriptions of the geography and socio-pragmatics of standards of usage. In accordance with more refined corpus-linguistic methods, a revised edition of the pluricentric *Variantenwörterbuch des Deutschen* (Lenz et al. 2016) was published. Meanwhile, the 'pluri'-debate has since cooled somewhat, with several scholars on either side conceding to the validity of the pluricentric attitudinal focus as well as the pluriareal usage-based approach (e.g. Niehaus 2015: 159–161; de Cillia & Ransmayr 2019: 41). The choice of a model more and more seems to indicate a preference:
   a. for a listener-based pluricentric methodology focused on perception or a speaker-based pluriareal methodology focused on language production,
   b. for theory-driven pluricentric spaces or data-driven pluriareal spaces, and
   c. for established pluricentric or progressionist pluriareal terminology.

Both models share the idea of geographic variation within standard German as well as the promotion of a liberal, tolerant language policy toward this variation. Subsequently, the models can be reconciled with each other to exploit their full explanatory strength if we not only gather more empirical data on language use, perception, and attitudes in the future, but also make more conscious efforts to include *all* these aspects in a theory of geographic variation in standard languages. In this chapter, I propose a theoretical integration for standard German: I present the most relevant empirical findings according to the nature of their approach (Section 2) and then introduce the idea that language ideologies can unite pluricentricity and pluriareality (Section 3). I combine the concept of centers of frequency in language use with a theory of social meaning of variation, namely the indexicalization and *enregisterment* of linguistic variants (cf. Agha 2007) during which ideological centers are established. Language ideologies lie at the heart of enregisterment, i.e. sets "of beliefs about language articulated by users as a rationalization or justification of perceived language structure and use" (Silverstein 1979: 193). Hence, (explicit) attitudes and perceptions are the superficial appearance of underlying, presupposing ideologies. Examples of national indexicalization and relevant ideologies in Section 4 will demonstrate the usefulness of such an approach. National enregisterment may be just one of several possibilities of indexicality but it has been effective, for instance in official codification (cf. Niehaus to appear). With regard to the "pluri"-debate, my approach bridges the gap between pluricentric and pluriareal notions of normativity. To underline this, it seems appropriate not to favor any of the two in terminology.

Chapter 4. Regiocentric use and national indexicality   69

This is not to say that the idea of including enregisterment is something new (cf. also Auer 2013, 2021; Lenz et al. 2022). However, there is still not only a lack of empirical analyses, but also a need for theoretical elaboration concerning the interaction of use, attitudes, and ideology.

My integrational approach draws on some basic ideas in Reiffenstein (2001) and Auer (2013, 2021). However, it reconceptualizes "centers" on the levels of usage and indexicality which not only help to distinguish different notions of norms, but also to see that pluricentricity and pluriareality do not exclude but complement each other. Although the examples stem from standard German, the general outline may also prove fruitful for other "bigger" standardized languages or universal models of standardization.

2. A short summary of empirical findings on geographic variation in standard German

2.1 A speaker-based approach: Language use[3]

The most distinguishing geographic phenomenon in standard German use on all linguistic levels is the north-south-divide (Elspaß & Kleiner 2019: 161): The divide runs roughly along the Main river in southern Germany ("Mainlinie") and reflects an old dialect border — northernly Central German vs. southernly Upper German — as well as a former hegemonic sphere of political powers, namely Prussia vs. Habsburg in the 19th century. Examples include prevocalic /z/ in the onset ([s] in the south, [z] in the north), everyday vocabulary (e.g. 'boy', *Bub* in the south, *Junge* in the north, 'curtain/drape', *Vorhang* in the south, *Gardine* in the north), and the auxiliary verb for present or past perfect of positioning verbs like *sitzen, stehen, liegen* ('to sit', 'to stand', 'to lie'), i.e. *sein* 'to be' in the south, *haben* 'to have' in the north (Elspaß & Kleiner 2019: 162–163).

In Austria, Switzerland, and South Tyrol, southernly variants often reach a considerably higher frequency than in South Germany (cf. Elspaß & Kleiner 2019: 171–180). In addition, Bavaria's tradition of federalist self-confidence in media and politics has helped establish a typical standard use within southern Germany, e.g. the qualities of /r/, [r], [ɾ] and [ʀ], administrative terms in education like *Extemporale* 'short, unannounced written test', *Schulaufgabe* 'long, announced written test at school' or *Unterschleif* 'cheating at assignments or tests', and the mor-

---

3. See Elspaß (this volume) for a similar and more extensive description. Analyses of standard use typically rely on model texts and respective speakers such as newspaper reports for written standards and TV news for spoken standards (cf. Ammon 1995: 79–80).

phology of some administrative terms, e.g. *Parteiverkehr* 'business/office/opening hours' and *Klasslehrer/-leiter* 'homeroom teacher'[4] (cf. Elspaß & Kleiner 2019: 168–169).

In the central western areas, East Belgium and Luxembourg often conform with the usage in bordering areas of central western Germany; however, they tend to retain 'older' western variants more strongly, like [χt] for <rt> (instead of [rt]/[ɐ̯t]), e.g. in *hart* 'hard', *Sport* 'sports', *kurz* 'short' (cf. Elspaß & Kleiner 2019: 166–167).

In north-eastern and central eastern Germany, 'relict' lexical variants of the former German Democratic Republic (GDR) are still widespread: This goes, again, for administrative terms such as *Fleischer* 'butcher' but also everyday items such as *Klammeraffe* 'stapler' or *Broiler* 'grilled chicken', and in terms of grammatical variation the subjunctive use of *trotzdem* 'nevertheless' is most common here (cf. Elspaß & Kleiner 2019: 167).

In sum, an overwhelming majority of variants either cross borders, thereby covering large areas, or concentrate in smaller, intra-national regions.

2.2 Listener-based approaches: Perception and attitudes

Speaker-based approaches rest on the assumption that a sufficient frequency indicates general acceptance and normativity within a speech community (e.g. Dürscheid et al. 2011: 133). Indeed, speakers and listeners may tolerate the frequent use of geographic variants in standard language contexts. But that does not answer the question of whether those speakers, let alone listeners, also regard those features to be standard, and if so, to which degree (cf. Niehaus 2015: 162; Auer 2021: 45). Let us therefore turn to perceptual and attitudinal data. Most studies[5] have focused on testing the national categories German, Austrian, and Swiss standard German, yet, even within this paradigm, "questions concerning areal-national and social positioning of the [...] standard are yet to be satisfactorily addressed" (Koppensteiner & Lenz 2020: 49).

One can observe a general paradox in attitudes toward geographic variation in standard German (cf. Schmidlin 2011: 283): On the one hand, geographic variants of standard German receive a positive evaluation in metalinguistic commentary, i.e., speakers perceive distinguishable national standards and tend to rate their "own" national standard favorably in terms of social attractiveness.

On the other hand, standard variants other than northern Germany's are often treated with intolerance in normative action such as teachers' corrections

---

4. Otherwise *Parteienverkehr* and *Klassenlehrer/-vorstand*.
5. With the notable exceptions of Kehrein (2009) and Schmidlin (2011).

at school. This has been described as *asymmetric* pluricentricity where Germany *dominates* over the other areas via a supra-regional sociolinguistic prestige of its standard German (cf. e.g. Ammon 1995: 300). One frequently attested example is that Austrian and Swiss speakers more willingly tolerate standard variants from Germany while they tend to correct so-called 'austriacisms' and 'helvetisms' – we can interpret this as a reflection of perceived sociolinguistic inferiority toward speakers from Germany (cf. Ammon 1995: 436–447; Schmidlin 2011: 200).

Austrians, particularly East Austrians, are critical of Germany's dominant role and stress the existence and equality of an Austrian national standard (cf. Schmidlin 2011: 259, 284). Compared to local or regional non-standards, standard German in general is a sign of education, competence, eloquence, and proficiency but also of unappealing artificiality and snobbery to many Austrians (cf. e.g. Kaiser et al. 2019: 352). The majority of Austrian speakers seem to think that *Austrian German* is colloquial (everyday) speech and varies between dialect and standard (cf. de Cillia & Ransmayr 2019: 125–126). If Austrian speakers adhere to this idea, they consider *Austrian German* an integral part of their national identity even if – or precisely because – this includes what they consider "incorrect" or "non-standard" variants (cf. de Cillia & Ransmayr 2019: 225). This paradox influences Austrians' negative ratings of their own lexical standard items (cf. Pfrehm 2011). In comparison, many Swiss speakers perceive Germany's standard German as the only "correct" standard since their language of group identity is not Swiss standard German but an individual's Swiss German dialect, *Schweizerdeutsch* (cf. Ammon 1995: 301; Koller 1999; Scharloth 2005: 261–262). This also explains why Swiss speakers often state that standard German is a "foreign language" and regard Swiss German dialect as their "mother tongue" (cf. Watts 1999: 74). This "ideology of dialect" (Watts 1999) triggers Swiss speakers' negative attitudes toward standard German, regardless of its origin, at the level of social attractiveness (cf. e.g. Studler 2019: 408). Yet, attitudes of Swiss speakers can depend on intra-individual factors, e.g. their education and personal experiences over the courses of their lives, and more positive attitudes toward Swiss standard German are also attested (cf. Oberholzer 2017: 146–147).

What about speakers from Germany? Apart from a few studies such as Schmidlin's (2011), we still lack sufficient evidence. A *Binnendeutsch*-attitude which regards all geographic variation in standard German as "incorrect" or "dialect" still is supposedly widespread in Germany. Researchers often assume a disregard for any geographic variation among Germans (cf. Clyne 1995: 22; Auer 2013: 20, 2021: 34). Schmidlin's evidence (2011: 259) points in that direction.

The result is a north-south-divide in the perception of "correctness" and prestige, with northern Germany being most closely associated with standard pronunciation (at least among educated participants, cf. Kehrein 2009). On the level of language perception, Herrgen (2015:155) argues that an ongoing "denationalization" can be observed since nowadays northern standard German speech is universally favored, after a phase of assumed national pronunciation norms in the second half of the 20th century. In the case of Austria, however, Koppensteiner & Lenz (2020:73–74) were able to show that this preference is restrained by how 'standardness' is contextualized, e.g. 'pureness' elicits higher ratings of preference for northern German speech than 'suitability for Austrian news broadcasting.'

2.3 Summary

Setting aside methodological and methodical differences, one could summarize the findings as follows: On the one hand, both national and regional usage can be observed, with the latter being more common, much in line with the pluriareal model. On the other hand, there is a relevant effect of nationality on perception and attitudes, and some standard variants – even if few in number – do symbolize national identity (cf. also Schmidlin 2017:48), much in line with pluricentric theory. The following integrative approach tries to reconcile the respective manifestations of norms. Moreover, the importance of socially meaningful geographic spaces for perception and attitudes will be theoretically accounted for by utilizing enregisterment and recognizing power in discourse,[6] especially in mass media discourse and in educational policy.

3. An integrative approach using regiocentricity and enregisterment

3.1 The starting point: Enregisterment according to Auer (2013, 2021)

Auer (2013) analyzes the pluricentric enregisterment of standard variation with a focus on Swiss and Austrian standard German registers. He uses Agha's concept of *enregisterment*, i.e. "processes and practices whereby performable signs become recognized (and regrouped) as belonging to distinct, differentially valorized semiotic registers by a population" (Agha 2007:81). In a semiotic process of *indexicalization*, speakers attach social meaning(s) such as courtesy, modernity, sloppiness, correctness, authenticity, geospatial origin etc. to certain linguistic features. One form of indexicality in meta-linguistic discourses of speakers is that linguistic fea-

---

6. All human practices in which "language, actions, interactions, ways of thinking, believing, valuing and using various symbols, tools, and objects" serve "to enact a particular sort of socially recognizable identity" (cf. Gee 2005:21).

tures can be associated with stereotypes of speakers and become part of a stylized *register*. A community of speakers stereotypes its "own" register in order to perform group identity. Psychologically speaking, the group must eliminate factual similarities with "other" groups as well as factual differences among members of their "own" group (*erasure*, cf. Irvine & Gal 2000: 38). In other words, they establish stereotypes of out-group speakers (hetero-stereotypes) and of in-group speakers (auto-stereotypes).

For standard variation in German, this means that speakers can, for instance, enregister their "own" national variety: They create a list of linguistic features they consider indices of their national identity, passed on in interaction, popular collections, or — in terms of language planning — in codices relevant to implementation at school.[7] During this discursive process, they tend to omit or *erase* factual in-group variation which opposes national categories (cf. Auer 2013: 41), i.e. innernational differences (cf. de Cillia & Ransmayr 2019: 224). Speakers enregister variants which they perceive as salient (cf. Auer 2013: 32) since those refer to a relevant linguistic ideology. This could, for example, be the idea that national borders should have an effect on language use and determine a speaker's identity. I define saliency broadly as a type of conspicuity for physiological (predominantly auditive), cognitive (contrast-perceiving) or sociolinguistic (emotional-affective) reasons, e.g. speech rate, passive/active linguistic competence, or psychological needs satisfaction, respectively (cf. Auer 2014: 9–14). The latter type of saliency is likely the most urgent motivation for enregisterment (cf. Auer 2014: 9–14).

Among other reasons, Auer utilizes enregisterment to explain the geographic variation in standard German because he is critical of the term "center". He argues that center is often understood to refer to a nation, but evokes the image of several central locations that "radiate" into a periphery: Germany's standard radiates into every other nation or region, most intensively into East Belgium and Luxembourg, Switzerland's standard radiates into Liechtenstein, and Austria's standard radiates into South Tyrol (cf. Auer 2021: 32–35). The radiation refers to speakers' attitudes towards standards as well as their orientation towards codices. In Austria, for example, a "dual standard" has emerged, consisting of a perceived supraregional standard on the one hand, the *Duden* from Germany, and a national standard on the other hand, the *Österreichisches Wörterbuch* (ÖWB), (cf. Auer 2021: 34; Lenz et al. 2022: 46).

However, Auer argues that we still cannot define clear locations which establish and cultivate norms such as national capitals, nor can we detect a central group of speakers other than "standard speakers", at least not without an elitist

---

7. Ultimately, the register becomes part of a 'communicative memory', later 'cultural memory' (cf. Assmann 2008).

focus on educated speakers (Auer 2021: 35). Hence, pluricentricity "fails to cover the variety of multi-standard languages in the world today" and "presupposes the existence of various centres with their peripheries, without providing a clear and meaningful definition of these centres" (Auer 2021: 35). In a first step, I will try to define what a center could be and distinguish between usage centers and ideological centers.

3.2 Regional pluricentricity revisited: Usage centers

Firstly, I propose to utilize *regiocentricity* (cf. Niehaus 2015)[8] in order to clarify the centers of language use: *Regiocentricity* refers to quantitative "core" areas (*centers*) where certain standard variants are most frequent. These are areas where it is safe to assume that the most similar norms of usage will be at work. The concept is comparable to regional pluricentricity (cf. Reiffenstein 2001) which stresses underlying and overlapping regional structures in otherwise plurinational contexts. However, regiocentricity does not take "center varieties" for granted but further specifies centers by quantification, namely "areas of density" ("the most *dense* form", cf. e.g. Millar 2005: 1; Berruto 2010: 229) or "usage patterns" (Schneider 2022: 471). In these areas, a frequency peak of specific phonetic, spelling, lexical, grammatical, and pragma-linguistic variants occurs and creates a geospatial cluster (cf. Niehaus 2015: 164). Based on the current empirical evidence (see 2.1), some areas can be seen as *usage centers* in the sense of frequency clusters, namely "the North" (northern Germany, north-western Germany in particular), "the West" (central western Germany, East Belgium, Luxembourg, parts of south-western Germany [esp. the Baden region]), "the East" (northern and central East Germany, i.e. the former GDR), and "the South" (all of southern Germany, Austria, Switzerland, Liechtenstein, South Tyrol as well as Bavaria, Austria, and Switzerland taken separately). As can be seen, all of these centers overlap with others. Moreover, empirical analyses reveal further geographical specifics, e.g. a west-east-divide in Austria, and a highly frequent use of several variants per center (cf. Elspaß & Kleiner 2019: 171). As yet, Switzerland seems to be the area with the

---

8. *Regio-* emphasizes sub- and transnational variation as the more frequent type of "center" in language use but can also indicate a national distribution of variants on a more global scale (e.g. one nation as a regional center in Europe). This could avoid the terminological pitfalls of the 'pluri'-debate. I will use the term subsequently for structures in language use, although readers not wholly comfortable with this may prefer "regionally pluricentric" ('regional pluricentricity'), "pluriareal" ("pluriareality") or even "multiple" ("multi-standard") without grievous consequences for the overarching argument.

highest number of nation-exclusive variants (cf. Eichinger 2005: 156–158 for lexis; Niehaus 2015: 161 for syntax).

3.3 Enregisterment in *ideological centers*

Secondly, the emergence of socially meaningful geographic standards is yet to be explained in more theoretical and empirical detail (cf. Auer 2021: 45), especially with regards to the different forms of a linguistic nationalization in German since the late 19th century (cf. von Polenz 1999: 412, Reiffenstein 2001).

As Auer (2021: 44) notes, use, ideology, and indexicality interact: An ideology is based on perceived (salient) language use, allowing for an indexicalization of variants. During enregisterment, language use is either "blown up" or "shrunk" via ideology and indexicalization (cf. Auer 2021: 44). Salient features are either perceived as more widespread or more restricted than empirical evidence suggests.

I argue that in most cases the perception is orientated to a factual usage center. This interaction of use and ideology is mediated through attitudes, strengthening or weakening tendencies in actual language use such as a nationalization of standard usage. In other words: Regiocentric "core" areas either are the cause or the consequence of enregisterment. The idea of any geographic enregisterment will more easily appeal to speakers whose language use overall corresponds to a usage center. During subsequent processes of enregisterment, the most influential speakers are any kind of "ideology brokers" (Blommaert 2005: 520). In the case of standard registers, special attention must be paid to individual and institutional norm authorities and their self-legitimization efforts in public discourses, e.g. in codification, mass media, and language policy in educational institutions. Ideology brokers normally establish an *ideological center* in discourse – a center in a metaphorical sense. Broadly speaking, an ideological center is a center of perceived "correct or authentic language use by some individuals" (Langer 2021b: 85). An ideological center could, for example, be a prototypical text or source, e.g., a codex, concerned with sociolinguistic topics or objects to which other metalinguistic artifacts regularly refer to explicitly or implicitly. The discourse may change over time and include new objects and topics, but at each given time the discourse revolves around some "core" issues, e.g. certain fields of lexis. Ideological centers may overlap with each other, just as usage centers. For instance, multiple standard codices within the same language are ideological centers. In settings of geographical standard variation, it is likely that different ideological centers originate in different geographic spaces. This is the case with Austria's "dual standard" (Auer 2021: 34).

3.4 Terminology and preliminary framework

Auer (2013, 2021) — in a traditional pluricentric turn — defines centers solely based on attitudes and codification despite "regional pluricentricity" being an "undisputed fact" in language use (Auer 2013: 40). This resembles Ammon (1995: 212–213) who uses a model of "region of use vs. region of validity/prestige" in which validity eventually trumps use. I believe that we need to address the different notions of normativity more cautiously by looking more closely at how they interact with each other and establish usage and ideological centers. Moreover, I am convinced a truly integrational approach must not favor one or the other.

Ammon's model is an apt starting point to incorporate the previous findings in a single framework, but falls short of a comprehensive inclusion of the interaction of use and indexicality. Moreover, the processual character of any kind of norm has to be made more explicit than in his model.

For this, I utilize the terminological differentiations in Pickl (2020), as they are useful in distinguishing the different types of normativity. Pickl distinguishes emic ideological *criteria* like pureness, correctness, authenticity, and etic, variational *factors* of language use like age, gender, geographical space (cf. Pickl 2020: 238). Both make for the selection of features which must be considered part of a standard language. This also means that a standard language consists of varieties as well as registers.[9]

An etic regiocentric standard *variety* in language use corresponds to a usage center, identified via density and frequency in model texts such as newspaper reports.

The enregisterment of linguistic features establishes an emic standard *register* which corresponds to an ideological center, identified via analysis of metalinguistic discourse such as the identification of indexicalized features and ideology brokers. Note that neither center is predefined but must be identified via empirical analysis.

In my approach, attitudes do not contribute directly to the formation of a standard. In other words, attitudes alone do not suffice for measurements of a variety or a register. They do, however, influence the choice of language use as well as the ideological selection of features. As the examples will show, they function as a perceptional mediator which modifies (confirms or corrects) acts of language use as well as acts of indexicality, built on specific cognitive, affective, and conative *constraints*.[10] For example, the use of a previously unknown geographic variant in a standard context may lead a speaker to rethink his or her attitude

---

9. Similarly pointed out by Lenz et al. (2022: 32).
10. On the trilogy of cognitive, affective, and conative parts of a theory of mind cf. e.g. Hilgard (1980); this tripartite concept has its limitations (cf. Koppensteiner & Lenz 2020: 50) but will suffice for a first differentiation.

towards geographic variation, which in turn can be reflected in a correction of ideology, i.e. a more strict or a more liberal view of correctness. Note that this is not a comprehensive take on attitudes which needs more empirical evidence in order to become clearer in theory. The important point is that language attitudes should neither be viewed as an overly ideologically biased aspect which is theoretically unsuitable for any definition of standard, nor as the empirical backbone of standard; they assume a middle position in which they reveal the specifics of how perception influences language use as well as enregisterment.

Thus, we need all three aspects – use, attitudes, and indexicality – to get "the full picture" of a standard language. I have provided a basic summary of these aspects in Figure 4.1.

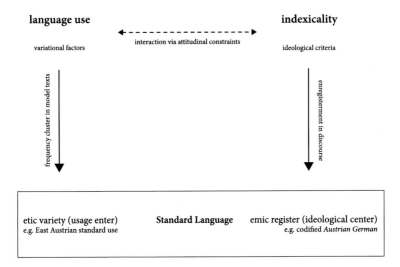

Figure 4.1 An integrational approach toward geographic variation in standard German

I would like to illustrate the approach subsequently in two examples of nationalization in standard German, namely: (1) supra-regional nationalization and (2) specific nationalization, such as in Austria. That being said, enregisterment processes are highly sensitive to context. As far as standard German is concerned, enregisterment need not stop at the national level. For instance, Bavaria is a usage center of standard German and, from time to time, shows certain efforts of enregisterment such as Zehetner's dictionary (cf. Zehetner 2018) and the promotion of a Bavarian-centered *Südhochdeutsch* 'Southern Standard German' (Bund Bairische Sprache 2024). Still, the development of Bavaria into a full-fledged ideological center is unlikely without an implementation in regional administration and educational institutions as well as other political action against the contemporary indexicalization of "Bavarian" as a nonstandard repertoire of regional folklore (cf. Niehaus 2021: 73–74).

4. Examples

4.1 Supra-regional nationalization

The historical linguistic ideology all further beliefs build on is monocentrism, which is in line with the idea of *Binnendeutsch* (cf. von Polenz 1999: 412–419).

In Germany, national enregisterment supports this view up to today: Northern 'German standard German' counts as 'actual' and 'good' German (cf. von Polenz 1999: 416). The idea goes back to the 19th century pan-Germanic nationalist ideology of *Sprachnation* where language, ethnicity, and national territory were inseparable — the *one nation, one language ideology* (cf. von Polenz 1999: 413; Millar 2005: 17–18; Stevenson et al. 2018: 16). The result of the nationalist movement in German-speaking areas was the only German-by-name nation state of the 19th century, the German Empire (1872–1918), dominated by the northern kingdom of Prussia. In the wake of these events, German ideology brokers (from Prussia) played a crucial part in the first codifications of pronunciation and official spelling (cf. von Polenz 1999: 413). Despite a few concessions to geographic variation, the most relevant ideological criterion was uniformity. Prussian language use and norm authorities dominated the perception of a 'uniform' standard German. While the notion of *nation* has long since shifted away from pan-Germanism (Langer 2021b: 79), the idea of monocentrism continues to be perpetuated in various ways.

If Germans perform a public national group identity at all, they tend to stylize a uniform standard (cf. von Polenz 1999: 416), while regional group identity can be indexed via regional standard, dialect, or regiolect features (cf. e.g. Niehaus 2021: 73). The conceptualizations of standard on display here — uniform vs. regional — conflict only from an etic perspective such as a researcher's outsider perspective. From an emic perspective, a speaker's insider perspective, they do not contradict each other — after all, different identities in different contexts are construed (cf. Niehaus 2021: 75). The ideological "blow-up" of northern, "Prussian" features to supra-regional features and the disregard for geographic standard variation are, for instance, evident in regional schoolbooks in Germany (cf. Maitz 2015). This perceived supra-regional, but factual northern, German standard is also what speakers often call "pure" or "real" *Hochdeutsch* 'lit.: High German' (cf. Koppensteiner & Lenz 2020: 56–57).

Monocentrism is also still present in Austria and Switzerland, especially with standard pronunciation. Perceptional data on the 'dialectness' of usage-based standards (e.g. Kehrein 2009) and the 'best' spoken German (cf. e.g. Schmidlin 2011: 268–270) reveals the supra-regional linguistic ideology is still at work in German-speaking countries. Maitz (2015: 208) has called this ideology *Hanoverism*, i.e.

the belief that the 'best', 'purest' and 'most correct' spoken German is northern German, to be more exact: the German spoken in the north-western town of Hanover.[11] Besides, many speakers are under the impression that people in the culture and media industry, and more educated people speak the 'best' German (cf. Schmidlin 2011: 272–275). This linguistic *elitism*, often combined with *Hanoverism*, seems to be prevalent in Germany but is also common in other German-speaking areas (cf. Schmidlin 2011: 275, Koppensteiner & Lenz 2020: 51). A negative conative constraint of Austrians' and Swiss' attitudes toward "national" standard variants concerns social status and follows the monocentric idea (cf. Lenz et al. 2022: 47), resulting in corrections toward a perceived supra-regional, factual northern German standard. The latter is said to be spreading in general usage — especially phonetic and lexical variants seem to radiate into "the South", although more empirical evidence is needed to back such claims (cf. e.g. de Cillia & Ransmayr 2019: 226). Furthermore, perceived supra-regional German indexes "seriousness" and "professionality" in several situations most forcefully. This indexicality is probably due to the early introduction of northern linguistic norms in educational institutions, e.g. in Austrian schools in the 18th century, and the subsequent feelings of inferiority in southern areas and nations (cf. Stevenson et al. 2018: 60–62). In that sense, Austrian speakers today can utilize "Prussian" variants to index "supra-regional standardness". Yet, they can also utilize lexemes perceived as distinctive for Germany such as *Treppe*, 'stairs' or *Tschüs!* 'bye-bye!' either to create new forms not common in Germany, e.g. *Treppe-rl* 'small stairs', *ver-tschüss-en* 'to say bye-bye' (cf. Pichler 2015: 195–208), or to exploit the "Germaness" of these variants and ironize transnational linguistic competency (cf. Glauninger 2015: 46–47; Niehaus 2024). In these latter cases, monocentrism may still be the basic concept but feelings of inferiority are highly unlikely.

The current perceptual and attitudinal data do not hold up to a general cognitive structure of "pluricentric enregisterment". The idea of pluricentricity remains comparatively rare, in Germany as well as in Austria and Switzerland (cf. Herrgen 2015: 155; de Cillia & Ransmayr 2019: 115, 224; Studler 2019: 416–417). Monocentrism is still effective for historical reasons. (Northern) Germany and respective discursive artifacts such as the *Duden* codex can be regarded as the crucial ideological center of this ideology.

However, attitudinal evidence shows a cognitive and affective saliency of national accents, i.e. to recognize national accents and attribute emotional evaluations to them respectively. This is linked to the specific nationalization explained in the next section.

---

11. Strikingly, speakers do not conceptualize a location of the "best" *written* German (cf. Schmidlin 2011: 277).

4.2 Specific nationalization

Post-war politics in Austria and, to a lesser degree, in Switzerland called for the need to distance oneself from Germany's *Reichsdeutsch* and establish a distinct national form of German. The perception of Germany's overpowering normative dominance was maintained but modified. In line with the equation of *nation* and *state*, both countries, especially Austria, took an opposing stance toward the pan-Germanic *Sprachnation* (cf. von Polenz 1999: 416; Niehaus to appear) using the ideological criterion of "Non-Germanness". Until today, asymmetric pluricentricity anchors in a national double stereotyping, i.e. an over-generalized comparison of 'us' (Austrians, Swiss) vs. 'the others' (Germans). Speakers from Austria and, less pronounced, from Switzerland contrast "their" respective standard German to a monolithic *German German* while Germans supposedly do not usually reflect on any national features in standard German (cf. Auer 2013: 41). Standard German variants which index national identity often stem from regiocentric use, i.e. socially meaningful standard variants are variants used in specific intranational usage centers. In Austria, East Austrian or Viennese features can be considered *Demonstrationsaustriazismen* 'showcase austriacisms' of national identity (cf. Ammon 1995: 154–155, 204–206) even with speakers who are not from that area (cf. Niehaus 2024). In Switzerland, more rural variants index national identity, especially the north-eastern Swiss uvular variants [x]/[χ] (cf. Christen 2019: 246, 255). Austrian and Swiss speakers often stereotype features of 'the North' to stylize *German German* (von Polenz 1999: 418). This includes pragmatics, e.g. "fast and loud delivery" or directness with complaints – both index rudeness as opposed to Swiss and Austrian indirectness and politeness (cf. Auer 2013: 37). Additionally, specific idiomatic expressions are utilized as a phonetic iconization of a perceived German efficiency like *ruck zuck* 'in no time', *zack zack* 'hurry up! chop chop!' as opposed to a laid-back feeling in Austria and Switzerland (cf. Auer 2013: 37). The ideology at hand refers to a common social hetero-stereotype of Germans and their presumably hegemonic and inconsiderate demeanor (cf. Ammon 1995: 214–225 for Austria, 305–316 for Switzerland).

Linguistic stereotyping *erases* the regional or even local origins of most variants (usage centers) and is a crucial phase in national enregisterment. Intricacies start here since Austrians and Swiss speakers not only utilize standard features to enregister a national form of German but also – or in the case of Swiss often exclusively – non-standard features (cf. Auer 2013: 41), which conforms with attitudinal studies (see 2.2). Hence, standard features do not constitute a separate "language" of identity but act as a supplement within a national register in Agha's sense (cf. Agha 2007). From an etic perspective, the structural differentiation between "language", "dialect", or "colloquial speech" is of vital importance. From an emic perspective, the relevance of such a distinction is highly sensitive to context. Even within a standard language context, speakers can mix their in-group codes to index that non-standard is part of their national identity (cf. Glauninger 2015: 44–46), a performance which does not establish a "national standard variety" but a "national register". For instance, the register of *Austrian German* in popular YouTube videos draws on perceived national standard variants as well as East Austrian non-standard features. Moreover, YouTube influencers assign an ironic "language" status to *Austrian German*, not to postulate a separate language, but to clarify to their viewers that national identity is not solely a question of a national standard variety but of all linguistic repertoires (cf. Niehaus 2024).

Austrian national enregisterment is dominated by East Austria, in particular Vienna, which has been the capital of today's Austria and its predecessors as well as the center of national mass media. In addition, an official device of language planning, the ÖWB, has been endorsing a Viennese-centered enregisterment of *Austrian German* since its inception in post-war Austria (cf. Stevenson et al. 2018: 61, Langer 2021a: 6; Niehaus to appear). The ÖWB is still a mandatory dictionary at school and an important symbol of national independence from Germany (cf. Ammon 1995: 128). It includes not only standard variants but also colloquial or dialect features, with a strong focus on East Austrian usage. In addition, national educational tools such as schoolbooks are licensed in Vienna. The focus on language planning discourse for Vienna and its norm authorities explains why some East Austrian features have become enregistered as "showcase" austriacisms and why East Austria has considerable power in the discourse on national linguistic identity. The existence of such an ideological center consequently also explains why East Austrians tend to have more positive attitudes toward a national form of German than West Austrians. Such attitudes can be regarded as the visible surface of the interaction between language use and indexicality. East Austrians accept the idea of a monolithic Austrian German more often than West Austrians (cf. de Cillia & Ransmayr 2019: 140–141), even though the Western Austrian usage center is sufficiently similar to the Eastern usage center. However, due to these similarities, West Austrians still can pick up on the national enregisterment and respective register for ideological reasons – such as national belonging – so that West Austrian claims of authority in national codification efforts are directed at Viennese norm authorities and their artifacts such as the ÖWB as the ideological center (cf. Niehaus to appear). The power in discourse in this example "radiates" from East Austria, particularly Vienna, into West Austria. Even speakers from other regions in Austria can use register features to affirm themselves of their *Austrianness*, and intensified language contact through higher inner-Austrian mobility acts as a "catalyst" for East Austrian features in everyday use. The consequence is an "ideological blow-up" of regional East Austrian to national Austrian features (cf. Auer 2021: 44), a linguistic nationalization first in discourse, then in actual use.

To give an example: The ÖWB indicates which variants are 'non-domestic', 'neighborly' *German German* (cf. Ammon 1995: 181–196). This suggests that the latter variants may be common in Austria but should not be used since they are not 'authentic', i.e. autochthonous, Austrian features: The ÖWB, therefore, attempts to purify *Austrian German* (cf. Ammon 1995: 183–184) from stylistic use which builds on monocentric ideas (see Section 4.1). The history of *Jänner* 'January' is an example of such a purification. *Jänner* nowadays is one of the rare absolute 'austriacisms' (cf. Lenz et al. 2016: 354). Scheuringer (1998) observes that *Januar* had overtaken *Jänner* but when the former was marked 'non-domestic' by the ÖWB it fell out of use in school textbooks and *Jänner* superseded *Januar*.

Austria, and to a lesser degree also Switzerland, have developed a *Nationalvarietäten-Purismus* 'purism of national variety' (cf. Ammon 1995: 184–186). This includes, for example, opposing the influence of *Piefkinesisch* 'German German (derog.)' in Austria (cf. Stevenson et al. 2018: 127). An emotional-affective constraint for social attractiveness based on nation-purist criteria is at work here and has created a national standard (cf. Auer 2021: 34, 39–45; Lenz et al. 2022: 47), which now can be fiercely demanded from German migrants in Austria and leads to explicit discriminatory attitudes from some Austrian speakers (cf. Greth & Köllen 2016). In any case, national enregisterment "radiates" from ideological centers and ideology brokers to peripheral discursive areas, encouraging use among fellow nationals while discouraging use among others. For instance, the codification of features as "Austrian" or "Swiss" German discourages use among South Germans, notwithstanding any shared standards of usage in the larger "South" usage center. There is one last caveat — the empirical evidence so far suggests that processes of national enregisterment are more apparent in Austria than in Switzerland. I would argue that this is because Switzerland has not established a clear ideological center. This may be not only due to its official multilingualism, but also due to its stronger federalism which is said to foster a certain *Kantönligeist* 'mentality of particularism (neg.).' On the other hand, the impression of a more fiercely promoted *Austrian German* could also be a mere artifact of the present research focus on Austria's 'dual standard'.

5. Summary and outlook

As we have seen, enregisterment analyzes and explains the discrepancy between regional standards in language use and perceived national standard varieties. It was argued that national enregisterment concentrates on features of usage centers within a nation and that a usage center will correspond to an ideological center.

The focus on language ideologies also resolves a common paradox in attitudes — a speaker may display a certain sympathy toward national variation in standard German in some contexts, but intolerance toward it in others. The intra-individual co-existence of monocentrism and national purism is also why 'pureness' cannot be equated with 'standardness' in attitudinal studies (cf. Koppensteiner & Lenz 2020: 73–74). Although perceived *German German* receives higher ratings of "pureness" among Austrian listeners (in accordance with monocentrism), it can still be regarded as inadequate for standard contexts like Austrian newscasting (in accordance with national purism). Finally, enregisterment also accounts for the changing notions of *nation* during the standardization of German as the two examples of nationalization illustrate. I hope to have shown that my approach considers the differing aspects of normativity and therefore allows for pluriareal as well as pluricentric analyses.

Future pluriareal research, while already sufficiently capturing language use, should focus more on attitudes and indices to explain geographic structures, i.e. cross-check the social relevance of such structures: Why are only certain geographical structures relevant in standard variation, despite the data-driven approach? How exactly do federal states, districts, dialect continua, economic catchment areas etc. shape the picture of frequency centers? Why should "linguistic justice" (Oakes 2021) not only apply to national standards but any geographical standard?

Vice versa, pluricentric research underpins national linguistic symbolism and attitudes toward standard variation but would benefit from acknowledging statistical measurements of usage centers and seeing them not as a theoretically inferior type of normativity but as a *different* type of normativity. This would also lead to a higher sensitivity toward different contexts of identity construction. After all, national identity is of immediate indexical relevance first and foremost in bi-national or international contexts as given in the examples of enregisterment above.[12]

I am convinced that future endeavors in that vein would facilitate a terminological solution of the 'pluri'-debate. As said before, this first draft needs further refinement through empirical evidence. The approach could also be applied onto other "bigger" standardized languages. This holds especially true with nations and regions which share a common language with various standards and a geographic closeness, ideally a direct border: Spanish in the Americas, Dutch in Europe, and World Englishes in various neighboring nations and regions make for promising cases. In a similar fashion, the ideas laid out here may also prove fruitful for diachronic analyses, e.g. the standardization of "national languages"

---

12. A point also made by Auer (2013: 41).

within the historical south Slavic dialect continuum or the historical northern Germanic dialect-continuum in Scandinavia where usage-based centers may not always match ideological centers (cf. e.g. Höder 2017 for the case of standard Norwegian *nynorsk*). In particular, the "radiation" of density in use as well as of power in discourse seems to connect well with the notion of "gravity" in language change (cf. Chambers & Trudgill 1998), a thought which could be explored further. An integrational approach could also help to resolve the debate on "epicenters" in World Englishes (cf. e.g. Schneider 2022; Schneider, this volume) if we accept the different types of *norms* as part of the picture of a standard language and include ideologies more rigorously. In addition, an approach including enregisterment would also contribute to revisions of Haugen's standardization model in the vein of Ayres-Bennett's recent modifications (cf. Ayres-Bennett 2021: 51–55). In particular, codification procedures should be seen as enregisterment processes (cf. Androutsopoulos & Busch 2020: 14; Niehaus to appear).

As for pluricentricity and pluriareality, the issue of terminology remains. Recently, "pluricentricity/-areality" has been used by some scholars (e.g. Dürscheid & Schneider 2019, Schmidlin to appear), and Auer (2021) has proposed the more neutral "multi-standard". I think both attempts are a step in the right direction. Whatever terminology we eventually prefer, pluricentricity and pluriareality should not struggle for dominance in sociolinguistic paradigms but see each other's benefits and limitations. I hope to have demonstrated that a stronger theoretical focus on language ideologies is an invaluable addition in that respect, and that enregisterment is a necessity of a future, more robust, sociolinguistic theory of standard languages.

References

Agha, Asif. 2007. *Language and Social Relations.* Cambridge: Cambridge University Press.

Ammon, Ulrich. 1995. *Die deutsche Sprache in Deutschland, Österreich und der Schweiz. Das Problem der nationalen Varietäten.* Berlin, New York: De Gruyter.

Ammon, Ulrich, Hans Bickel, Jakob Ebner et al. 2004. *Variantenwörterbuch des Deutschen. Die deutsche Standardsprache in Österreich, der Schweiz und Deutschland sowie in Liechtenstein, Luxemburg, Ostbelgien und Südtirol.* Berlin, New York: de Gruyter.

Androutsopoulos, Jannis & Florian Busch (ed.). 2020. Register des Graphischen. *Register des Graphischen* (Linguistik — Impulse und Tendenzen 87), 1–29. Berlin, Boston: De Gruyter.

Assmann, Jan. 2008. Communicative and Cultural Memory. In Astrid Erll & Ansgar Nünning (eds.), *Cultural Memory Studies. An International and Interdisciplinary Handbook* (Media and Cultural Memory / Medien und Kulturelle Erinnerung 8), 109–118. Berlin, New York: De Gruyter.

Auer, Peter. 2013. Enregistering pluricentric German. In Augusto Soares da Silva (ed.), *Pluricentricity. Language Variation and Sociocognitive Dimensions* (Applications of Cognitive Linguistics 24), 19–48. Berlin, Boston: De Gruyter.

Auer, Peter. 2014. Anmerkungen zum Salienzbegriff in der Soziolinguistik. *Linguistik Online*, vol. 66, 7–20, (16 August 2021).

Auer, Peter. 2021. Reflections on linguistic pluricentricity. *Sociolinguistica*, vol. 35, 29–47.

Ayres-Bennett, Wendy. 2021. Modelling Language Standardization. In Wendy Ayres-Bennett & John Bellamy (eds.), *The Cambridge Handbook of Language Standardization* (Cambridge Handbooks in Language and Linguistics), 27–64. Cambridge: Cambridge University Press.

Berruto, Gaetano. 2010. Identifying dimensions of linguistic variation in a language space. In Peter Auer & Jürgen Erich Schmidt (eds.), *Language and space. An international handbook of linguistic variation. Volume 1: Theories and methods.* (Handbook of Linguistics and Communication Science / Handbücher zur Sprach – und Kommunikationswissenschaft 30.4), 226–241. Berlin, Boston: De Gruyter.

Blommaert, Jan. 2005. Language Ideologies. In Keith Brown (ed.), *Encyclopaedia of Language and Linguistics*. Oxford: Elsevier. 510–523.

Bund Bairische Sprache. 2024. Südhochdeutsch. https://www.bund-bairische-sprache.de/s%C3%BCdhochdeutsch/

Chambers, Jack K. & Peter Trudgill. 1998. *Dialectology*, 2nd edn. (Cambridge Textbooks in Linguistics). Cambridge: Cambridge University Press.

Christen, Helen. 2019. Alemannisch in der Schweiz. In Joachim Herrgen & Jürgen Erich Schmidt (eds.), *Sprache und Raum. Ein internationales Handbuch der Sprachvariation. Band 4: Deutsch / Language and Space. An International Handbook of Linguistic Variation. Volume 4: German* (Handbook of Linguistics and Communication Science / Handbücher zur Sprach – und Kommunikationswissenschaft 30.4), 246–279. Berlin, Boston: De Gruyter.

de Cillia, Rudolf & Jutta Ransmayr. 2019. *Österreichisches Deutsch macht Schule. Bildung und Deutschunterricht im Spannungsfeld von sprachlicher Variation und Norm*. Wien: Böhlau.

Clyne, Michael G. 1982. Österreichisches Standarddeutsch und andere Nationalvarianten: Zur Frage Sprache und Nationalidentität. In Leslie Bodi, & Philip Thomson (eds.), *Das Problem Österreich. Interdisziplinäre Konferenz über Geschichte, Kultur und Gesellschaft Österreichs im 20. Jahrhundert*, 54–67. Melbourne: Monash University.

Clyne, Michael. 1995. *The German language in a changing Europe*. Cambridge: Cambridge University Press.

Dürscheid, Christa, Stephan Elspaß & Arne Ziegler. 2011. Grammatische Variabilität im Gebrauchsstandard: das Projekt „Variantengrammatik des Standarddeutschen". In Marek Konopka, Jacqueline Kubczak, Christian Mair, František Štícha & Ulrich H. Wassner (eds.), *Grammatik und Korpora 2009. Dritte Internationale Konferenz. Mannheim 22.–24.09.2009* (Korpuslinguistik und interdisziplinäre Perspektiven auf Sprache/Corpus Linguistics and Interdisciplinary Perspectives on Language. 1), 123–140. Tübingen: Narr.

Dürscheid, Christa & Jan Georg Schneider. 2019. *Standardsprache und Variation* (narr starter). Tübingen: Narr.

Eichinger, Ludwig M. 2005. Norm und regionale Variation. Zur realen Existenz nationaler Varietäten. In Alexandra N. Lenz & Klaus J. Mattheier (eds.), *Varietäten – Theorie und Empirie* (VarioLingua 23), 141–162. Frankfurt a. Main: Peter Lang.

Elspaß, Stephan & Stefan Kleiner. 2019. Forschungsergebnisse zur arealen Variation im Standarddeutschen. In Joachim Herrgen & Jürgen Erich Schmidt (eds.), *Sprache und Raum. Ein internationales Handbuch der Sprachvariation. Band 4: Deutsch / Language and Space. An International Handbook of Linguistic Variation. Volume 4: German* (Handbook of Linguistics and Communication Science / Handbücher zur Sprach – und Kommunikationswissenschaft 30.4), 159–184. Berlin, Boston: De Gruyter.

Gee, James Paul. 2005. *An introduction to discourse analysis: Theory and method*, 2 edn New York & London: Routledge.

Glauninger, Manfred. 2015. (Standard-)Deutsch in Österreich im Kontext des gesamtdeutschen Sprachraums. Perspektiven einer funktional dimensionierten Sprachvariationstheorie. In Alexandra N. Lenz & Manfred M. Glauninger (eds.), *Standarddeutsch im 21. Jahrhundert – Theoretische und empirische Ansätze mit einem Fokus auf Österreich* (Wiener Arbeiten zur Linguistik 1), 11–57. Göttingen: V&R Vienna university press.

Greth, Julia & Thomas Köllen. 2016. Perceived Anti-Germanism in Austria. *Studies in Ethnicity and Nationalism*, vol. 16, 40–62.

Herrgen, Joachim. 2015. Entnationalisierung des Standards. Eine perzeptionslinguistische Untersuchung zur deutschen Standardsprache in Deutschland, Österreich und der Schweiz. In Alexandra N. Lenz & Manfred M. Glauninger (eds.), *Standarddeutsch im 21. Jahrhundert – Theoretische und empirische Ansätze mit einem Fokus auf Österreich* (Wiener Arbeiten zur Linguistik 1), 139–164. Göttingen: V&R Vienna university press.

Hilgard, Ernest R. 1980. The trilogy of Mind: Cognition, affection, and conation. *Journal of the History of the Behavioral Sciences*, vol. 16, 107–117.

Höder, Steffen. 2017. Dialekte und konkurriende Standards: Indexikalitätsressourcen im Norwegischen. In Lieselotte Anderwald & Jarich Hoekstra (eds.), *Enregisterment. Zur sozalen Bedeutung sprachlicher Variation* (Kieler Forschungen zur Sprachwissenschaft 8), 189–205. Peter Land: Frankfurt a. Main.

Irvine, Judith T. & Susan Gal. 2000. Language ideology and linguistic differentiation. In Paul V. Kroskrity (ed.), *Regimes of Language: Ideologies, Polities, and Identities*, 35–83. Santa Fe, New Mexico: School of American Research Press.

Kaiser, Irmtraud, Andrea Ender & Gudrun Kasberger. 2019. Varietäten des österreichischen Deutsch aus der HörerInnenperspektive: Diskriminationsfähigkeiten und sozio-indexikalische Interpretation. In Lars Bülow, Ann Kathrin Fischer & Kristina Herbert (eds.), *Dimensions of Linguistic Space: Variation – Multilingualism – Conceptualisations. Dimensionen des sprachlichen Raums: Variation – Mehrsprachigkeit – Konzeptualisierung*, 341–362. Wien: Peter Lang.

Kehrein, Roland. 2009. Dialektalität von Vorleseaussprache im diatopischen Vergleich – Hörerurteil und phonetische Messung. *Zeitschrift für Dialektologie und Linguistik*, vol. 76,14–54.

Kellermeier-Rehbein, Birte. 2014. *Plurizentrik. Eine Einführung in die nationalen Varietäten des Deutschen*. Berlin: ESV.

Kleiner, Stefan. 2011–present. *Atlas zur Aussprache des deutschen Gebrauchsstandards (AADG)*. Unter Mitarbeit von Ralf Knöbl. http://prowiki.ids-mannheim.de/bin/view/AADG (16 August 2021).

Koller, Werner. 1999. Nationale Sprach(en)kultur in der Schweiz und die Frage der „nationalen Varietäten des Deutschen". In Andreas Gardt, Ulrike Haß-Zumkehr & Thorsten Roelcke (eds.), *Sprachgeschichte als Kulturgeschichte* (Studia Linguistica Germanica 54), 133–170. Berlin, New York: De Gruyter.

Koppensteiner, Wolfgang & Alexandra N. Lenz. 2020. Tracing a standard language in Austria using methodological microvariations of Verbal and Matched Guise Technique. *Linguistik Online*, vol. 102, 47–82.

Langer, Nils. 2021a. Review of: Stefan Dollinger. 2019. The Pluricentricity Debate. On Austrian German and other Germanic Standard Varieties (Routledge Focus). Abingdon: Routledge. *Zeitschrift für Rezensionen zur germanistischen Sprachwissenschaft*, 1–8.

Langer, Nils. 2021b. Pluricentricity and minority languages: the difficult case of North Frisian. *Sociolinguistica*, vol. 35, 73–90.

Lenz, Alexandra N., Ulrich Ammon & Hans Bickel. 2016. *Variantenwörterbuch des Deutschen. Die Standardsprache in Österreich, der Schweiz, Deutschland, Liechtenstein, Luxemburg, Ostbelgien und Südtirol sowie Rumänien, Namibia und Mennonitensiedlungen*. Berlin, Boston: De Gruyter.

Lenz, Alexandra N., Barbara Soukup & Wolfgang Koppensteiner (eds.). 2022. Standard German in Austria from the folk perspective: Conceptualizations, attitudes, perceptions. *Standard Languages in Germanic-speaking Europe: Attitudes and Perception*, 23–57. Oslo: Novus.

Maitz, Péter. 2015. Sprachvariation, sprachliche Ideologien und Schule. *Zeitschrift für Dialektologie und Linguistik*, vol. 82, 206–227.

Millar, Robert McColl. 2005. *Language, Nation and Power*. Basingstoke: Palgrave Macmillan.

Moser, Hugo. 1959. Neuere und neueste Zeit. Von den 80er Jahren des 19. Jahrhunderts zur Gegenwart. In Friedrich Maurer & Friedrich Stroh (eds.), *Deutsche Wortgeschichte*, Band 2, zweite, neubearbeitete Auflage, (Grundriss der germanischen Philologie 17), 445–560. Berlin: De Gruyter.

Niehaus, Konstantin. 2015. Areale Variation in der Syntax des Standarddeutschen. Ergebnisse zum Sprachgebrauch und zur Frage Plurizentrik vs. Pluriarealität. *Zeitschrift für Dialektologie und Linguistik*, vol. 82, 133–168.

Niehaus, Konstantin. 2021. Regionale Identitäten im mehrsprachigen Bayern. Eine soziolinguistische Annäherung. *Zeitschrift für Dialektologie und Linguistik*, vol. 88, 57–84.

Niehaus, Konstantin. in press. Double standards in Austria? Enregistering 'Austrian German' and 'German German' since the late 20th century. In Stephan Elspaß, Imke Mendoza, Bernhard Pöll & Erik Schleef (Hgg.): *Double Standards. Codified norms and norms of usage in European languages (1600–2020)* (Historical Sociolinguistics). Frankfurt am Main [u. a.]: Lang.

Niehaus, Konstantin. 2024. Enregistering 'Austrian German' on YouTube. A qualitative sociosemiotic analysis. *Zeitschrift für Angewandte Linguistik*, vol. 80, 61–102.

Oakes, Leigh. 2021. Pluricentric linguistic justice: a new ethics-based approach to pluricentricity in French and other languages. *Sociolinguistica*, vol. 35, 49–71.

Oberholzer, Susanne. 2017. Sprachgebrauch und Spracheinstellungen in der Deutschschweiz. Pfarrpersonen als sprachbewusste Sprecherinnen und Sprecher im Fokus. *Linguistik online*, vol. 85, 127–151, (16 August 2021).

Österreichisches Wörterbuch (ÖWB) = Pabst, Christiane M., Herbert Fussy & Ulrike Steiner. 2016. *Österreichisches Wörterbuch. Vollständige Ausgabe mit dem amtlichen Regelwerk*. Herausgegeben im Auftrag des Bundesministeriums für Bildung. Wien: Österreichischer Bundesverlag.

Pfrehm, James. 2011. The Pluricentricity of German: Perceptions of the Standardness of Austrian and German lexical Items. *Journal of Germanic Linguistics* 23(1). 37–64.

Pichler, Inés. 2015. *Bundesdeutsches Wortgut in der österreichischen Pressesprache. Von Abitur bis Zicken-Zoff*. (Schriften zur deutschen Sprache in Österreich 43). Frankfurt a. Main: Lang.

Pickl, Simon. 2020. Factors of selection, standard universals, and the standardisation of German relativisers. *Language Policy* 19(2). 235–258.

Von Polenz, Peter. 1999. *Deutsche Sprachgeschichte vom Spätmittelalter bis zur Gegenwart*. Bd. III: 19. und 20. Jahrhundert. (de Gruyter Studienbuch). Berlin, New York: De Gruyter.

Reiffenstein, Ingo. 2001. Das Problem der nationalen Varietäten. Rezensionsaufsatz zu Ulrich Ammon: Die deutsche Sprache in Deutschland, Österreich und der Schweiz. Das Problem der nationalen Varietäten. Berlin, New York 1995. *Zeitschrift für deutsche Philologie*, vol. 120, 78–89.

Scharloth, Joachim. 2005. Asymmetrische Plurizentrizität und Sprachbewusstsein. Einstellungen der Deutschschweizer zum Standarddeutschen. *Zeitschrift für Germanistische Linguistik*, vol. 33, 236–267.

Scheuringer, Hermann. 1998. Deutsche, insbesondere süddeutsche Wortgeschichte anhand des Fallbeispiels Jänner / Januar. *Sprachwissenschaft*, vol. 23, 263–280.

Schmidlin, Regula. 2011. *Die Vielfalt des Deutschen. Gebrauch, Einschätzung und Kodifizierung einer plurizentrischen Sprache*. Studia Linguistica Germanica 106. Berlin, New York: De Gruyter.

Schmidlin, Regula. 2017. Normwidrigkeit oder Variationsspielraum? Die Varianten des Deutschen als sprachliche Zweifelsfälle. In Winifred V. Davies, Annelies Häcki Buhofer, Regula Schmidlin, Melanie Wagner & Eva Lia Wyss (eds.), *Standardsprache zwischen Norm und Praxis. Theoretische Betrachtungen, empirische Studien und sprachdidaktische Ausblicke* (Basler Studien zur deutschen Sprache und Literatur 99), 41–60. Tübingen: Narr Francke Attempto.

Schmidlin, Regula. To appear. German pluricentricity/pluriareality. In Joshua Bousqeutte & Simon Pickl (eds.), *The Oxford Handbook of the German Language*. Oxford: Oxford University Press.

Schneider, Edgar. 2022. Parameters of epicentral status. *World Englishes*, vol. 41, 462–474.

Silverstein, Michael. 1979. Language structure and language ideology. In Paul R. Clyne, William F. Hanks & Carol L. Hofbauer (eds), *The elements: A parasession on linguistic units and levels*, 193–247. Chicago: Chicago Linguistic Society.

Stevenson, Patrick, Kristine Horner, Nils Langer & Getrud Reershemius. 2018. *The German-speaking World. A Practical Introduction to Sociolinguistic Issues*, 2nd edn. (Routledge Language in Society). Abingdon: Routledge.

Studler, Rebekka. 2019. Ambivalente Spracheinstellungen und was dahintersteckt: Mentale Modelle im diglossischen und plurizentrischen Kontext der Deutschschweiz. In Lars Bülow, Ann Kathrin Fischer & Kristina Herbert (eds.), *Dimensions of Linguistic Space: Variation – Multilingualism – Conceptualisations. Dimensionen des sprachlichen Raums: Variation – Mehrsprachigkeit – Konzeptualisierung*, 407–450. Wien: Peter Lang.

Variantengrammatik 2018 = *Variantengrammatik des Standarddeutschen. 2018. Ein Online-Nachschlagewerk*. Verfasst von einem Autorenteam unter der Leitung von Christa Dürscheid, Stephan Elspaß und Arne Ziegler. Open-access publication. http://mediawiki.ids-mannheim.de/VarGra/index.php/Hauptseite (16 August 2021).

Watts, Richard J. 1999. The ideology of dialect in Switzerland. In Jan Blommaert (ed.), *Language Ideological Debates* (Language, Power and Social Process 2), 67–103. Berlin, New York: De Gruyter.

Wolf, Norbert Richard. 1994. Österreichisches zum österreichischen Deutsch. Aus Anlaß des Erscheinens von: Wolfgang Pollak: Was halten die Österreicher von ihrem Deutsch? Eine sprachpolitische und soziosemiotische Analyse der sprachlichen Identität der Österreicher. *Zeitschrift für Dialektologie und Linguistik*, vol. 61, 66–76.

Zehetner, Ludwig. 2018. *Bairisches Deutsch. Lexikon der deutschen Sprache in Altbayern*, 5th edn. Regensburg: edition vulpes.

CHAPTER 5

Pluricentricity versus pluriareality?
Areal patterns in the English-speaking world

Edgar W. Schneider
University of Regensburg, Germany | National University of Singapore, Singapore

This paper investigates the issue of what data from the English-speaking world can contribute to the ongoing debate on the notions of "pluricentricity" versus "pluriareality" — and to the interpretation of English(es) as pluricentric or pluriareal, respectively. After brief definitions and discussions of the core notions, areal distributions in the English-speaking world — which can be viewed as evidence for either perspective — are systematically screened and exemplified. This includes differences between national varieties of English and evidence for "epicentric" linguistic influences on the one hand, and areal distributions on local, regional, supra-national, and global scales on the other. I conclude that both notions do not exclude each other; rather, each captures and highlights different aspects of reality. "Pluriareality" describes language production, while "pluricentricity" focuses on perception.

Keywords: epicenter, language perception, language production, national varieties, pluriareality, pluricentricity, regional dialects, Southern American English, World Englishes

1. Introduction

As the present volume shows, the last few years have seen an intense debate on the validity and applicability of the competing notions of "pluricentricity" and "pluriareality" (see, most recently, Dollinger 2019a, 2019b, Muhr 2020). The key point is the role of national boundaries and nation states in the presence, emergence, and interpretation of linguistic differences and the understanding of language varieties. Essentially, pluricentricists believe that national varieties of languages need to be recognized as distinct entities, and national boundaries constitute, or tend to become, linguistic boundaries as well. In contrast, adherents of the pluriareality position argue that dialect boundaries and areal distributions of linguistic features tend to disregard state boundaries and that nation states are not primary determinants of linguistic differences. The discussion has been particularly strong in German linguistics and has been fueled by Austrian linguists whose agenda is very strongly the defense of the autonomy of Austrian German against German German (Dollinger 2019a, 2019b); but, of course, it touches upon fundamental questions of language evolution, attitudes, and the impact of language policy.

The purpose of this paper is to assess the contribution of language variability in the English-speaking world to the issues under discussion. In English linguistics, this distinction has not figured prominently so far, to the best of my knowledge. The notion of pluricentricity is known and is associated with the name of the late Australian linguist Michael Clyne (especially in his 1992 book). Leitner (1992) was the first to suggest that English should be considered a pluricentric language, and a small number of later publications enquired into the nature of pluricentricity and possible epicentric influences in English-speaking nations (Leitner 2010; Hoffmann et al. 2011; Hundt 2013; Schneider 2011a, 2013, 2014a; Gries & Bernaisch 2016; Bernaisch & Peters 2022). In contrast, to my knowledge, outside of the context of the present volume, the conference from which it stems, and work by Dollinger (esp. 2019a), the term "pluriareality" has not been adopted by scholars investigating the English language.

I will first consider and compare the core notions under discussion (regarding definitions, conceptual frames, research traditions and applications) and will ask whether they may overlap or exclude each other mutually. In the main part, I present pertinent areal patterns of distribution from the English-speaking world (national, epicentric, local, regional, supra-regional, and global ones) as examples and ask whether they can be seen as supporting either the pluricentric or the pluriareal perspective. I conclude with an overall assessment which argues that the distinction between language perception and production (favoring pluricentric versus pluriareal views, respectively) plays a primary role in understanding the relationship between these two notions.

2. Pluricentricity versus pluriareality: Competing notions

2.1 "Pluricentricity" — an ambiguous notion

The term "pluricentricity" and the concept of some languages being "pluricentric" was introduced by Kloss (1978) and popularized by Clyne (1992). Clyne defined a pluricentric language as one which has several "(epi-)centers", which, in turn, he defines as "a national variety with at least some of its own (codified) norms"

(Clyne 1992:1). Cases in point include English, with British, American, Canadian, Australian and more varieties of their own (Leitner 1992); German, with distinct norms in Germany, Austria, and Switzerland; Portuguese, which branches into a European-Portuguese and a Brazilian form, and, a fairly young manifestation to which Clyne devotes some attention: Serbian and Croatian, which formerly were regarded as Serbo-Croatian but have come to be posited as two distinct languages after the break-up of former Yugoslavia.

On closer inspection, however, it turns out that the notion of pluricentricity is fuzzy, somehow related to standardization and nationhood but not precisely defined (Schneider 2013); it is a graded property that has been assigned, more or less but rather loosely, to a variety of languages (Muhr & Meisnitzer 2018). In fact, I hold that, without this having been recognized so far, it is clearly an ambiguous concept, with two distinct readings (by implication, the same applies to its main manifestation, the notion of "epicenter").

A weak reading implies little more than the existence of different national varieties of a language, each with norms of their own. This is Clyne's original understanding quoted above, "languages with several interacting centres" (1992:1). The examples which he offers for English (Singapore, Malaysia, India, West Africa and other so-called "New Englishes") are in line with what has been recognized and described in the vibrant field of "World Englishes" (see e.g. Schneider 2007, 2020; Schreier et al. 2020). A focus on national varieties has clearly characterized this discipline from its beginnings to the present day (e.g. Kachru 1992; Schneider 2007; Buschfeld & Kautzsch 2020; and many more),[1] mostly without resorting to the concept of pluricentricity, however. One exception is Leitner (1992), who attributes the concept of pluricentricity to various Englishes around the world, though without any further discussion or evidence.

In addition, there is a strong reading which views pluricentricity not only as co-existence but as unilateral influence, exerted from large, important "epicenters" to smaller, adjacent varieties, thus employing an earthquake metaphor, with pressure waves diffusing from the center to the vicinity and periphery. This perspective views the "relationship between national varieties as a dynamic and interactive one" (Clyne 1992:2), including dominance relationships and possible convergence processes. The core assumption is, as Peters states, that "notional epicenters exercise some influence over the surrounding environment" (2009:108;

---

1. However, the recent decade or so has seen a decreased emphasis on nationally distinct varieties and a greater focus on increasingly blurring boundaries and transnational flows of linguistic resources (Blommaert 2010; Seargeant & Tagg 2011; Schneider 2020: 232–235; and many contributions to Schreier et al. 2020) — a trend which has not yet informed the pluricentricity debate. See Section 4.4. below.

Hundt 2013:182), which implies the spread and adoption of features from one variety into another, adjacent one (Hundt 2013:183–184). Clyne (1992) discusses a few possible components of pluricentricity along these lines (and so does Hundt 2013). He also recapitulates a proposal brought forward by Ammon (1989), who postulates different degrees of impact, i.e. "full centres", "nearly full", "semi-", and "rudimentary" centers (without any more detailed discussion, application, or exemplification, however).

2.2 "Pluriareality" — A controversial notion

The notion of pluriareality was posited and advanced forcefully for the first time by Scheuringer (1996:152). When investigating dialect differences or similarities along the Bavarian-Austrian border (in the adjacent cities of Simbach and Braunau, to be exact) and, more widely, in the Bavarian-Austrian dialect region, he identifies "Räumlichkeitsmuster unterhalb der staatlichen Ebene", ('areal patterns below the national level'), in addition to "Ein-Räumlichkeit" ('uni-spatiality'), forms shared all across the German-speaking region. Consequently, against "das staatsorientierte *plurizentrische Muster*" ('the state-oriented pluricentric pattern') he claims German to be "*pluriareal*" (152; italics in original). Pluriareality thus highlights feature distributions or similarities while disregarding national boundaries, i.e. forms which exist in areas smaller than a state or transcending state borders.

Over the last few years, this notion has been employed and revitalized by a group of linguists who have investigated variant choices in German syntax on the basis of large-scale electronic text corpora compiled from regional newspapers (Niehaus 2015; Elspaß et al. 2017). Their cross-national investigation has identified a wide range of patterns and preferences, with varying regional choices of syntactic variants in German. The areal distributions which they have pointed out are totally independent of state boundaries; they find not a single full correspondence between a syntactic variant and a nation (Elspaß et al. 2017:88). Instead of a codified national standard, they highlight the importance of shared usage, which, in their data, is found to be independent of political entities (although they do concede that nationhood is one possible determinant of linguistic variability (Niehaus 2015:138). Consequently, they advocate a pluriareal perspective against the pluricentric model, which they essentially reject as strongly nation-oriented and ideologically motivated (Niehaus 2015:135–138).

Some linguists vehemently oppose this position, especially Dollinger (2019a, 2019b), since it is supposed to neglect the independence of "non-dominant" national varieties, such as Austrian German. Pluriareality is accused of being no more than geographical variation (Dollinger 2019a:63) — which may be true but is not a deficiency, since practically all languages are known to vary regionally.

Instead, pluricentricity is strongly advocated, highlighting nations as "imagined communities" ((2020: 51), a defensible but politically dangerous concept since it may invite an overly constrained national focus and attitude) and forms (mostly a small set of lexical choices) which are indeed almost or completely aligned with nationhood. For example, the first month of the year is *Jänner* in Austria but *Januar* in Germany, and Dollinger (2019: Chapter 8) points out further Austrianisms such as *Tormann* 'goalkeeper' as opposed to *Torwart*, or *hudeln* 'act hastily'. Such distributions clearly exist, but they are largely constrained to a small set of vocabulary choices, while it is equally uncontroversial that the vast majority of linguistic choices on all language levels disregard national boundaries. In dialect geography, it is uncontroversial that Austrian German is a south-eastern dialect of Bavarian, which, in turn (and including Austrian speech), is linguistically clearly distinguished from central and especially northern German dialects (König 1981: 230–231). Dollinger (2019a) frames the relationship between Austrian German and German German (and some linguists who work on these varieties) as an antagonism, the need being to defend the integrity and identity of the smaller against the larger variety; in my view, in an increasingly integrative Europe and world this is a position which may invite narrow and dangerously nationalist perspectives.

This is not the place to enter a prolonged debate on the many theoretical points which Dollinger (2019a, 2019b) raises, many of which I find empirically unsubstantiated. Briefly, I do not think it is justified to accuse the pluriarealist position of "atheoretical empiricism" (64). In the philosophy of science, collecting data and looking for patterns represents a well-respected inductive (Aristotelian) procedure (Nickerson 2010). The alternative deductive (Platonist) approach of positing a theory and then testing whether it can be falsified is advocated here, following the philosopher Karl Popper (Dollinger 2019a: 112); it is equally respectable but also difficult to apply, and here seems misapplied. It all depends on how one formulates one's hypotheses. I do not agree that Popper's knowledge theory renders pluriareality "conceptually empty" (Dollinger 2019b: 104–105): a hypothesis stating that "There exist areal linguistic distributions disregarding national boundaries" is clearly valid and has not been falsified. Conversely, a claim such as "national boundaries determine linguistic differences" can easily be falsified (for instance by pointing out regional distributions which do not observe state boundaries), while a more realistic, hedged version, something like "some linguistic differences observe national borders," can be upheld.

There are two points in Dollinger (2019a, 2019b) that I find strongly relevant and would like to highlight, however.

One is the claim that national borders will have a diversifying effect over time: "the dynamic quality of the border and attitudinal and cognitive effects among speakers on both sides of the border," creating "dialect diversification" (2019b: 100). It is predicted, therefore, that dialects in neighboring towns on different sides of borders (like Braunau in Austria and Simbach in Germany, or Vancouver in Canada and Bellingham in the USA) will diverge over time. Dollinger (2019a: 44) quotes some evidence to that end — which shows that boundaries do have an effect (though this does not imply that it is the only or the strongest one, or that it is valid all across the board).

Secondly, Dollinger suggests that speaker attitudes are the decisive "lynchpin" (2019: Chapter 7) for distinguishing varieties, and he holds that a small number of salient different types (like the *Jänner – Januar* distinction mentioned earlier) are decisive and justify positing independent varieties, whereas the large number of shared tokens and forms are argued not to count ("the number of differences is quite irrelevant, yet the weight that speakers assign to a possibly small set of features is," (Dollinger 2019a: 73)). I do not see any solid justification for these claims; who is entitled to state what is or is not irrelevant? Language attitudes are just one component of language knowledge; important, but to my mind, secondary to structural knowledge, usage, and performance. And what one considers important or not is purely a matter of subjective choice, especially when objective parameters like type frequency are discarded.

2.3 Testing and assessment strategies

So, what would be arguments in favor of one or the other perspective? Is it possible to test or empirically substantiate whether the pluricentric or the pluriareal perspective is stronger, and which has more explanatory power?

Both hypotheses make different predictions as to how linguistic features will be areally distributed (or, more accurately, which areal distributions matter). Pluricentricity, based on the wider, weak position, predicts that there will be clear linguistic distinctions between national varieties, and the strong reading also predicts that evidence of linguistic influence from an "epicenter" on neighboring varieties should exist. Arguments pro-pluriareality, in contrast, will be fuzzy distinctions between national varieties and evidence of areal distributions which are independent of national boundaries, operating on a local, regional, or transnational space.

An interesting and important point in need of discussion is the relationship between the two core terms discussed here and the formality dimension of language variability between standard and nonstandard usage.[2] It is well known that

---

[2] This point was raised by the editors of this volume in the reviewing process, and I am grateful to them for bringing it up.

languages tend to vary strongly "on the ground", the level of local dialects, less so on the regional level, and hardly at all on the formal, standard level (Trudgill 1974: 42). The focus in this debate is on the role and importance of national boundaries, hence on national varieties, and these are strongly associated with formal usage and standard varieties — but not exclusively so. For example, when we talk about British English or American English we think of (primarily) the formal core of grammar and lexis and national pronunciation norms (commonly labelled Received Pronunciation or General American, respectively), but, clearly, we also know that this is not all. British English includes all kinds of regional or urban dialects, and American English comprises, say, Southern speech or African American English. The same applies here. The notion of pluricentricity highlights national varieties (and hence standards), but even Clyne's classic definition quoted at the beginning of this chapter defines these varieties as "with *at least some* of its own (codified) norms" (Clyne 1992: 1, emphasis mine) — which implies that not all features of pluricentric varieties are codified norm elements. Similarly, Dollinger (2019a), who strongly advocates pluricentricity and looks into Austrian-German lexical distinctions, discusses forms such as *anpatzen* 'make disreputable' (2019a: 84–85), *hudeln* (2019a: 86–89), or, on the level of syntax or phraseology, *es geht sich (nicht) aus* (2019a: 90–91) which are clearly nonstandard / dialectal and unacceptable in formal contexts. Conversely, the concept of pluriareality, with its focus on transnational, local or regional features (see, for example, Scheuringer 1996 on Braunau vs. Simbach dialect features) appears to be more focused on nonstandard usage, but this is clearly not necessarily the case. For example, the important work on pluriareality in the syntax of German referred to earlier (Niehaus 2015; Elspaß et al. 2017) describes regional preferences between syntactic choices which clearly are all on the standard level (like *froh über / um etwas, am / auf dem Foto, Dies weil / obwohl / nachdem, immer noch / noch immer, dass er hat kommen können / dass er kommen hat können / dass er kommen können hat*, and many more); and while there is a lot of local and regional nonstandard lexis, there are also words which are clearly standard items but not nationally constrained (consider words like *Semmel* or *Samstag* in German, which are broadly southern, shared at least by Austria and Bavaria). Thus, the two notions in question cannot and should not be compared with a limitation to standard forms only.

In the following sections I will work out arguments, facts and constitutive criteria supporting either of these competing alternatives. I will look into feature distributions in English which operate on several levels of scale, areal patterns from the local via regional, national, and transnational to global ones, and will assess their relative importance.

3. Evidence for pluricentricity

3.1 National varieties

3.1.1 *British English versus American English*

At the heart of the debate lie national varieties as symbols of nationhood, and this applies most evidently to today's global lead varieties, British English (BrE) and American English (AmE). An important phase in the origins of AmE appears to be in line with the predictions made by pluricentricists, since the branching off of the variety was also a deliberate move pushed in the US after independence. The 1770s saw an extensive debate on not only political but also the possibility of linguistic independence; a distinct "Federal English" was called for as a symbol of self-reliance by many public figures, including Thomas Jefferson. In a speech in 1786, Noah Webster, a leading figure of this movement, proclaimed that "as an independent nation, our honor requires us to have a system of our own, in language as well as government" (cf. Schneider 2007: 276–277). In reality, though, this desire was soon reduced to some persistently used spelling differences. To what extent the two main "metropolitan" varieties really differ is an interesting, partly controversial question.

Table 5.1 illustrates the "traditional view" of differences between BrE and AmE as found in Strevens (1971) or Tottie (2002: 92), which is fully in line with the pluricentric perspective. There is a set of clear qualitative differences, i.e. British speakers use one form, Americans another.

Table 5.1 BrE – AmE differences: Traditional view

BrE	AmE
pavement	*sidewalk*
petrol	*gas*
autumn	*fall*
...	...
non-rhotic (cf. *car, card*)	rhotic (/r/ in *car, card*, ...)
/ɑ:/ in *dance, staff, can't*, ...	/æ/ in *dance, staff, can't*, ...
...	...

Such clear-cut distinctions are a rare exception, however; mostly, distributions are more complex. For example, *fall* occurs in British English as well but is dialectal there; some Americanisms are entering BrE (and Briticisms are used in AmE for effect); some regions of AmE are non-rhotic, and vice versa; etc. (cf. Strevens 1971; Algeo 2006; Tottie 2002; and more).

(1) a. *Avoid queuing — Customers not requiring a receipt should pin their cheque to the payment counterfoil and post here*
b. *Don't wait in line — If you don't need a receipt, attach your check to the bill and put it in the slot here*
c. *For check payment only. Insert bills and payments here if you do not want receipt*

Example (1) from Algeo (1989) is a nice illustration of a more realistic perspective preferred in more recent writings. When living in England, Algeo came across (1)a., an instruction for a specific payment modality, and found this odd and "labyrinthly British". So, he asked American friends how they would express the same situation, and synthesized responses in b. as an American equivalent. And then, back home in Athens, GA, he came across c., a real sign with the very same meaning. His conclusion is that BrE is more "ornate", formal, complicated, like a command; while AmE, by comparison, is laconic, more direct, and less formal. Most importantly, the example shows that, except for a small set of lexical items (like *queue* or *counterfoil*), the differences between both varieties are not a yes/no-matter but rather a question of tendencies, preferences, and frequency differences.

And this is precisely what more recent, corpus-based research has shown empirically. On both sides of the Atlantic, essentially the same expressions and patterns are used, but frequencies and preferences of choices vary greatly. Algeo (2006) showed this extensively for vocabulary and phraseology, Mittmann (2004) for prefabricated phrases, and the contributions to Rohdenburg & Schlüter (2009) for a range of grammatical patterns. Table 5.2, culled from these sources, shows a small selection of choices illustrating this relationship: all forms are used everywhere, but there are strong and consistent frequency preferences. The noun *specialty* and the predication *have a sleep* are predominantly (though not exclusively) British; to downplay the importance of something British speakers prefer *fair enough* and Americans *no big deal*; with *you'd better* versus *you better* the preference relationship is less strong but also clearly visible.

Table 5.2 Lexical and phraseological preferences in BrE and AmE (normalized frequency per 100 million words)

	BrE	AmE
specialty	57.8	2.6
have a sleep	5.7	0.9
fair enough	450	10
no big deal	15	140
you'd better	290	110
you better....	350	520

Thus, recent evidence, based on extensive corpus screenings, shows that the differences between the main national varieties of BrE and AmE are not qualitative or clear-cut (with very few, mostly lexical exceptions) but a matter of different modes of expression, of varying tendencies and preferences — and this is evidently in line with pluriareal rather than pluricentric thinking.

The situation is complicated even further when considering two related dichotomies, the relationship between standards and varieties and the perception versus production perspectives. Comparisons of BrE and AmE typically focus on the respective standard, norm varieties. To some extent, however, these are conventionalized abstractions, perceived as uniform and monolithic while the down-to-earth reality is much more complicated and messy; linguistic homogeneity is a myth. British English is normally understood as a "standard" grammar and vocabulary and associated with "Received Pronunciation" (RP) as the norm and target of teaching around the globe — but Trudgill (2002: 171) estimated that RP is spoken by only 3% of the British population, and any visitor talking to, say, a Yorkshire farmer will notice that the school English one has studied is a far cry from what is encountered in reality. Similarly, for the US, as Kretzschmar (2004) points out, the concept of "General American" has been promoted and upheld, "presumed …[to be a] 'default' form of American English [and] relatively unmarked" (262) — but Kretzschmar claims that such a form is non-existent but only "characterized negatively, by the suppression of identifiable regional and social variants" (268). So, the perception of standard varieties is an idealization; in reality and in language production, an immense amount of variability on all levels prevails.

3.1.2 *National varieties on a global scale*

The same question can be asked on a global scale, regarding "World Englishes": are there any clear-cut distinctions between national varieties? There have been many empirical comparisons of varieties (e.g. Hundt & Gut 2012; Collins 2015), usually based on large-scale electronic corpora. These are well known in corpus linguistics. The most widely used tools are the components of the "International Corpus of English" (ICE) project (https://www.ice-corpora.uzh.ch/en.html), with one million words per variety, and the Corpus of Global Web-Based English of 1.9 billion words from twenty different countries (GloWbE; https://www.english-corpora.org/glowbe/). These sources (and others) offer a huge potential for comparative investigations. I illustrate this and document the nature of the results found by briefly showcasing two examples from my own earlier work.

The subjunctive in English is a relatively rare, historically residual form, marked mainly by the lack of a verbal suffix in the third person singular (e.g. *They demanded that he come*). It is widely claimed to be mainly an American form, while BrE expresses the same hypothetical meaning by means of a modal (*… that he should come*; cf. Schneider 2011b). Table 5.3 shows the absolute token frequencies

Table 5.3 Comparative frequencies of the subjunctive in varieties of English (after Schneider 2011b: 169)*

Variety	Source	N subj.	% subj.	N should	% should
AmE 1991	Frown	94	89.5	11	10.5
PhilE 1990s	ICE-PHI	62	86.1	10	13.9
AmE 1961	Brown	116	85.9	19	14.1
AusE	ACE	78	72.9	29	27.1
NZE	WCNZE	70	66.7	35	33.3
BrE 1991	FLOB	44	39.6	67	60.4
InE	Kolhapur	35	30.2	81	69.8
BrE 1961	LOB	14	12.6	91	87.4

* Abbreviations used in Table 5.3: AmE = American English; PhilE = Philippine English; AusE = Australian English; NZE = New Zealand English; BrE = British English; InE = Indian English; ICE-PHI = ICE-Philippines corpus; ACE = Australian Corpus of English; WCNZE = Wellington Corpus of New Zealand English; FLOB = Freiburg remake of the LOB corpus; LOB = Lancaster-Oslo-Bergen Corpus. For discussions and applications of the corpora see Biber & Reppen (2015).

and the relative proportions of either variant in eight different varieties (partly the same national forms at different times; first column) represented by different corpora (column two). Findings show that indeed the subjunctive is predominant in AmE and rare in BrE, and increasing in both varieties (compare the 1961 to 1991 data), but again there is no qualitative distinction. Philippine English, an offspring of AmE, is very similar to this variety in its frequency of employing the structure; conversely, Indian English resembles BrE, while the Englishes of Australia and New Zealand are in between, perhaps becoming Americanized. So national varieties of English align themselves along a British — American dimension, partly based on history. Most importantly for the present context, however, there is gradual fluctuation between national varieties, and absolutely no clear-cut distinction.

My second, concise example is from Schneider (2018: 52). Certain impersonal constructions were found to occur more frequently in BrE than in postcolonial varieties, perhaps due to their syntactic complexity. Figure 5.1, based on GloWbE data, shows that for the construction *seems to me,* this can be broadly generalized to the relationship between first-language and second-language varieties: the form is common in the US, Britain, Australia, etc., but less frequent in India, Sri Lanka (SL), etc. But again, we find a cline of gradations, of different national preferences for this construction, but no qualitative division.

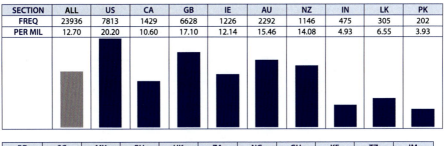

Figure 5.1 Frequency of *seems to me* in 20 national varieties of English (based on GloWbE; from Schneider 2018: 52)

Thus, while grammatical and phraseological preferences obviously do not observe national boundaries, the question remains: do words behave differently? Is there nationally distinctive lexis? Table 5.4 probes into this, based on frequency observations from GloWbE. The first block of forms compares three pairs of "classic" lexical distinctions between BrE and AmE, and finds very strong preferences (though, again no absolute distinctions): *pavement, windscreen* and *nappies* are predominantly found in BrE and *sidewalk, windshield* and *diapers* in AmE – but each form does occur in the other variety as well, though much less frequently. The second block documents words which are considered nationally distinctive: *Pakeha* 'person of European descent' and *kauri* 'kind of tree' are characteristically New Zealand items; *lakh* '100.000' is common in India; *kiasu* 'eagerly competitive' in Singapore, *dim sum* 'small dishes' in Hong Kong, and *stubbie* 'small bottle' and *breakie* 'breakfast' in Australia. The frequency distributions of these items in the national sections of GloWbE strongly (though also not absolutely) confirm the strong association of words with national language varieties: each word occurs very frequently in its own language variety, and rarely (but still present) in the BrE and AmE corpora.

Table 5.4 Frequencies of select lexical items in BrE, AmE and other national varieties (token frequencies and [in parentheses] frequencies normalized to words-per-million [wpm]; based on GloWbE)

Frequency in GloWbE	Other variety		GB	US
pavement			2546 (10.3)	1215 (4.8)
sidewalk			450 (1.8)	2718 (10.7)
windscreen			693 (2.7)	68 (.3)
windshield			180 (.7)	700 (2.8)
nappies			1071 (4.2)	59 (.2)
diapers			218 (.9)	1513 (6.0)
Pakeha	NZ:	1835 (31.3)	9 (.0)	1 (.0)
kauri	NZ:	808 (13.8)	17 (.1)	6 (.0)
lakh	Ind:	6791 (99.9)	63 (.2)	18 (.1)
kiasu	Sing:	162 (5.5)	1 (.0)	0 (0)
dim sum	HK:	529 (17.7)	116 (.5)	102 (.4)
stubbie	Aus:	19 (.2)	4 (.0)	1 (.0)
breakie	Aus:	10 (.1)	2 (.0)	0 (0)

It should be noted that there would of course be many different ways and many possible sets of data to illustrate the basic claims made in this section. I have chosen to point out some quantitative tendencies for select features on the levels of morphosyntax and lexis. Recent research has tended to employ sophisticated statistical machinery to investigate relationships between varieties and to bring out new patterns. For example, Bohmann (2019) analyzes a huge amount of aggregate data quantitatively and highlights the importance of stylistic over geographical factors as a predictor of linguistic variation, and many other studies could be chosen to illustrate this type of approach (including some mentioned in the present context, such as Gries & Bernaisch (2016)). It is worth asking, however, whether statistical modeling yields stronger insights than conventional qualitative and quantitative documentation and theoretical modelling, as Hundt (2020) does. In the present context, the basic point is clear and robust, and confirmed by quantifying and aggregate studies: there are varying frequency preferences of specific features across different national varieties of English; most of these are persistent but inconspicuous tendencies, and just a small number are more focused and noticeable; but there are practically no clear-cut qualitative differences between national varieties of English.

3.2 Epicentric influences

This section looks into the "strong" reading of the notion of pluricentricity, the claim that "various regionally relevant norm-developing centres have emerged that exert an influence on the formation and development of the English language in neighbouring areas" (Hoffmann et al. 2011: 258; Hundt 2013: 182). Possible examples suggested include Australian, Indian, and Singaporean English influencing their respective neighboring regions (Hundt 2013: 182). Hundt (2013) offers an extensive and convincing discussion of the topic, and she ultimately remains very skeptical: "the concept is far from straightforward, both on theoretical and on methodological grounds" (182). She believes that the concept has "immediate intuitive appeal" but is not really useful because of "theoretical pitfalls and methodological stumbling blocks" (201). For a serious documentation of epicentric influences, we lack methodological standards, evidence of the functional equivalence of variants in different varieties, a proof of external influence rather than parallel developments, and an assessment of attitudes involved.

In addition to Hundt's (2013) fundamental paper, a few studies have attempted to investigate specific instances of influences of "new epicenters" on neighboring varieties.

Hoffmann et al. (2011) ask whether Indian English constitutes a possible epicenter for varieties across South Asia. Extralinguistic, supportive evidence is provided, for instance, by the observation that Sri Lanka adopts Indian language teaching material (259). The crucial question is, however, whether "degrees of similarity" (i.e., purely synchronic data) are sufficient to establish diachronic impact (261). On the basis of a comparison of light verb constructions across South Asian varieties, the authors conclude that their findings are "compatible with the hypothesis that IndE is a model variety … in the region" (261) but no more than that; there is no real, solid evidence: "our data do not allow any substantial conclusions as far as the epicentre hypothesis is concerned" (276). Similarly, Lange

(2020) believes that the notion of Indian English as a possible epicenter has "intuitive plausibility" (255). She surveys five structures and finds "a possible 'trickle-down effect'" (i.e., higher frequencies in India than in neighboring varieties) but views this as "a necessary, but not a sufficient condition for stipulating epicentre status". Accordingly, she states the "issue [remains] unresolved" (255).

One other possible case in point is Australia, which, as noted already by Clyne, is "conducting a more aggressive export campaign of its variety" (Clyne 1992: 5), attempting to establish it on the Pacific Rim, including parts of Asia (similarly Leitner 2010). Peters (2009) conducts an explicit (though thematically limited) investigation of the issue and finds anecdotal evidence that appears to confirm the weak epicentric influence of Australian English in New Zealand, if only on the lexical level, "dated through historical lexicography" (109). Table 5.3 shows *breakie* to occur 10 times (.10 wpm) in the Australian segment of GloWbE, and the other components of this corpus also show it weakly in Asia (6 times in Malaysia [.21 wpm], twice in Singapore [.07 wpm]) and New Zealand (twice, .03 wpm). The evidence for *stubbie* is similar in principle (wpm .18 in AusE) but weaker: it is also found twice in New Zealand (.03 wpm) and once in Hong Kong (.04 wpm).

A recent collection (Bernaisch & Peters 2022) probed more deeply into the issue of epicentric relations in the English-speaking world, offering a few more suggestive case studies, some attempts at testing the hypothesis statistically, and arguments for a prototypical character of the notion, composed of several constitutive parameters (Schneider 2022). It does not refer to the concepts of pluricentricity or pluriareality, however.

3.3   Intermediate summary – Pluricentricity: National varieties and putative epicenters

So, what is the overall impression regarding the distinctness of national varieties of English? Evidence for the importance of national boundaries is weak: differences are mostly fuzzy, and surface as tendencies and frequency-based preferences; there are hardly any clear-cut, sharp qualitative distinctions. A small-scale possible exception are select lexical items, typically those associated with local cultures (e.g. *pakeha, kauri, lakh, kiasu, stubbie, breakie*). Unless these become internationalisms known more widely but associated with a particular region and culture (like *dim sum*), they are almost completely confined to their respective native varieties. So, there is only very limited support for the weak version of pluricentricity – unless, as with Dollinger (2019a) as quoted in 1.2, the vast majority of the evidence is discarded as irrelevant and the focus is exclusively on select distinctive types, not frequently used shared tokens. Similarly, support for the notion of epicenters as influencing other varieties turns out to be questionable. There are some indicators but there has only been quite limited empirical substantiation, so the strong reading of "pluricentricity" remains a viable hypothesis but so far has not been backed by solid evidence.

4. Evidence for pluriareality: Non-national patterns

As stated earlier, support for the validity of the concept of pluriareality may be provided by showcasing all kinds of areal distributions which disregard national boundaries. Consequently, this section will inquire into the systematicity and cohesiveness of distributions on various levels of scale, beginning with the smallest, local one.

4.1 Areality: The local scale

The discipline of dialect geography has investigated regional language variation since the late nineteenth century, and has identified many dialect regions and types of distributions. Very often, the focus of research has been the speech habits of one particular locality, as for example in Hedevind's (1967) study, *The dialect of Dentdale in the West Riding of Yorkshire*. Analyzing a single local dialect, e.g. the speech of a village, was a rather popular type of dissertation topic in much of the twentieth century, typically with a diachronic orientation, comparing localized speech forms with Middle English origins. Local and regional lexical distributions are widely documented in regional dictionaries such as Cassidy et al. (1985–2013).

(2) [hɔɪ tɔɪd ən ðə saʊnd sɔɪd] 'high tide on the Sound side'

More recent and modern sociolinguistic research has of course also often focused on specific, linguistically interesting localities. A well-known example in American sociolinguistics is the dialect of Ocracoke, a small island off the coast of North Carolina, which has been intensively investigated and documented by Walt Wolfram and his team since the 1990s (Wolfram & Schilling-Estes 1997). Over centuries of isolation, Ocracoke has developed a conservative, distinctive dialect locally known as "brogue". Example (2) illustrates the dialect's signature phrase and feature, a strongly backed onset of the /aɪ/ diphthong, which islanders like Rex O'Neal enjoy performing (e.g. on video documentaries produced by the *North Carolina Language and Life* project, e.g. Hutcheson & Wolfram 2006). During the summer months, the island is swamped by well-to-do tourists now, so, with fishing no longer being the main source of revenue of the community, the ancestral men's traditional standing is threatened, and they strengthen such local dialect features as signs of belonging and local identity.

4.2 Areality: The regional scale

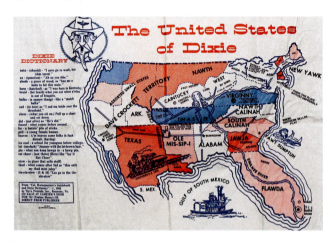

Figure 5.2 The United States of Dixie (restaurant place mat)

There is a strong association between cultural regions and their respective dialects, and I illustrate this by looking at the most distinctive cultural region of the United States: the American South. A strong regional identity prevails, traditionally associated with social stereotypes such as a "good ol' boy" and "redneck" identity, hunting and fishing as favorite pastimes, love of country music, conservatism and importance of religion (the "bible belt") and a rustic but down-to-earth, good-hearted character (cf. Schneider 1986). (It should be noted, though, that these stereotypes express an exclusively white and largely male and rural perspective which disregards the African American experience and the deeply rooted racism in the region.) The southern dialect, marked by features such as a distinct second-plural pronoun *y'all* or the "southern drawl" (a tendency to diphthongize or triphthongize short vowels), constitutes a strong symbol of areal identity. Figure 5.2, a place mat found in southern restaurants,[3] illustrates both several linguistic features and a number of cultural stereotypes (such as the "southern belles" or the illegal "moonshining" of whiskey). The dialect has been extensively documented and investigated (e.g. Nagle & Sanders 2003). In a broad case study, Schneider (2020: 90–99) presents text samples and feature discussions. Example (3) also shows a nicely concise illustration: in less than three seconds at the beginning of a country song, as many as five dialect features can be identified (the lack of a subject, the reduction of *have* to [ə], no postvocalic /r/ in *heard*, the high front vowel merger before nasals in *pin/pen*, and final consonant deletion in *drop*).

---

3. The image was created by a company named Tip 'Twinkle in Roanoke, VA, in 1966, which seems to have gone out of business a long time ago. I have attempted but not been able to track a copyright holder.

(3) [kəd ə hɜːd ə pïn drɒ] *'You could have heard a pin drop...'*
(initial 3 seconds of the song "Tonight the heartache's on me", by The Dixie Chicks (e.g. on YouTube: https://www.youtube.com/watch?v=tmVisJfKkBA, last accessed 21 February 2024)

4.3 Areality: The transnational scale

Some areal distributions of linguistic forms and features are clearly "transnational", i.e. transcending national boundaries and spreading across several nation states. Such spatial patterns are related to so-called "sprachbund" phenomena in general and typological linguistics. We find regionality, historical processes, and multilingualism in interaction, so such areal distributions are often caused by shared substrate languages, social histories, or cultural roots (cf. Velupillai 2012: 51, 411–415). A clear case in point is the Caribbean, where substantial linguistic similarities across many nations can be observed (e.g. Alleyne 1980). Most importantly, this relates to characteristically creole features (such as preverbal markers for tense and aspect) and the socio-stylistic cline from basilects via mesolects to acrolects (Roberts 1988).

Another good example for transnational linguistic distributions is South-East Asia. There are (at least) two evident reasons for this: the political union in the region, ASEAN (the Association of South-East Asian Nations), decided to establish English as its "sole official language" in Article 34 of its Charter of 2009, a factor which clearly boosts its further diffusion in the region (Kirkpatrick 2010). Secondly, many of the nations in the region (or strong population segments there) are Malay-speaking, so cross-linguistic influences from Malay and similarities between these Englishes have been reported (Percillier 2016) despite the fact that the status of English varies greatly (English is a foreign language in Indonesia, a second language in Malaysia, and a strong second or even first language for many in Singapore).

(4) **B:** Come to think of it, okay *lah* ... he also *kena* play out *lor*.
C: By who?
B: He *kena* sabotage *what*, the airport ...
(selection from a "Singlish" conversation; from Schneider 2020: 169–170)

(5) **A:** [on the phone] Hello, where you now? You want to kena firing from me is it?
B: ... At PJ, wait me lah
A: ... faster lah ...
(Transcript of selection of school assignment YouTube clip from Malaysia "Manglish VS Proper English ~ ??!!" (https://www.youtube.com/watch?v=WoNk4dFCHZA, after 53 seconds; accessed 21 February 2024)

Examples (4) from Singapore and (5) from Malaysia illustrate such transnationally shared features – in this case the emphatic discourse particle *lah* and the so-called "*kena*-passive", a typical regional construction of English in Singapore and Malaysia, transferred from Malay but adjusted grammatically (for example, semantically it obligatorily implies an adversative reading of the predicate). Both features are shared between the informal Englishes of Singapore and Malaysia (see Schneider 2020: 169–173 for a comprehensive discussion and explanation of more features). In a comment to (5) on YouTube, one lay observer rightly states "lol singlish and manglish kinda same leh.. ;p" (and that's exactly the point I am trying to make here).

4.4 Areality: The transnational and global scale

It is not at all difficult to show that substantial linguistic similarities across Englishes also prevail both transnationally and globally. English has come to be the world's leading language and is now rooted in some 100 countries around the globe as a national, second, co-official or otherwise internally used language (see the map in Schneider 2020: 64). The discipline of World Englishes has investigated and described these processes extensively (see Schneider 2007, 2020; Schreier et al. 2020; and many more), and comprehensive documentation of structural properties of these varieties is available in monumental handbooks and projects (most importantly, Schneider et al. 2004; Kortmann & Lunkenheimer 2012). Space limitations prevent a more comprehensive discussion of these exciting phenomena, but it is absolutely clear that there is a huge number of transnational feature distributions of various kinds, and for various reasons. For example, "angloversals" are widespread non-standard structural patterns, such as multiple negation (*I don't know nothing*) or the lack of inversion in questions (*You're coming?* or *where you now?* in (7)). Areal typological similarities, as mentioned earlier, include the *kena*-passive exemplified in (6) and (7) or a widespread lack of articles, found widely across Asia. High-contact varieties display typical properties including a frequent lack of inflection (in contact with analytic languages, e.g. China English) or preverbal markers (in creole varieties). Many second-language varieties show simplification phenomena, e.g. a reduction of vowel distinctions to only five or seven vowel phonemes or a preference for finite over non-finite clauses (*... want that ...*; Steger & Schneider 2012).

Figures 5.3 and 5.4, produced by mapping software that comes with the respective projects and publications, visualizes two select transnational or even global linguistic distributions on the levels of pronunciation and grammar, respectively. As Figure 5.3 shows, many varieties in the Caribbean, in (mostly West) Africa and on the Pacific Rim, but also in the UK, pronounce words like *trap* or *cat* with a low open /a/ vowel. According to Figure 5.4, the tendency to use progressives with stative verbs is equally, or even more, widespread on a global scale.

Furthermore, transnational and global areal patterns can also either encompass huge geographical spaces or be understood as fuzzy diffusion patterns – both will be illustrated briefly.

The best example of large-scale, transnational, but nevertheless sub-global entities, is the growing notion of "Asian Englishes". English has been growing and becoming institutionalized vigorously across Asia, and substantial similarities in developmental trajectories, social settings, sociolinguistic, and structural consequences have been observed (see Schneider 2014b). Consequently, awareness of this topic is now reflected by a specialized journal (*Asian Englishes*, founded in 1999), a new Handbook (Bolton et al. 2020), and many other publications (e.g. Kirkpatrick & Wang 2020).

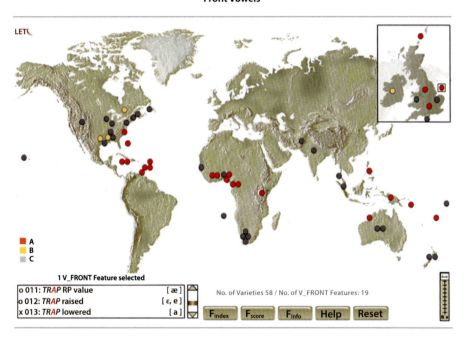

Figure 5.3 Varieties in which /æ/ is lowered to /a/ (produced by the CD-ROM Kortmann & Schneider 2004; online at http://www.varieties.mouton-content.com/)
Legend: "A" = "pervasive (possibly obligatory) or at least very frequent;" "B" = "exists but... rarely ...;" "C" = "does not exist ...."

Recent scholarship increasingly tends to shy away from focusing on norms and national varieties, instead emphasizing transnational feature distributions and language forms as migrant global linguistic resources, with boundaries becoming increasingly fuzzy (Schneider 2020: 232–235). There is a growing

Figure 5.4 Varieties in which progressives are used with stative verbs (feature 88, e.g. *I'm liking this.*) (produced with *eWAVE*: https://ewave-atlas.org/; cf. Kortmann et al. 2020)
Legend: square: Traditional L1 varieties; tilted square: High-contact L1 varieties; downward triangle: English-based Pidgins; upward triangle: English-based Creoles; circle: Indigenized L2 varieties.
red = feature is pervasive or obligatory; orange: feature is neither pervasive nor extremely rare; dark yellow: feature exists, but is extremely rare; light yellow: attested absence of feature; white: no information on feature is available.

awareness of the importance of transnational links, migration, and heterogeneity, and a decreasing interest in norms and national entities in a globalizing world. Substantial applications of such thinking can be found in discussions of Pennycook's (2007) "Transcultural Flows", Blommaert's (2010) "Sociolinguistics of Globalization", Meierkord's "Interactions across Englishes" (2012), or the spread of grassroots Englishes (Meierkord & Schneider 2020). Finally, another context that operates transnationally and strengthens ties between various localities is the internet, the impact of cyberspace. Figure 5.5 presents an example: "Nairaland" is an online community of (mainly but not exclusively) Nigerians serving expatriates, and, in doing so, it disseminates Nigerian English and Nigerian Pidgin globally to wherever Nigerians or other interested community members reside, totally disregarding boundaries and political entities.

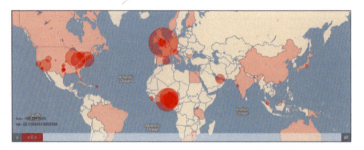

Figure 5.5 Activity in the Nairaland community by region (from Mair 2013: 267)

All of these observations and distributions are obviously fully in line with the pluriareal view.

4.5 Areality in perception: Perceptual Dialectology

All of these statements on areal distributions relate to observed linguistic usage, i.e. performance and production. On the other hand, there are also shared regularities of perception, speakers' awareness of linguistic forms, and distributions. Speakers of a language have a concept of linguistic areas. They know, for instance, that, in a neighboring village, different words are used or that in different regions people talk differently, and this is in fact a rather popular topic of discussion amongst laypersons. The linguistic branch of "perceptual dialectology", founded by Dennis Preston, investigates such beliefs systematically (Preston 1989). Preston asked respondents to draw dialect maps. Figure 5.6 serves as an example; it shows American dialect regions as assessed by a respondent from Chicago. Preston then aggregated such maps and calculated regions where the "worst" or "most pleasant" English is spoken. In the present context it is noteworthy that practically all the distributions representing speakers' beliefs on areal patterns disregard political divisions.

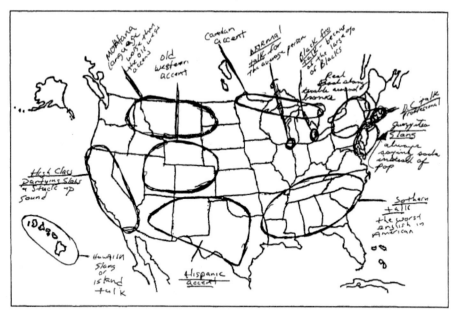

Figure 5.6 Map of US dialects drawn by a Chicago respondent (Preston 1996: 307)

4.6 Intermediate summary – pluriareality

Weighing the evidence presented in Sections 4.1 to 4.5, we find that there are plenty of varying regional distributions of linguistic features that are local, regional, transnational or global. Areal patterns disregarding national boundaries are perfectly normal and, in fact, predominate when looking at linguistic similarities. This clearly supports a fundamentally pluriareal interpretation of regional linguistic distributions.

5. Pluricentricity or pluriareality? Weighing the arguments and evidence

In sum, what do the general observations on areal distributions in the English-speaking world imply on the basic dichotomy that is at stake in this paper and this volume?

Evidence for the weak reading of pluricentricity, the claim that there are distinct national norms, is mostly negative: national boundaries are hardly ever linguistic boundaries. Instead, comparisons of feature distributions in and across national varieties show that a set of consistent quantitative usage tendencies and varying preferences, shared by speakers through usage entrenchment, constitute a variety's distinct character. There is a very minor set of exceptions to this rule: typically, there is a very small number of lexical choices, mostly cultural terms, which are indeed almost (though, again, not fully) exclusively used in specific nations.

Evidence for the strong reading of pluricentricity, the assumption of epicentral influence of some nations on their neighbors, has been postulated and investigated for a few possible cases, notably Indian English and Australian English. Weak similarities and some anecdotal observations have suggested the possibility of influences, but little more than that. Ultimately, the evidence is inconclusive; no solid proof of epicentral diffusion has been presented so far.

In contrast, the evidence for pluriareality, the existence of feature distributions across or below national boundaries, is overwhelming. All the examples presented in Section 4 illustrate that there are many such patterns, on all levels of scale, and they represent just a minute selection from very many more possible cases. Certainly, Dollinger is right in stating that "pluri-areal is a synonym for geographical variation" (2019a: 63), but I do not understand why this fact should render the concept "an empty concept, a non-concept" (63). Pluriareality, i.e. geographical variation, is an important determinant of actual human linguistic performance.

Is there a need to decide between the two core concepts compared here, to debunk one at the expense of the other? I do not see any need for such a choice. I believe the relationship between both notions is not "either … or" but "both … and", depending on perspective and framework. Both terms highlight different aspects of the same reality, especially when we factor in the reality of consistently variable linguistic production as against the conceptual categorizations imposed by perception and socially ingrained language attitudes. In a complex and fuzzy world, the human mind seeks order and recognizable categories. Language production thrives on this complexity, while perception and cognition seek simplified, familiar entities.

Thus, the concept of pluricentricity focuses on national identity, distinctness along national lines, attitudes as products of language policy, and the construction of norms. In the English-speaking world, we encounter the concept and awareness of national varieties, but, outside of formal usage and higher-level education contexts, this is not something that many speakers care about. Furthermore, some of the debate results from a confusion of the term's weak and strong interpretations. Hence, pluricentricity appears a meaningful but weak concept, one that can be upheld but is not really necessary or very important for an understanding of how language works.

In contrast, the notion of pluriareality focuses on usage and on distributions of dialect forms. In English it clearly describes an important aspect of linguistic reality, since it characterizes very many feature distributions. It is not clear whether, based on Occam's razor, the term as such is needed, since it seems not any more informative than the established fact of geographical variation in language. Hence, pluriareality seems a meaningful, strong concept, but possibly a superfluous term, since it is questionable whether it adds value to established linguistic theorizing.

Ultimately, however, I hold that the relationship between these two notions is essentially a matter of perspective. Pluriareality is a term which adequately describes language production, the distribution of linguistic forms in space. It is essentially another term for regional variation, disregarding nationhood, and thus may be terminologically redundant, but it clearly captures an important aspect of linguistic performance and reality. In contrast, pluricentricity, especially in its weak meaning, operates purely in language perception, highlighting and recognizing some (select and rare, mostly lexical) properties of national varieties. It seems defensible, but also insufficiently informative, since it fails to capture the vast majority of observed phenomena of areal linguistic variability. It may also be seen as a problematic concept since it lends itself primarily to nationalistic perspectives and exploitation.

References

 Algeo, John. 1989. Queuing and other idiosyncracies. *World Englishes* 8. 157–163.
 Algeo, John. 2006. *British or American English? A handbook of word and grammar patterns.* Cambridge: Cambridge University Press.

Alleyne, Mervyn C. 1980. *Comparative Afro-American. An historical-comparative study of English-based Afro-American dialects of the new world*. Ann Arbor: Karoma.

Ammon, Ulrich (ed.). 1989. Towards a descriptive framework for the status / function / social position of a language within a country. *Status and function of language and language varieties*, 21–106. Berlin: De Gruyter.

Bernaisch, Tobias & Pam Peters (eds.). 2022. Linguistic epicentres in World Englishes. Special Issue of *World Englishes* 41(3).

Biber, Douglas & Randi Reppen. 2015. *The Cambridge handbook of English corpus linguistics*. Cambridge: Cambridge University Press.

Blommaert, Jan. 2010. *The sociolinguistics of globalization*. Cambridge: Cambridge University Press.

Bohmann, Axel. 2019. *Variation in English world-wide: Registers and global varieties*. Cambridge: Cambridge University Press.

Bolton, Kingsley, Werner Botha & Andy Kirkpatrick (eds.). 2020. *The handbook of Asian Englishes*. Hoboken, NJ: Wiley Blackwell.

Buschfeld, Sarah & Alexander Kautzsch (eds.). 2020. *Modelling world Englishes: A joint approach to postcolonial and non-postcolonial Englishes*. Edinburgh: Edinburgh University Press.

Cassidy, Frederic G. et al. 1985–2013. *Dictionary of American regional English*. 6 vols. Cambridge, MA: Harvard University Press.

Clyne, Michael (ed.). 1992. Pluricentric languages: Introduction. *Pluricentric languages: Differing norms in different nations*, 1–10. Berlin: De Gruyter.

Clyne, Michael (ed.). 1992. *Pluricentric languages. Differing norms in different nations*. Berlin, New York: Mouton de Gruyter.

Collins, Peter. 2015. *Grammatical change in English world-wide*. Amsterdam: Benjamins.

Dollinger, Stefan. 2019a. *The pluricentricity debate: On parallels, differences and distortions in German versus English and other languages*. London: Routledge.

Dollinger, Stefan. 2019b. Debunking "pluri-areality": On the pluricentric perspective of national varieties. *Journal of Linguistic Geography* 7(2). 98–112.

Elspaß, Stephan, Christa Dürscheid & Arne Ziegler. 2017. Zur grammatischen Pluriarealität der deutschen Gebrauchsstandards – oder: Über die Grenzen des Plurizentrizitätsbegriffs. *Zeitschrift für deutsche Philologie* 136. 69–91.

Gries, Stefan Th. & Tobias Bernaisch. 2016. Exploring epicentres empirically: Focus on South Asian Englishes. *English World-Wide* 37. 1–25.

Hedevind, Bertil. 1967. *The dialect of Dentdale in the West Riding of Yorkshire*. Upsala: Appelberg.

Hoffmann, Sebastian, Marianne Hundt and Joybrato Mukherjee. 2011. Indian English – an emerging epicentre? A pilot study on light-verbs in web-derived corpora of South Asian Englishes. *Anglia* 128. 258–280.

Hundt, Marianne. 2013. The diversification of English: Old, new and emerging epicentres. In Daniel Schreier & Marianne Hundt (eds.), *English as a contact language*, 182–203. Cambridge: Cambridge University Press.

Hundt, Marianne. 2020. On models and modelling. *World Englishes* (Early View).

Hundt, Marianne, & Ulrike Gut. 2012. *Mapping unity and diversity world-wide*. Amsterdam: Benjamins.

Hutcheson, Neal & Walt Wolfram. 2006. *Voices of North Carolina*. DVD. Raleigh, NC: The Language and Life Project, www.talkingnc.com. (21 Feb., 2024.)

Kachru, Braj B. (ed.). 1992. *The other tongue: English across cultures*. 2nd edn. Urbana, Chicago: University of Illinois Press.

Kirkpatrick, Andy. 2010. *English as a lingua franca in ASEAN. A multilingual model*. Hong Kong: Hong Kong University Press.

Kirkpatrick, Andy & Wang Lixun. 2020. *Is English an Asian language?* Cambridge: Cambridge University Press.

Kloss, Heinz. 1978. *Die Entwicklung neuer germanischer Kultursprachen seit 1800*, 2nd edn. Düsseldorf: Schwann.

König, Werner. 1981. *dtv-Atlas zur deutschen Sprache*. München: dtv.

Kortmann, Bernd, & Edgar W. Schneider. 2004. Varieties of English. *CD-ROM: A multimedia reference tool*. Berlin, New York: Mouton de Gruyter. http://www.varieties.mouton-content.com/

Kortmann, Bernd & Kerstin Lunkenheimer (eds.). 2012. *The Mouton world atlas of variation in English*. Berlin, Boston: Mouton de Gruyter.

Kortmann, Bernd, Kerstin Lunkenheimer & Katharina Ehret (eds.). 2020. *The electronic world atlas of varieties of English*. Zenodo. . http://ewave-atlas.org. (9 August, 2021.)

Kretzschmar, William R. 2004. Standard American English pronunciation. In Edgar W. Schneider, Kate Burridge, Bernd Kortmann, Rajend Mesthrie & Clive Upton (eds.), *A handbook of varieties of English*. Vol. 1: *Phonology*, 257–269. Berlin, New York: Mouton de Gruyter.

Lange, Claudia. 2020. English in South Asia. In Daniel Schreier, Marianne Hundt & Edgar W. Schneider (eds.), *The Cambridge handbook of world Englishes*, 236–262. Cambridge: Cambridge University Press.

Leitner, Gerhard. 1992. English as a pluricentric language. In Michael Clyne (ed.), *Pluricentric languages: Differing norms in different nations*, 179–237. Berlin: De Gruyter.

Leitner, Gerhard. 2010. Developmental stages in the formation of epicentres of English. In Oriana Palusci (ed.) *English, but not quite: Locating linguistic diversity*, 17–36. Trento: Tangram Edizioni Scientifiche.

Mair, Christian. 2013. The world system of Englishes: Accounting for the transnational importance of mobile and mediated vernaculars. *English World-Wide* 34. 253–278.

Meierkord, Christiane. 2012. *Interactions across Englishes. Linguistic choices in local and international contact situations*. Cambridge: Cambridge University Press.

Meierkord, Christiane & Edgar W. Schneider (eds.). 2020. *World Englishes at the grassroots*. Edinburgh: Edinburgh University Press.

Mittmann, Brigitta. 2004. *Mehrwort-Cluster in der englischen Alltagskonversation. Unterschiede zwischen britischem und amerikanischem gesprochenem Englisch als Indikatoren für den präfabrizierten Charakter der Sprache*. Tübingen: Narr.

Muhr, Rudolf. 2020. Pluriareality in sociolinguistics: A comprehensive overview of key ideas and a critique of linguistic data used. In Rudolf Muhr & Juan Thomas (eds.) *Pluricentricity theory beyond dominance and non-dominance*, 9–78. Graz, Berlin: PLC Press.

Muhr, Rudolf & Benjamin Meisnitzer (eds.). 2018. *Pluricentric languages and non-dominant varieties worldwide*. Berlin, Berne: Peter Lang.

Nagle, Stephen & Sara Sanders. 2003. *English in the Southern United States*. Cambridge: Cambridge University Press.

Nickerson, Raymond S. 2010. Inference: deductive and inductive. In Neil J. Salkind (ed.), *Encyclopedia of research design*, vol. 2, 593–596. Thousand Oaks: Sage.

Niehaus, Konstantin. 2015. Areale Variation in der Syntax des Standarddeutschen: Ergebnisse zum Sprachgebrauch und zur Frage Plurizentrik vs. Pluriarealität. *Zeitschrift für Dialektologie und Linguistik* 82(2). 133–168.

Pennycook, Alastair. 2007. *Global Englishes and transcultural flows*. London, New York: Routledge.

Percillier, Michael. 2016. *World Englishes and second language acquisition. Insights from Southeast Asian Englishes*. Amsterdam: Benjamins.

Peters, Pam. 2009. Australian English as a regional epicentre. In Thomas Hoffmann & Lucia Siebers (eds.), *World Englishes – Problems, properties and prospects*, 107–124. Amsterdam: John Benjamins.

Preston, Dennis. 1989. *Perceptual dialectology. Nonlinguists' views of areal linguistics*. Dordrecht: Foris.

Preston, Dennis. 1996. Where the worst English is spoken. In Edgar W. Schneider (ed.), *Focus on the USA*, 297–360. (VEAW G16) Amsterdam: Benjamins.

Roberts, Peter A. 1988. *West Indians and their language*. Cambridge: Cambridge University Press.

Rohdenburg, Günter, & Julia Schlüter. 2009. *One language, two grammars? Differences between British and American English*. Cambridge: Cambridge University Press.

Scheuringer, Hermann. 1996. Das Deutsche als pluriareale Sprache: ein Beitrag gegen staatlich begrenzte Horizonte in der Diskussion um die deutsche Sprache in Österreich. *Die Unterrichtspraxis / Teaching German* 29(2). 147–153.

Schneider, Edgar W. 1986. 'How to Speak Southern' – An American English dialect stereotyped. *Amerikastudien / American Studies*, 425–439.

Schneider, Edgar W. 2007. *Postcolonial English. Varieties around the world*. Cambridge: Cambridge University Press.

Schneider, Edgar W. 2011a. The pluricentricity of English: Centrifugal forces. In Augusto Soares da Silva, Amadeu Torres & Miguel Goncalves (eds.), *Línguas Pluricêntricas. Variação Linguística e Dimensões Sociocognitivas. Pluricentric languages. Linguistic variation and sociocognitive dimensions*, 109–124. Braga: Publicações da Faculdade de Filosofia Universidade Católica Portuguesa.

Schneider, Edgar W. 2011b. The subjunctive in Philippine English. In Maria Lourdes Bautista (ed.), *Studies in Philippine English*, 159–173. Manila: Anvil.

Schneider, Edgar W. 2013. The pluricentricity of English today — and how about non-dominant varieties? In Rudolf Muhr, Carla Amorós Negre, Carmen Fernández Juncal, Klaus Zimmermann Emilio Prieto und Natividad Hernández (eds.), *Exploring linguistic standards in non-dominant varieties of pluricentric languages / Explorando estándares lingüísticos en variedades no dominantes de lenguas pluricéntricas*, 45–54. Frankfurt, Wien: Peter Lang.

Schneider, Edgar W. 2014a. Global diffusion, regional attraction, local roots? Sociocognitive perspectives on the pluricentricity of English. In Augusto Soares da Silva (ed.), *Pluricentricity. language variation and sociocognitive dimensions*, 191–226. Berlin, New York: De Gruyter Mouton.

Schneider, Edgar W. 2014b. Asian Englishes — into the future: a bird's eye view. *Asian Englishes* 16. 1–8.

Schneider, Edgar W. 2018. The interface between cultures and corpora: Tracing reflections and manifestations. *ICAME Journal* 42. 25–60.

Schneider, Edgar W. 2020. *English around the world. An introduction*, 2nd edn. Cambridge: Cambridge University Press.

Schneider, Edgar W. 2022. Parameters of epicentral status. *World Englishes* 41. 462–474.

Schneider, Edgar W., Bernd Kortmann, Kate Burridge, Rajend Mesthrie, & Clive Upton, (eds.). 2004. *A handbook of varieties of English*. Vol. I: *Phonology*. Vol. 2: *Morphology and syntax*. Berlin, New York: Mouton de Gruyter.

Schreier, Daniel, Marianne Hundt & Edgar W. Schneider (eds.). 2020. *The Cambridge handbook of world Englishes*. Cambridge: Cambridge University Press.

Seargeant, Philip and Caroline Tagg. 2011. English on the internet and a 'post-varieties' approach to language. *World Englishes* 30(4). 496–514.

Steger, Maria & Edgar W. Schneider. 2012. Complexity as a function of iconicity: The case of complement clause constructions in New Englishes. In Bernd Kortmann & Benedikt Szmrecsanyi (eds.), *Linguistic complexity: Second language acquisition, indigenization, contact*, 156–191. Berlin, New York: Mouton de Gruyter.

Strevens, Peter. 1971. *British and American English*. London: Collier-Macmillan.

Tottie, Gunnel. 2002. *An introduction to American English*. Malden, MA, Oxford: Blackwell.

Trudgill, Peter. 1974. *Sociolinguistics. An introduction to language and society*. Harmondsworth: Penguin.

Trudgill, Peter (ed.). 2002. The sociolinguistics of modern RP. *Sociolinguistic Variation and Change*, 171–180. Edinburgh: Edinburgh University Press.

Velupillai, Viveka. 2012. *An introduction to linguistic typology*. Amsterdam: John Benjamins.

Wolfram, Walt & Natalie Schilling-Estes. 1997. *Hoi toide on the Outer Banks. The story of the Ocracoke Brogue*. Chapel Hill, NC, London: University of North Carolina Press.

CHAPTER 6

The pluricentricity vs. pluriareality debate
What postcolonial diffusion and transnational language contact can tell us

Sarah Buschfeld
TU Dortmund University, Germany

The notions "pluricentricity" and "pluriareality" are hotly debated conceptions, in particular among linguists aiming to conceptualize the spread and standards of the German language (e.g. Dollinger 2019a, 2019b; Elspaß et al. 2017; Muhr 2013, 2020; Scheuringer 1996). The present chapter aims to shed light on this controversy from an Anglophone perspective. Drawing on examples of general linguistic distribution patterns and language use in Southeast Asia and Southern Africa, I discuss what the two notions can contribute to our understanding and conceptualization of the English language. The conclusion, however, will be far from satisfactory for the strict proponents of the two approaches: I argue that both are valid approaches and not necessarily mutually exclusive. Only a joint perspective can shed conclusive light on the spread, conceptualizations, and standards of supra-national languages such as English (and probably also German). Further, I will argue that in times of ongoing globalization, these conceptions become increasingly obsolete, requiring more flexible approaches to linguistic variation — at least if we take on the global perspective.

Keywords: globalization, multilingualism, Malaysian English, Indonesian English, Namibian English, Singapore English, South African English

1. Introduction

The notions "pluricentricity" and "pluriareality" have been hotly debated conceptions, in particular among linguists aiming to conceptualize the spread, norms, and standards of the German language (e.g. Dollinger 2019a, 2019b; Elspaß et al. 2017; Muhr 2013, 2020; Scheuringer 1996). In this context, particularly the concept of pluricentricity has also been applied and discussed against the background of the English language (e.g. Clyne 1992; Leitner 1992; Schneider, this volume). Pluriareal approaches to English are still rare. Dollinger (2019a) is one of the very few to discuss this issue for the anglophone world.

The present chapter aims to address this controversy from the Anglophone perspective. I briefly introduce the two notions and then focus on what the Anglophone perspective has contributed so far to the discussion (Section 2). Drawing on linguistic features as well as general distribution patterns and language use in Southeast Asia and the area of Southern Africa, I discuss in how far English should be conceptualized as a pluriareal or a pluricentric language, with Singapore and the Republic of South Africa as potential epicenters for their neighboring regions (Sections 3.1, 3.2, 4.1). I then turn towards the global perspective and discuss what recent approaches to World Englishes contribute to our understanding and the conceptualization of the two approaches and the English language (Section 4.2.). As discussed in Section 4, my overall observations indicate that the two approaches are not as mutually exclusive as the heated debate between the two camps would suggest. In fact, the debate appears to mainly revolve around ideologically-loaded questions of standards, norms of correctness, and acceptance of speech forms (as in the case of Austrian German vs. German German). However, we can only fruitfully continue the scientific discussion if we resolve these ideological tensions. In this respect, I will propose that only a joint perspective, combining the major assumptions of the two approaches, can shed conclusive light on the spread, conceptualizations, and standards of supra-national languages such as English or German. Beyond that, I will argue that in times of globalization and widespread multilingualism, these conceptions (and in particular their clear-cut separation) become increasingly obsolete – at least if we take on the global perspective: nation state boundaries may persist (and certainly have an important influence on identity conceptions and linguistic practices) but communities of practice do not necessarily adhere to such boundaries, and distinctions between languages and dialects become increasingly blurred in times of massive language contact and linguistic restructuring.

2. Pluricentricity vs. pluriareality: Two competing approaches?

Approaching the existing debate, the central question that comes to mind is: Are the two notions "pluricentricity" and "pluriareality" really two competing approaches? From what has been reported in the literature so far, the answer appears to be clear. As Dollinger (2019a: 1) states, "'Pluri-areality' directly contradicts the established concept of pluricentricity in its fundamental assumptions of how national varieties are to be modelled." Following an early publication on the topic and introduction of the term "pluricentricity" by Kloss (e.g. 1967, 1978), the concept was spread with groundbreaking contributions by Michael Clyne (1984, 1992, 1995), Gerhard Leitner (1992), and Ulrich Ammon (1995) in the 1980s and early 1990s. According to Kloss (1978: 67), a language is pluricentric if it has different cultural centers that are politically and culturally independent from one another. He further assumes that a language is pluricentric if it is used in different independent nations. Clyne defines a language as pluricentric if it is "a national variety with at least some of its own (codified) norms" and several "(epi-)centers" (Clyne 1992: 1).

As Schneider (2013, see also this volume) points out, the notion of pluricentricity is a fuzzy, ambiguous concept, with at least two readings. The "weak reading" follows the assumption that different national varieties of a language exist which all hold norms of their own. The examples listed by Clyne (1992) include Singapore, Malaysia, India, West Africa, and other postcolonial varieties of English. The "strong reading" of the concept relates to the idea of the existence of larger epicenters which exert a unilateral influence on smaller, neighboring "versions" of a language. I deliberately avoid terms such as "variety" or "dialect" here since these would suggest inferiority of these speech forms to the epicentral one, which exactly is one of the core issues so hotly debated in the field.

The notion of "pluriareality" was introduced and first advocated by Scheuringer (1996). It goes beyond the nation state in that it considers the distribution and use of linguistic features (e.g. lexical, phonological, and morphosyntactic) across national boundaries. A number of studies have shown that areal distributions of speech forms, such as, for example, to be found along the German-Austrian border, are independent of nation states and are used on both sides of the border (e.g. Elspaß et al. 2017: 88; Niehaus 2015). Proponents of the pluriareal approach thus view the pluricentric model as strongly ideologically motivated with a too strong focus on the nation state (e.g. Niehaus 2015: 135–138). As Dollinger (2019a: 1–2) concludes: "Pluricentricity refers to the development of multiple standards, often national standards of a given language, while 'pluriareality' downplays, if not negates, any national level."

Even though variation and standards of the German language have been at the heart of this debate, it is by no means the only language identified as pluricentric in the literature. Clyne (1995: 20) lists English, French, Swahili, Spanish, Arabic, Bengali, and Chinese as instances of pluricentric languages (see Muhr 2016a, 2016b for further examples). Dollinger (2019a) expands the perspective to the Anglophone world and also includes some other languages such as Dutch, Luxembourgish, Norwegian, Swedish, and Danish. His primary aim, however, is to make the case for pluricentricity and debunk the notion of pluriareality. Apart from this, the notions have not been extensively discussed for the context of English – Leitner (1992) relates the concept of pluricentricity to the English language but does not empirically assess or discuss the situation.

A number of later publications have discussed epicentric influences of varieties of English on neighboring varieties (e.g. Leitner 2010; Hundt 2013; Schneider 2013, 2014; Bernaisch & Peters 2022). Originating in the earth sciences, the term denotes "the point on the earth's surface directly above the origin of an earthquake," or in a slightly more general sense, "the place that has the highest level of an activity" (Cambridge Dictionary 2014: epicenter). The metaphorical connection to language is obvious. Hundt (2013: 185) identifies two main characteristics of epicenters:

1. Epicenters are endonormatively stabilized in the sense of Schneider's notion of endonormative stabilization as the main characteristic in phase 4 of his Dynamic Model (2003, 2007).
2. They serve as the linguistic model for other varieties.

Schneider (2014: 201) identifies further criteria that come with endonormativity and thus are also indexical for epicenter status, namely formal acceptance of a variety in a specific region, homogeneity, codification, literary attestation, and an "attractor function for other varieties in a certain region (i.e. when learners from other regions acquire the variety in question)." American English (AmE) is, in many ways, the prime example of older epicenters of English, but Australian or New Zealand English have also been discussed as epicenters in the Antipodean area. In addition to that, Hundt (2013: 186) introduces "emerging epicentres" to the debate; these are "epicentres [...] that have developed their own endo-normativity (e.g., IndE (Indian English) and SinE (Singaporean English)) but whose status as a potential (local) norm-providing center has only recently attracted linguists' attention" (my additions; see also Heller et al. 2017). South Africa might also be a case in point (Schneider 2014), but has, to my knowledge, not been discussed on empirical grounds. The discussion of Namibian English (NamE) as an offspring of South African English (SAfE) implicitly entails this idea (e.g. Maho 1998: 166–169; Trudgill & Hannah 2002: 28, 33; see also Stell 2014: 227).

3. English from postcolonial diffusion to globalization

As the discussion above has shown, a number of English varieties have been identified and discussed as potential epicenters for the Anglophone world, which would support the strong reading of pluricentricity. However, reservations towards this approach exist, based both on empirical investigations of feature distributions and use in varieties of English and their neighbors, and on methodological considerations. As Schneider (this volume) puts it: "There are some indicators but there has only been quite limited empirical substantiation, so the strong reading of "pluricentricity" remains a viable hypothesis but so far has not been backed by solid evidence." Moreover, the global dissemination of English clearly shows characteristics that fuel the pluriareal approach, since in a number of postcolonial localities, linguistic features transcend national borders, such as in the neighboring countries Singapore and Malaysia. Therefore, the picture is far from conclusive.

In what follows, I draw on two sets of examples from the World Englishes paradigm, one set based on Southern Africa, more precisely SAfE and NamE,[1] the other one entailing South-East Asian varieties of English, namely SingE, and Malaysian (MalE), and Indonesian English (IndonE). I discuss what the data imply for the discussion at hand. In both cases, I focus on similarities and differences in linguistic features characteristic of the Southeast Asian varieties and the two Southern African varieties and discuss in how far Singapore and South Africa can be conceptualized as epicenters for the respective neighboring varieties MalE and IndonE, and NamE.

3.1 Singapore English: Emerging epicenter standard or southeast Asian Englishes continuum?

Singapore English (SingE), spoken in Singapore, a sovereign city-state in Southeast Asia located between Malaysia and Indonesia, is one of the most widely researched varieties of English. It has been mainly analyzed and discussed as a second-language (L2) variety since this is its historical origin. Nowadays, however, English is increasingly acquired and spoken as a first language (L1) by major cohorts of the younger generation: Census data report an increase in use of English as a home language for five- to nine-year-olds from 34.1% in 2000 to 51.5% in 2010 (Singapore Department of Statistics 2001, 2010, 2011), and to 70.1% in 2020 (Singapore Department of Statistics 2021).

Modern Singapore pursues a policy of multiracialism, which promotes equal status among the different ethnic groups. It is characterized by a co-existence of many different languages, of which four, Mandarin, Tamil, Malay, and English,

---

1. I would like to thank Markus Bieswanger, Alexander Kautzsch, and Anne Schröder, who were part of the research team that collected the data the study draws on. I would also like to thank the student assistants at Bielefeld University, most notably Jens Thomas, Daniela Kauschke, Lisa Schumacher, and Frederic Zähres, as well as Jill Mazzetta at the University of Regensburg, for transcribing and editing the data and transcripts. Lastly, I would like to thank all those who supported us during the data collection process, most notably Sarala Krishnamurthy, Ernest Olivier, Ronel Louw, and Reiner and Gillian Stommel.

have been designated as official languages. English was included due to its ethnic neutrality in hopes that it would uphold and guarantee this multiracial equality (Wee 2004: 1019). In fact, "English is the only common bond shared by everybody" (Schneider 2007: 156).

However, the linguistic situation in Singapore is not only complex in terms of multilingualism and which languages are acquired and spoken when and with whom. The question of how many varieties of SingE really exist has not been conclusively answered yet. SingE is used as both an L1 and an L2, and in a variety of domains, both formal and informal. For many years, the situation has been described as diglossic between a standard and a non-standard, colloquial variety of English, viz. Standard Singapore English (SSE) and Colloquial Singapore English (CSE/Singlish) (esp. Gupta, e.g. 1989, 1994). A variety of other approaches exist but cannot be discussed in detail. It seems that the diglossic approach does not meet recent linguistic realities and that no two homogenous varieties of SingE exist. However, the existence of a clearly identifiable, homogenous standard – or several regional standards (cf. the notion of "regional pluricentricity" or "second level pluricentricity"; Auer 2014: 44; Muhr 2018: 40–42) – would be the prerequisite for a pluricentric approach. And, indeed, such a standard appears to exist in Singapore – at least from a language-political and ideological/attitudinal perspective. In 2000, the government launched the so-called "Speak-Good-English" movement as a measure to counter the usage of CSE/Singlish and promote the use of standard speech and thus SSE. Furthermore, SSE has been discussed as a potential, newly emerging epicenter for norm orientation in the Southeast Asian region (cf. the discussion in Hundt 2013). The increase of English as a home language in Singapore, and thus the ever-growing cohorts of young people speaking English as (one of) their L1(s), seems to be in line with this claim. The other characteristics mentioned by Schneider (2014b: 184), viz. "endonormativity, manifested via formal acceptance, homogeneity, codification, literary attestation, and [...] attractor function for other varieties" seem to be at least mostly met, too. These observations would clearly promote the long-standing conception of English as a pluricentric language. However, when it comes to actual language use and if we compare the use of linguistic characteristics between Singapore and some of its neighboring countries, we see how the pluriareal approach is the more suitable framework.

First of all, in particular the more recent literature on SingE has pointed towards a stronger linguistic heterogeneity than often assumed. Buschfeld (2020), for example, shows that variation in the realization of specific features in L1 child SingE are not only observable between but also within speakers. The children in her study produce both, features that have so far been conceptualized as standard but also non-standard speech forms in the same conversational event. Even though the pluricentricity/pluriareality debate revolves around the standards of a language, findings of non-standard language use are also relevant for the discussion at hand for the following, (partly) interrelated reasons: First of all, pluriarealists traditionally have included non-standard speech forms in their investigations, too (cf. the work by Elspaß et al. 2017; Niehaus 2015; Scheuringer 1996). And this makes sense, since no speaker would ever produce standard features only and "not all features of pluricentric varieties are codified norm elements" (Schneider, this volume). Therefore, the strict separation between standard and non-standard speech forms is an artificial construct at best, with standards being "conventionalized abstractions [...] while the down-to-earth reality is much more complicated and messy" (Schneider, this volume). Furthermore, the use of non-standard speech forms in the children investigated by Buschfeld (2020) partly outweighs the use of the standard variants, a finding which Buschfeld interprets as indicative of ongoing language change. SingE has clearly emancipated itself from alleged BrE or AmE standards and the linguistic characteristics the children produce may well be the standard variants of the future (see Ronan & Buschfeld 2024) and may become part of Singapore's potential epicentral influence on other countries.

In this respect, it has repeatedly been observed that the Englishes in Singapore and Malaysia, Singapore's direct neighbor, seem to have much in common; they have even been described in a single approach (e.g. Ooi, ed. 2001; Platt & Weber 1980). Drawing on Buschfeld's (2020) corpus of current L1 children's SingE, I compare the realization of past tense endings between the varieties as an example. SingE allows for two strategies beyond the standard marking of regular and irregular verbs via -ed endings or *Ablaut*-processes. These are the use of bare verb forms (Examples 3 and 4) and a specific, Chinese-derived structure in which *finish* serves as the past tense marker (Example 5).[2]

(1) Child (5;6, female, Chinese): [...] he took some [...] sticks and then [...] he **make** a [/] a stick house.

(2) Child (5;4, male, Indian): but he couldn't. And then he took a ladder and **climb** up the [/] the chimeney [=chimney].

(3) Child (5;2, female, Chinese): She **tie finish** her [...] shoes.

(Buschfeld 2020: 147–148)

---

2. The data in the corpus come from nineteen female and eighteen male children aged 1;4 to 12;1. Twenty of the children are of Chinese ancestry, nine are of Indian ancestry, and three are of "mixed" ancestry. The notation X;Y used here refers to year(s) and month(s), respectively, i.e. 1;4 = 1 year and 4 months. Please note that Buschfeld could not recruit any Malay families for this project for a variety of practical reasons.

Looking into the distribution of these realizations, we see that the Chinese children make more frequent use of the local structures than the Indian children. With regular verbs, the former use 52.7% unmarked and 3.6% verb-*finish* structures, while the Indian children use 29.3% and 1.5%, respectively. With irregular verb forms, the percentages are slightly lower, viz. 45% of unmarked verbs and 1.2% of verb-*finish* structures for the Chinese children and 22.4% and 0.3% for the Indian children, respectively (Buschfeld 2020: 196–197; see similar results for her investigation of the realization of subject pronouns, Chapter 6).

When compared to Buschfeld's results, Percillier's (2016: 73) comparative study of SingE, MalE, and IndonE, three Englishes spoken in immediately neighboring geographical regions, shows much lower frequencies of non-standard past tense marking in SingE. Of course, this may well be due to the fact that the data come from adult speakers of SingE (both L1 and L2) and are of a rather acrolectal nature (see the National Institute of Education Corpus of Spoken Singapore English (NIECSSE), Deterding & Low 2001; and the Grammar of Spoken Singapore English Corpus (GSSEC), e.g. Lim & Foley 2004). Still, this observation as well as Percillier's comparison of the realization of past tense marking in the three varieties has revealed three important findings for the discussion at hand. First of all, all three varieties exhibit non-standard past tense marking of a very similar kind. Verbs are either bare, i.e. uninflected for past tense similar to what has been found by Buschfeld (2020) for Singapore, or speakers use an auxiliary to indicate a completed action (Percillier 2016: 71–79). The use of *already* as adverbial past tense marker has also been attested by Buschfeld (2020: 206–207); Percillier, however, does not report the use of the LEXV+*finish* structure.

These strong similarities between the varieties can, on the one hand, be explained as epicentral influences of SinE on its neighbors. However, what is surprising against the background of the assumption that Singapore would be the epicenter for its neighboring countries is that the rate of non-standard past tense marking is lowest in Singapore (<10%) and highest in the Indonesian data (>50%) (Percillier 2016: 73).[3] It can be argued that in an epicentral approach this should be the other way around. On the other hand, shared feature use between the countries can be ascribed to shared social and cultural histories and similarities in the language contact scenarios in these locations, i.e. the other languages being spoken alongside English. Such explanations of areal distributions of language are at the heart of pluriareal approaches (e.g. Velupillai 2012; see also Schneider, this volume).

---

3. Note that this applies to a number of the linguistic features investigated by Percillier (e.g. page 81 and the overview on 121).

When looking into what the differences between the varieties in Percillier's investigation and between Percillier's and Buschfeld's study may tell us,[4] we also have to take into consideration potential quantitative changes in the varieties. The Singapore data used in Percillier's study were mostly collected in the 1990s, the Indonesian data in 2009. The huge differences may therefore be the result of ongoing language change in the regions. This interpretation would also explain the much higher numbers of non-standard verb forms in Buschfeld's study, which do not correspond at all to what Percillier has found for Singapore. Two studies by Buschfeld (2017a on subject pronoun realization and 2017b on past tense marking; see also Ronan & Buschfeld 2024), comparing her child data to the spoken ICE-Singapore component, for which the data were also collected in the early 1990s, confirm the differences found in comparison to Percillier's study. Of course, age-grading, i.e. the possibility that children simply produce less formal speech than adults but that the differences will level out with adulthood, needs to be taken into consideration, too. However, the differences between adult and child SingE appear to be too strong to be simply the result of age-grading (see Ronan & Buschfeld 2024 for further details). This may indicate that the use of originally non-standard SingE features has grown stronger in the last 30 years and that to conclusively answer the question whether SingE has had epicentral effect on its neighboring varieties one has to compare recent speech data from the different contexts to earlier findings.

In addition to that, one has to consider changes in speaker attitudes when it comes to language use and norms of correctness. As pointed out above, some 20 years ago, the government aimed to exert a strong influence on the Singaporean people to use "correct", acceptable English, i.e. SSE, which was, back then, assumed to be very close to BrE. However, governmental control and thus their influence has weakened over time and thus the strong stance against using CSE. This shows how general language attitudes might change over time and with them norms of correctness and standards.

Another interesting trend that has been observed for SingE that might shed light on the pluricentricity/pluriareality debate is the commodification of Singlish. As Wee (2020: 117) states "Singlish is becoming increasingly commodified as a cultural product that is exportable." Singlish is promoted on internet channels such as YouTube, non-Singaporeans can learn Singlish in online tutorials, and films and series featuring Singlish-speaking characters have increasingly gained

---

4. Even though Percillier draws on different corpora (NIECSSE, GSSEC, ICE-Malaysia, and self-collected data for Indonesia), he has attempted to select comparable data sources for his study (2016: 37–42) and the strong differences in the frequencies of the non-standard features are not very likely to be the results of a corpus effect only.

international recognition as can be observed, for example, from the Netflix series *Orange is the New Black*. Not only does this issue of commodification lead to different dynamics in language attitudes and practice (Wee 2020: 117–118), i.e. the acceptance of originally non-standard SingE features in and outside the country, it also adds further layers of complexity to the discussion at hand. Can we really pursue a strict epicentral approach taking into consideration such complex linguistic states and diffusion patterns? How is the notion of "standard" really linked to the phenomenon, in particular since the conceptual boundaries between standards and non-standards are often of an ideological nature and fuzzy. Furthermore, today's vernacular features may well develop into tomorrow's standards, as has often been attested in the history of English (e.g. Barber 1997: 166–168 on the third person singular present; Kohnen 2014: 176 on the progressive) and as seems to be the case for SingE. In the discussion, I will come back to the question what all this ultimately suggests for the pluricentricity/pluriareality debate.

3.2 Namibian English: A product of South African epicentral influence?

As a next step, I approach the topic from the recipient perspective looking into whether and how Namibia might have been under epicentral influence from South Africa. Namibia and South Africa are neighboring countries and share a direct historico-political connection via South Africa's mandate over Namibia (known as Southwest Africa at the time) following World War I (for further details, e.g. Buschfeld 2014). With the end of World War I, Germany lost all colonial possessions, which is why the formerly German territories were redistributed to other countries. Namibia fell under a C-class mandate, a category assigned to former German territories, "thought least able to govern themselves" (Wallace 2011: 217) by the League of Nations. The mandate was formally granted to Britain but administered by South Africa, even if against the will of the United Nations, after World War II. However, South Africa refused to give up control over Namibia and employed its apartheid system in both states. After years of political struggles, the South West African People's Organization (SWAPO) formed and started a war of independence against South African domination. Namibia finally gained independence in 1990.[5]

With independence, English was introduced as the sole official language of Namibia, which was a surprising decision against the background of Namibia's great linguistic diversity and the fact that it never was a British colony in the strict sense. South Africa's constitution, for example, stipulates eleven official languages.

---

5. For more detailed accounts of the history of Namibia see, e.g., Böhm (2003); Buschfeld & Kautzsch (2014); Deumert (2009); Wallace (2011).

Still, it would not be the first country that introduced English as its official language (a trend particularly strong in Africa and Asia), simply since English often was associated with ethnic neutrality so that the country did not have to decide in favor of one or a group of ethnic languages over others. Still, English was not completely new to the scene as it had been the language of SWAPO and the liberation movement (Frydman 2011: 183).

Due to its complex history and language political decisions, Namibia is ethnically and linguistically diverse. The majority of its population is what is traditionally referred to as "black," consisting of a number of ethnic groups (e.g. Ovambos (Namibia's majority), Kavangos, Hereros, Damaras/Namas, Caprivians, Bushmen, Basters, and Tswanas). About 6% of the population are white European, including mostly Afrikaners but also a number of Germans; 6.5% are of mixed African-European ancestry (Central Intelligence Agency 2021a). As a result, a number of indigenous and European languages are spoken in Namibia, i.e. sixteen Bantu languages, about nine Khoisan languages, and three West Germanic languages (Böhm 2003: 525; NIDS 2006: 42).

When compared to South Africa, it is characterized by a similar contact setting with similar African languages spoken in the two regions and with Afrikaans having been the language of apartheid and the lingua franca in both countries for a considerable amount of time. The historical depth and entrenchment of both Afrikaans and English, however, is different, which would allow for an epicenter interpretation of the relationship between South Africa and Namibia. In this respect, Schröder and Zähres (2020: 49) "suspect that South African forms of English may have had (and may still have) an influence on the development of English in Namibia." They expect that "South African forms of English [were] very likely to have served as a norm-providing model – probably alongside Standard British English and more recently Standard American English – during the colonial era, but also in the stabilization phase of NamE following independence" (Schröder & Zähres 2020: 49). Taking into consideration the criteria for epicenter status discussed in Section 2, this seems to be a well-founded assumption. To validate their claim, Schröder and Zähres report on findings from an earlier study by Kautzsch and Schröder (2016), who observe a merger of TRAP and DRESS and TRAP-DRESS-NURSE vowels.[6] They conclude that "[w]ith regard to these two mergers, the variation in NamE seems to parallel some aspects of South African English (SAfE) since the trap-dress merger has been reported for Broad White SAfE as well as Black SAfE" (Schröder & Zähres 2020: 50; see also Bowerman 2004: 937; Van Rooy 2004: 945). On the other hand, the findings in Kautzsch und

---

6. Such lexical sets were introduced to English linguistics by Wells (1982) to capture and describe groups of words that share the respective phonological feature under investigation.

Schröder (2016) reveal clear differences between the NamE data and findings for SAfEs when it comes to the realization and distribution of the KIT split and the NURSE-WORK split (see also Schröder & Zähres 2020: 50–51; Schröder et al. 2020). Unfortunately, I cannot go into further details within the framework of the present chapter, but I would like to compare one morphosyntactic feature between the two varieties as an example, viz. the extended use of the progressive, as investigated by Buschfeld (2021) and illustrated in Examples 1 and 2 (Buschfeld 2021: 178).

(4) Speaker (Damara, female, *1970): I'm having four brothers and one sister.

(5) Speaker (Ovambo, male, *1996): Yeah, I'm growing up here.

The Electronic World Atlas of Varieties of English (eWAVE; Kortmann et al. 2020) reports similar extended uses of the progressive for SAfE. Furthermore, it reinforces Buschfeld's (2021) observation that progressives are mostly extended to semantic verb classes that in standard BrE and AmE traditionally do not take progressive endings. Such forms are primarily reported for black speakers and less so for white speakers (see also, for example, Mesthrie 2004: 963, 975).

Other linguistic commonalities between SAfE(s) and NamE(s) have been identified by, for example, Steigertahl (2019: 282–288), who offers a direct and more detailed comparison of the two contexts. Still, she also identifies some features as unique to NamEs and concludes that the shared features "do [...] not imply that English(es) used by Black Namibians represents a sub-variety of SAE (SAfE)" (2019: 287; my addition).

For the debate at hand, it is important to note that for both contexts, the existence of different sub-varieties have been reported, mostly distributed along ethnic lines, for example White and Black SAfEs and NamEs. These differences could be interpreted as examples of regional pluricentricity / second level pluricentricity. Together with the shared historico-political relationship between South Africa and Namibia, and in particular Namibia's dependency on the neighboring country as well as geographical and demographic factors (with a land area of 823,290 sq km and a population of approximately 2.6 million Namibia is much smaller and less populated than South Africa with 1,214,470 sq km of land and a population of approximately 56.5 million (July 2020 est., Central Intelligence Agency 2021b)), the epicenter interpretation would then not be far to seek. However, shared linguistic characteristics and thus areal distributions of features across national borders due to a shared historical and sociocultural background as well as similar language contact scenarios favor a pluriareal explanation of the linguistic realities in Southern Africa. The epicenter interpretation can, once again, only be applied from a more ideological, abstract perspective and is even more difficult to empirically pin down than for the Southeast Asian example.

4. Discussion

4.1 What South Africa and Southeast Asia tell us about the pluricentricity/pluriareality debate

The results from the comparison of the Southeast Asian and South African contexts are far from conclusive for the debate. For both contexts, the historico-political and sociolinguistic developments and the geographical parameters would support an interpretation of SingE as an epicentral variety for MalE and IndonE, and South African English as an epicentral variety for NamE. Language attitudes and common perceptions of the existence of homogeneous national standards seem to confirm such an interpretation. However, clearly more research is needed to shed conclusive light on the question of what exactly constitutes an epicentral variety or sub-variety and what not. As Hundt aptly states, the concept of an epicenter "is far from straightforward, both on theoretical and methodological grounds" (2013: 182). The strong reading of pluricentricity is, therefore, hard to confirm but does not seem very likely. The weak reading, i.e. that different national varieties of a language exist which all hold norms of their own and are thus clearly delimitable from each other, is hard to verify on the basis of the above comparisons (cf. Sections 3.1 and 3.2). Schneider (this volume) concludes for a comparison of BrE and AmE that clear-cut distinctions between varieties are rather exceptional since "on both sides of the Atlantic essentially the same expressions and patterns are used, but frequencies and preferences of choices vary greatly". This seems to be true for the sets of varieties under observation as well, though some clear qualitative differences can be found between Asian and African varieties that range above questions of frequencies and preferences. When turning back to our examples and the comparisons of direct neighbors, however, we see how the pluriareal approach has much to offer to account for the distribution and use of linguistic characteristics. Even though SingE has often been nominally treated as a monolithic whole, more recent research has shown that SingE is characterized by sociolinguistic variation in general and ethnic variation in particular (e.g. Buschfeld 2020; Leimgruber 2013; Lim 2010). The same holds for SAfE, for which different ethnic varieties have been reported (White, Black, Indian, and Cape Flats South African English; e.g. the contributions in Kortmann & Schneider 2004). NamE can be conceptualized along similar lines with at least three existing sub-varieties (White, Black, and Baster NamE; Schröder & Zähres

2020; Buschfeld 2021). Even if this does not speak against a pluricentric interpretation in principle as the existence of different varieties inside a country has been conceptualized as "regional pluricentricity" or "second level pluricentricity" (cf. Auer 2014: 44; Muhr 2018: 40–42; see also Section 3.1), feature investigations which are needed to empirically come to terms with such variety-internal heterogeneity are more at the heart of pluriareal approaches. Also, even more importantly, such feature analyses, and in particular the comparison of SingE with MalE and IndonE and the comparison of SAfE with NamE, have revealed strong similarities between the varieties. At first sight, these may seem to support an epicentral and therefore pluricentric interpretation of the linguistic distributions and patterns in both contexts. However, the quantitative and qualitative differences of feature use between the varieties and thus fuzzy distributions across national boundaries, which often manifest as dialectal preferences and in non-standard language use, can far better be explained by the pluriareal position. They seem to be the result of different sociolinguistic realities in the countries under observation (e.g. SingE as an L1, IndoE as a learner English) and/or varying preferences by the population (see also Schneider, this volume, for a similar line of argumentation). This, once again, calls into question the strong epicentral conceptualization often taken for granted in World Englishes research (e.g. Leitner 1992; Mair 2009) and supports the pluriareal approach as it does not put the nation state and one allegedly homogenous standard variety of a language center stage.

As my observations have shown, the debate is very complex and cannot be resolved on the basis of the case studies and data bases at hand — but I pretty much doubt any case study or data set could, no matter how thorough and well-founded the investigation. In fact, as many contributions to the current volume point out, the two approaches do not seem to be as mutually exclusive and opposing as long assumed but nicely complement each other since "both of these models, in their intent and analyses, seem to largely be investigating different aspects of language use" (cf. the conclusion of this volume). While pluriarealists mostly focus on production, which is suitable to account for variation across borders (e.g. Elspaß, this volume), pluricentricists tend to stress aspects of language attitudes, perception, and awareness (e.g. Ransmayr, this volume). As the editors aptly state in the introduction to this volume, "both models weigh the importance of language production and perception to different degrees in capturing and conceptualizing linguistic variation (see also Ransmayr, this volume; Niehaus, this volume; Schneider, this volume)". However, both perspectives are important to account for the complex realities of linguistic developments, distributions, and variation and for our understanding of what constitutes a standard and might have an influence on other varieties of the same language and what not. The examples of Southeast Asia and Southern Africa discussed in this chapter have illustrated how these manifest in practice.

On the one hand, the case of Southeast Asia shows how language policies, attitudes, and perceptions have contributed to the shaping of SSE and its preference over CSE/Singlish in at least the official domains of language use. This has been an important milestone in the development and acceptance of SingE as a valid, fully-fledged L2 variety of English, inside and outside the country — and has, ultimately, led to the development of SingE as an L1 variety and a commodified good. Together with the many parallels that have been detected between SingE and other Southeast Asian varieties of English and the joint treatment of, in particular, SingE and MalE, this notion of an existing homogenous standard lends itself to a pluricentric interpretation. On the other hand, actual feature use is much fuzzier and seems to be more typologically, "sprachbund" motivated than determined by national boundaries. In addition to that, it has been argued that the difference between SSE and CSE/Singlish are not absolute and more to be viewed as a lectal continuum with language use being characterized by the use of more or less standard features, depending on the situation and speaker (group) (e.g. Buschfeld 2020: 11–15; Leimgruber 2013: 16–21). This also calls into question the absolute reliance on national standards, not only since more than one standard might exist in a particular territory but, more importantly, since the notion of standards seems to be more an abstract concept than corresponding to actual, everyday language use (see also Schneider, this volume). I am not trying to argue that the notion of a homogenous standard is always obsolete. As shown for Singapore, it may play an important role for the development and acceptance of varieties; it just seems a too gross abstraction from complex linguistic realities to account for actual language use, inside and outside the country. The same is true for the relationship of SAfE and NamE and other, comparable scenarios. Therefore, the one thing that can be safely concluded from the above observations is that only a joined perspective combining pluricentric and pluriareal aims, perspectives, and methodologies can shed conclusive light on the current debate.

However, the situation of the English language may be even more complex when it comes to its global dissemination and fragmentation into more or less mutually intelligible varieties or dialects than the situation of the German language. This aspect will briefly be discussed in the following section (Section 4.2).

4.2 The diffusion of English from a global perspective

When approaching the question from a global perspective by looking into current trends in the spread and use of the English language and its varieties, the picture, on the one hand, is even more complex and, on the other, much clearer when it comes to the present debate. In recent times, languages, and in particular the English language, transcend nation states, borders, and immediate neighbors. The worldwide spread and impact of AmE, which further complicates if not eludes any pluricentric interpretation, is a case in point here. As Schneider (2014: 201) puts it:

> Forms typical of American English have been documented in significant numbers in Australia, New Zealand, Singapore, Nigeria, South Africa, and so on. It goes without saying that all of this constitutes a challenge for the notion of pluricentricity, which implicitly rests upon the idea of rather clear-cut and distinct centers. In purely linguistic terms, there are different national varieties, but we are not faced with clear "centers" but rather with fuzzy focal points, networks of co-occurring forms and choices [...].

In this respect, AmE is often described as a "hyper-central variety" (Mair 2013: 261) and, indeed, AmE is one of the many factors influencing the current situation and use of the English language and has entered the majority of varieties of English (e.g. Burridge & Peters 2020 for Australia; Buschfeld 2020 for Singapore; Trüb 2008 for South Africa). On the one hand, this would clearly strengthen the epicentral approach towards the English language, assuming one, homogenous "hyper-center". On the other hand, AmE, too, is not a homogenous linguistic system and thus the epicentral approach would only hold on an abstract level of linguistic description. Also, if we assume that it enters the feature mix in other epicentral scenarios, for example in Southeast Asia or southern Africa, this means that varieties such as SingE or SAfE would not be the only epicenters influencing neighboring varieties. This corroborates the intuitive nature and validity of the term glocalization (Sharifian 2013), which has taken center stage in the World Englishes literature, and suggests that, at least for the English language, we might want to expand the notion of epicenter into heterocenter to describe the fact that some varieties may have more than one center. This would also accommodate the observation that defining epicenters — and the same would be true for the concept of pluricentricity — solely on the basis of the notion of standardness may be problematic since oftentimes no single and fixed standard exists, at least not from the perspective of actual language use and, in particular, not for a language like English.

The commodification of varieties of English as addressed for the case of Singapore in Section 3.1 is another relevant aspect contributing to the pluricentricity/pluriareality debate since it, too, offers support for both concepts. On the one hand, it corroborates the assumption that SingE has developed into an epicenter variety since its use in far away, even non-Asian contexts shows its economic and cultural power and influence on other varieties and their speakers. Interestingly in this context is the fact that in particular the traditional non-standard features of SingE have caught global attention and are spread, which, once more, calls into question the focus on standards in the pluricentricity/pluriareality debate, if not the notion of standardness as such. The latter observation is far from new but has, to my best knowledge, not yet been discussed as part of the current debate.

At the same time, the pluriareal approach holds even more explanatory power for accounting for the commodification of SingE as it goes beyond the nation state and considers the distribution and use of linguistic features across national borders. However, for the English context, this interpretation requires an extension, too. So far, the pluriareal approach has mainly been utilized in the debate about the spread and manifestations of the German language and its varieties and dialects, which are all spoken in continental Europe, a contiguous area of land. Potential varieties of German, such as, for example, spoken in Namibia (e.g. Deumert 2009), have, to my knowledge, not yet been included in the debate, probably since this part of the German-speaking world is detached from the contiguous rest. For scenarios of non-contiguous areas, pluricentricity has often been suggested as the best suited approach. The present chapter, however, has shown that this is not necessarily the case.

World Englishes research therefore requires a much wider approach. This may also be true for the dissemination, uses, and standards of the German language, but I will leave this to be decided by the experts in the discussion (see the various contributions to this volume). With the spread of English and its various forms, be they varieties, dialects, hybrid or mixed codes (e.g. Hinglish, Taglish, Spanglish, Camfranglais; Schneider 2016), international or national standards (keeping in mind the artificiality of these constructs), boundaries between languages are becoming more and more fuzzy and maybe even obsolete and cannot be captured in terms of the comparatively narrow concepts of pluricentricity and pluriareality. Both seem to be part of the complex realities of English (and presumably other languages) worldwide as are the notions of globalization, localization (glocalization), and heterocentricity. Concluding, I may want to speculate that in the future, national borders will become even more obsolete in linguistic discussions due to the strong dissemination of speech forms and language contact through the World Wide Web and other modern communication channels and so will notions which build their argument on purely national and standard-oriented grounds.

5. Conclusion

The present chapter has probed the two competing notions of pluricentricity and pluriareality against recent realities of the English language. Drawing on case studies from Southeast Asian and Southern African contexts, I have shown that both concepts have their validity in accounting for the development and dissemination of the English language but from different perspectives. The pluricentric approach revolves around language policies and attitudes, which, in turn, shape speakers' perceptions; the pluriareal approach holds the potential to better explain actual language use and the distribution of particular linguistic features. Both approaches, therefore, have their specific raison d'être, even though I agree with Schneider (this volume) that actual language use and performance should be given more weight and importance. Overall, the notion of pluricentricity is far more problematic for recent linguistic realities than the underlying conceptions of pluriareality. As the chapter has argued, actual language use normally does not reflect pure standard language so that the concept appears to rest upon rather abstract assumptions. In addition, it is not clear what can be considered a standard language feature at what times, in particular since languages evolve and standards may change. I would therefore suggest we leave behind ideologically loaded debates and move on to more fluid and flexible approaches towards languages and their various manifestations that, of course, include aspects of language perception as well as production – and maybe the best of both worlds in terms of the pluricentricity and pluriareality debate. These should take into account the partly contradictory global and local trends of recent linguistic developments, which manifest in internationalization via hyper-central varieties on the one hand and linguistic heterogeneity on the other. Furthermore, even if nation state boundaries may persist and certainly have an important influence on identity conceptions and linguistic practices, communities of practice do not necessarily adhere to such boundaries, and distinctions between languages and dialects become increasingly blurred in times of massive language contact and linguistic restructuring.

References

Ammon, Ulrich. 1995. *Die deutsche Sprache in Deutschland, Österreich und der Schweiz. Das Problem der nationalen Varietäten*. Berlin, New York: Walter de Gruyter.
Auer, Peter. 2014. Enregistering pluricentric German. In Augusto S. d. Silva (ed.), *Pluricentricity: Language variation and sociocognitive dimensions*. Berlin: De Gruyter.
Barber, Charles. 1997. *Early Modern English*. Edinburgh: Edinburg University Press.
Bernaisch, Tobias & Pam Peters (eds.) 2022. Linguistic epicentres in World Englishes. Special Issue of *World Englishes*, 41(3).
Böhm, Michael Anton. 2003. *Deutsch in Afrika. Die Stellung der deutschen Sprache in Afrika vor dem Hintergrund der bildungs – und sprachpolitischen Gegebenheiten sowie der deutschen auswärtigen Kulturpolitik*. Frankfurt/Main: Peter Lang.

Bowerman, Sean. 2004. White South African English: Phonology. In Bernd Kortmann & Edgar Schneider (eds.), *A Handbook of Varieties of English: A Multimedia Reference Tool. Volume 1: Phonology. Volume 2: Morphology and Syntax*, 931–942.

Burridge, Kate & Pam Peters. 2020. English in Australia — Extra-territorial influences. In Sarah Buschfeld & Alexander Kautzsch (eds.), *Modelling world Englishes. A joint approach to postcolonial and non-postcolonial varieties*, 202–227. Edinburgh: Edinburgh University Press.

Buschfeld, Sarah. 2014. English in Cyprus and Namibia: A critical approach to taxonomies and models of World Englishes and Second Language Acquisition research. In Sarah Buschfeld, Thomas Hoffmann, Magnus Huber & Alexander Kautzsch (eds.), *The evolution of Englishes: The Dynamic Model and beyond*, 181–202. Amsterdam: John Benjamins.

Buschfeld, Sarah. 2017a. From second to first language status: An apparent-time investigation of language change in Singapore English. Paper presented at the 10th conference of Studies in the History of the English Language (SHEL), Kansas, USA.

Buschfeld, Sarah. 2017b. The omission of past tense marking in Singapore English: An apparent time investigation of language change. Paper presented at the 23rd International Conference on Historical Linguistics (ICHL) at the workshop "The Loss of Inflection," San Antonio, Texas, USA.

Buschfeld, Sarah. 2020. *Children's English in Singapore: Acquisition, properties, and use*. London: Routledge.

Buschfeld, Sarah. 2021. The question of structural nativization in Namibian English: Some answers from extended uses of the progressive. In Anne Schröder (ed.), *The Dynamics of English in Namibia. Perspectives on an Emerging Variety*. Amsterdam: John Benjamins.

Buschfeld, Sarah & Alexander Kautzsch. 2014. English in Namibia: A first approach. *English World-Wide* 35(2). 121–160.

Cambridge Dictionary. 2014. https://dictionary.cambridge.org/de/worterbuch/englisch/epicenter. (9 Jan., 2021.)

Central Intelligence Agency. 2021a. *The World Factbook*. Namibia. https://www.cia.gov/the-world-factbook/static/b5ac4db93b3379cabced51723dda44c1/WA-summary.pdf (2 Sept, 2021.)

Central Intelligence Agency. 2021b. *The World Factbook*. South Africa. https://www.cia.gov/the-world-factbook/static/cc4e16e0616569c86a470890ccd01283/SF-summary.pdf (2 Sept., 2021.)

Clyne, Michael. 1984. *Language and society in the German-speaking countries*. Cambridge: Cambridge University Press.

Clyne, Michael (ed.). 1992. *Pluricentric languages. Differing norms in different nations*. Berlin, New York: Mouton de Gruyter.

Clyne, Michael. 1995. *The German language in a changing europe*. New York: Cambridge University Press.

Deterding, David. & Low Ee Ling. 2001. The NIE Corpus of Spoken Singapore English. *SAAL Quarterly*, no, 56, Nov. 2001, 2–5.

Deumert, Ana. 2009. Namibian Kiche Duits: The making (and decline) of a neo-African language. *Journal of Germanic Linguistics* 21(4). 349–417.

Dollinger, Stefan. 2019a. *The pluricentricity debate: On Austrian German and other Germanic standard varieties*. New York and London: Routledge.

Dollinger, Stefan. 2019b. Debunking "pluri-areality": On the pluricentric perspective of national varieties. *Journal of Linguistic Geography* 7(2). 98–112.

Elspaß, Stephan, Christa Dürscheid & Arne Ziegler. 2017. Zur grammatischen Pluriarealität der deutschen Gebrauchsstandards – oder: Über die Grenzen des Plurizentrizitätsbegriffs. *Zeitschrift für Deutsche Philologie* 136. 69–91.

Frydman, Jenna. 2011. A critical analysis of Namibia's English-only language policy. In Eyamba G. Bokamba, Ryan K. Shosted & Bezza Tesfaw Ayalew (eds.), *Selected proceedings of the 40th annual conference on African linguistics: African languages and linguistics today*, 178–189. Somerville MA: Cascadilla Proceedings Project. http://www.lingref.com/cpp/acal/40/paper2574.pdf. (10 Nov., 2014.)

Gupta, Anthea Fraser. 1989. Singapore Colloquial English and Standard English. *Singapore Journal of Education* 10(2). 33–39.

Gupta, Anthea Fraser. 1994. *The step-tongue. Children's English in Singapore*. Clevedon: Multilingual Matters.

Heller, Benedikt, Tobias Bernaisch, Stefan Th. Gries. 2017. Empirical perspectives on two potential epicenters: The genitive alternation in Asian Englishes. *ICAME Journal*, vol. 41. 111–144.

Hundt, Marianne. 2013. The diversification of English: Old, new and emerging epicentres. In Daniel Schreier & Marianne Hundt (eds.), *English as a contact language*, 182–203. Cambridge: Cambridge University Press.

Kautzsch, Alexander & Anne Schröder. 2016. English in multilingual and multiethnic Namibia: Some evidence on language attitudes and the pronunciation of vowels. In Christoph Ehland, Ilka Mindt & Merle Tönnies (eds.), *Anglistentag 2015 Paderborn: Proceedings*, 277–288. Trier: WVT.

Kloss, Heinz. 1967. Abstand languages and Ausbau languages. *Anthropological Linguistics* 9(7). 29–41.

Kloss, Heinz. 1978. *Die Entwicklung neuer germanischer Kultursprachen seit 1800*. Düsseldorf: Schwann.

Kohnen, Thomas. 2014. *Introduction to the History of English*. Frankfurt a.M.: Peter Lang.

Kortmann, Bernd & Edgar W. Schneider (eds.). 2004. *A Handbook of Varieties of English: A Multimedia Reference Tool. Volume 1: Phonology. Volume 2: Morphology and Syntax*. Berlin, Boston: De Gruyter Mouton.

Kortmann, Bernd, Kerstin Lunkenheimer & Katharina Ehret (eds.). 2020. The electronic world atlas of varieties of English. *Zenodo*. http://ewave-atlas.org. (30 Aug., 2020.)

Leimgruber, Jakob R. E. 2013. *Singapore English. Structure, variation, and usage*. Cambridge: Cambridge University Press.

Leitner, Gerhard. 1992. English as a pluricentric language. In Michael Clyne (ed.), *Pluricentric languages: Differing norms in different nations*, 179–237. Berlin: De Gruyter.

Leitner, Gerhard. 2010. Developmental stages in the formation of epicentres of English. In Oriana Palusci (ed.) *English, but not quite: Locating linguistic diversity*, 17–36. Trento: Tangram Edizioni Scientifiche.

Lim, Lisa. 2010. Migrants and 'mother tongues': extralinguistic forces in the ecology of English in Singapore. In Lisa Lim, Anne Pakir & Lionel Wee (eds.), *English in Singapore: Modernity and management*, 19–54. Hong Kong: Hong Kong University Press.

Lim, Lisa, & Joseph A. Foley. 2004. English in Singapore and Singapore English. In Lisa Lim (ed.), *Singapore English: A grammatical description*, 1–18. Amsterdam: John Benjamins.

Maho, Jouni Filip. 1998. *Few people, many tongues. The languages of Namibia*. Windhoek: Gamsberg Macmillan.

Mair, Christian. 2009. Corpus linguistics meets sociolinguistics: Studying educated spoken usage in Jamaica on the basis of the International Corpus of English. In Thomas Hoffmann & Lucia Siebers (eds.), *World Englishes – problems, properties and prospects: Selected papers from the 13th IAWE conference*, 39–60. Amsterdam: John Benjamins.

Mair, Christian. 2013. The world system of Englishes: Accounting for the transnational importance of mobile and mediated vernaculars. *English World-Wide* 34(3). 253–278.

Mesthrie, Rajend. 2004. Black South African English: Morphology and syntax. In Edgar Schneider & Bernd Kortmann (eds.), *A Handbook of Varieties of English: A Multimedia Reference Tool. Volume 1: Phonology. Volume 2: Morphology and Syntax*, 962–973.

Muhr, Rudolf. 2013. The pluricentricity of German today – struggling with asymmetry. In Rudolf Muhr, Carla Amorós Negre. Carmen Fernández Juncal, Klaus Zimmermann, Emilio Prieto & Natividad Hernández (eds.). *Exploring linguistic standards in non-dominant varieties of pluricentric lLanguages – Explorando estándares lingüísticos en variedades no dominantes de lenguas pluricéntricas*, 55–66. Frankfurt a.M.: Peter Lang.

Muhr, Rudolf (ed.). 2016a. *Pluricentric languages and non-dominant varieties worldwide. Part I: Pluricentric languages across continents. Features and usage*. Frankfurt: Peter Lang.

Muhr, Rudolf (ed.). 2016b. *Pluricentric languages and non-dominant varieties worldwide. Part II: The pluricentricity of Portuguese and Spanish. New concepts and descriptions*. Frankfurt: Peter Lang.

Muhr, Rudolf. 2018. Misconceptions about pluricentric languages and pluricentric theory – an overview of 40 years. In Rudolf Muhr & Benjamin Meisnitzer (eds.), *Pluricentric languages and non-dominant varieties worldwide: New pluricentric languages – old problems*, 17–56. Frankfurt: Peter Lang.

Muhr, Rudolf. 2020. Pluriareality in sociolinguistics: A comprehensive overview of key ideas and a critique of linguistic data used. In Rudolf Muhr & Juan Thomas (eds.), *Pluricentricity theory beyond dominance and non-dominance*, 9–78. Graz, Berlin: PLC Press.

NIDS – Namibia Inter-censal Demographic Survey 2006. http://www.npc.gov.na/publications/census_data/NIDS_report_final_revised_04%20August%202010.pdf. Last accessed: 17 July, 2012.

Niehaus, Konstantin. 2015. Areale Variation in der Syntax des Standarddeutschen: Ergebnisse zum Sprachgebrauch und zur Frage Plurizentrik vs. Pluriarealität. *Zeitschrift für Dialektologie und Linguistik* 82(2). 133–168.

Ooi, Vincent B.Y. (ed.). 2001. *Evolving identities: The English language in Singapore and Malaysia*. Singapore: Times Academic Press.

Percillier, Michael. 2016. *World Englishes and Second Language Acquisition. Insights from Southeast Asian Englishes*. Amsterdam: John Benjamins.

Platt, John & Heidi Weber. 1980. *English in Singapore and Malaysia: Status, features, functions.* Kuala Lumpur: Oxford University Press.

Ronan, Patricia & Sarah Buschfeld. 2024. From second to first language: language shift in Singapore and Ireland. In Mirjam Schmalz, Manuela Vida-Mannl, Sarah Buschfeld, & Thorsten Brato (eds.), *Acquisition and Variation in World Englishes: Bridging Paradigms and Rethinking Approaches*, 177–202. Berlin, Boston: De Gruyter Mouton.

Scheuringer, Hermann. 1996. Das Deutsche als pluriareale Sprache: Ein Beitrag gegen staatlich begrenzte Horizonte in der Diskussion um die deutsche Sprache in Österreich. *Die Unterrichtspraxis / Teaching German* 29(2). 147–153.

Schneider, Edgar W. 2003. The dynamics of New Englishes: From identity construction to dialect birth. *Language* 79(2). 233–281.

Schneider, Edgar W. 2007. *Postcolonial English. Varieties around the world.* Cambridge: Cambridge University Press.

Schneider, Edgar W. 2013. The pluricentricity of English today – and how about non-dominant varieties? In Rudolf Muhr, Carla Amorós Negre, Carmen Fernández Juncal, Klaus Zimmermann Emilio Prieto, & Natividad Hernández (eds.), *Exploring linguistic standards in non-dominant varieties of pluricentric languages / Explorando estándares lingüísticos en variedades no dominantes de lenguas pluricéntricas*, 45–54. Frankfurt, Wien: Peter Lang.

Schneider, Edgar W. 2014. Global diffusion, regional attraction, local roots? Sociocognitive perspectives on the pluricentricity of English. In Augusto Soares da Silva (ed.), *Pluricentricity. language variation and sociocognitive dimensions*, 191–226. Berlin, New York: de Gruyter Mouton.

Schneider, Edgar W. 2016. Hybrid Englishes: An exploratory survey. *World Englishes* 35(3). 339–354.

Schröder, Anne & Frederic Zähres. 2020. English in Namibia: Multilingualism and ethnic variation in the Extra – and Intra-territorial Forces Model. In Sarah Buschfeld & Alexander Kautzsch (eds.), *Modelling World Englishes. A joint approach to postcolonial and non-postcolonial varieties*, 38–62. Edinburgh: Edinburgh University Press.

Schröder, Anne, Frederic Zähres & Alexander Kautzsch. 2020. Ethnic variation in the phonology of Namibian English: A first approach to Baster English. *English World-Wide* 41(2). 193–225.

Sharifian, Farzad. 2013. Globalisation and developing metacultural competence in learning English as an International Language. *Multilingual Education* 3(1).

Singapore Department of Statistics. 2001. Census of Population 2000. Statistical Release 2: Education, Language and Religion. http://www.singstat.gov.sg/publications/ publications _and_papers/cop2000/cop2000r2.html. (29 Jan., 2014.)

Singapore Department of Statistics. 2010. Census of Population 2010. Demographic Characteristics, Education, Language and Religion. http://www.singstat.gov.sg/pubn /popn/c2010acr.pdf. (6 Nov., 2012.)

Singapore Department of Statistics. 2011. Census of Population 2010. Statistical Release 1: Demographic Characteristics, Education, Language and Religion. http://www.singstat .gov.sg/publications/publications_and_papers/cop2010/census10_stat_release1.html. (29 Jan., 2014.)

Singapore Department of Statistics. 2021. Census of Population 2020. Statistical Release 1: Demographic Characteristics, Education, Language and Religion. https://www.singstat.gov.sg/-/media/files/publications/cop2020/sr1/cop2020sr1.ashx. (19 April, 2024.)

Steigertahl, Helene. 2019. *English(es) in post-independence Namibia. An investigation of variety status and its implications for English language teaching*. Berlin: Peter Lang.

Stell, Gerald. 2014. Uses and functions of English in Namibia's multiethnic settings. *World Englishes* 33(2). 223–241.

Trudgill, Peter, & Jean Hannah. 2002. *International English: A guide to the varieties of Standard English*. Oxon and New York: Routledge.

Trüb, R. 2008. American English impact on South African English: An empirical analysis of its manifestations and attitudes towards it. Regensburg, DE: University of Regensburg PhD dissertation.

Van Rooy, Bertus. 2004. Black South African English: Phonology. In Edgar Schneider & Bernd Kortmann (eds.), *A Handbook of Varieties of English: A Multimedia Reference Tool. Volume 1: Phonology. Volume 2: Morphology and Syntax*, 943–952.

Velupillai, Viveka. 2012. *An introduction to linguistic typology*. Amsterdam: John Benjamins.

Wallace, Marion (with John Kinahan). 2011. *A history of Namibia*. London: C. Hurst & Co.

Wee, Lionel. 2004. Singapore English: Phonology. In Edgar W. Schneider, Kate Burridge, Bernd Kortmann, Rajend Mesthrie & Clive Upton (eds.), *A handbook of varieties of English. Volume 1: Phonology*, 1017–1033. Berlin: Mouton de Gruyter.

Wee, Lionel. 2020. English in Singapore: Two issues for the EIF Model. In Sarah Buschfeld & Alexander Kautzsch (eds.), *Modelling World Englishes. A joint approach to postcolonial and non-postcolonial varieties*, 112–132. Edinburgh: Edinburgh University Press.

Wells, John C. 1982. *Accents of English*. Cambridge: Cambridge University Press.

CHAPTER 7

A Scottish perspective on the pluricentricity/pluriareality debate

Andreas Weilinghoff
University of Koblenz, Germany

This study tests the implications of the pluricentric and pluriareal models with respect to prosody by analyzing the Scottish Vowel Length Rule (SVLR) in Scottish Standard English (SSE). Scotland is a particularly interesting example for the pluricentricity/pluriareality debate due to its linguistic and political situation. After a brief introduction of the context, this study applies linear mixed-effects modeling to account for variation in SVLR patterns while taking prosodic features as well as sociolinguistic factors into account. The findings are interpreted from the pluricentric and pluriareal perspectives and show that intralinguistic features rather than geographical factors influence variation in SVLR patterns. I therefore conclude that a mutual juxtaposition of the two approaches is neither necessary nor beneficial when it comes to modeling variation in standard languages.

Keywords: pluricentricity, pluriareality, prosody, suprasegmentals, Scottish Vowel Length Rule, Scottish Standard English, language-internal factors, language-external factors

1. Introduction

The approaches of pluricentricity and pluriareality model variation in standard languages from different perspectives. Whereas pluricentrists highlight the concept of different national standard varieties (Clyne 1989: 358), pluriarealists favor the view of regional usage standards (Elspaß et al. 2017). The present volume demonstrates that there is an intense debate between the adherents of the two approaches, especially in the field of German linguistics. In this debate, the concepts of pluricentricity and pluriareality are often opposed to one another (Dollinger 2019).

Numerous studies have been carried out against the background of the two approaches, with many of them analyzing and describing lexical, phraseological, and syntactic variation in standard languages (see e.g. Ruette et al. 2014; Niehaus

2015; Dollinger 2019). There are also some studies that have investigated variation of particular phonetic features (see e.g. Ashby et al. 2012; Lanwermeyer et al. 2019), yet, little research has tested the implications of the pluricentric and pluriareal models with respect to broader phonetic patterns prevalent in standard languages. In the present chapter, I will analyze a vowel quantity alternation pattern in Scottish Standard English (SSE), namely the Scottish Vowel Length Rule (SVLR), and discuss how linguistic variation on the suprasegmental level may tie into the concepts of pluricentricity and pluriareality.

I will first give a broad introduction into the context, describing the concepts of pluricentricity and pluriareality (Section 2), and will then demonstrate why Scotland is a very interesting case in the context of the current debate (Section 2.1). The introduction into the SVLR and the research questions of this study can be found in Section 2.2. I will then outline the methodology of the present investigation in Section 3 and state the results in Section 4. After a discussion of the results (Section 5), final conclusions are drawn in Section 6.

2. Pluricentricity, pluriareality and the interesting case of Scotland

Pluricentricity indicates that a language has more than one center which can provide a national variety with its own norms (Clyne 1989: 358). Thus, a pluricentric language does not have one monolithic standard variety, but several different national standards each with its own epicenter. A typical example are the two major reference varieties of English, namely British and American English (Schneider 2014: 197 ff.; Schneider, this volume), which have distinctive conventions for spelling, pronunciation, lexis, and grammar. Yet, there are also other national standard varieties that can be named in this context, namely Australian English, New Zealand English, Indian English, Singaporean English, South African English, Jamaican English (Schneider 2014: 201 ff.). Essentially, the concept of pluricentricity always entails a political sphere. Variation in standard languages is modelled and conceptualized on a predominantly national level. Thus, in German linguistics, pluricentrists argue for different Austrian, German, and Swiss standard varieties of German. Subnational regional variation, however, is often referred to as second level pluricentricity (Muhr 1997: 53).

By contrast, pluriareality emphasizes the importance of regional usage standards. Pluriarealists stress that they have a descriptive understanding of standard languages. Thus, the standard represents the particular language use in those formal contexts (e.g. newspaper articles) which are said to require standard language use (Elspaß et al. 2017: 2). Proponents of pluriareality do not think that national or political boundaries have a strong influence on variation in standard languages.

The concept is predominantly applied in German linguistics, and a contemporary project is the "Regional Variation in the Grammar of Standard German" (Elspaß et al. 2017). Based on the newspaper corpus in the aforementioned project, Niehaus (2015) could show that there are strong areal patterns in syntactic features of Standard German. Variation is not limited to nation states but presents itself on a smaller regional scale (Niehaus 2015: 164). He therefore dismisses a purely pluricentric approach to account for variation in standard languages.

Essentially, both approaches model variation in standard languages with a special focus on geography, emphasizing either national/political (pluricentricity) or regional/areal levels (pluriareality). Scotland is an interesting example in this context due to its current political status as well as its linguistic landscape and history.

2.1 The political status and linguistic history of Scotland

Scotland has been a fully independent kingdom for over seven centuries. The long period of independence is one of the reasons why Scotland retains a distinct national identity and why the country is highly autonomous in terms of its culture. The current political situation provides evidence for the autonomy of the country even though it remains a constituent part of the United Kingdom. Due to the processes of devolution, Scotland could form its own parliament as well as its own government since the end of the last century. As a result, some executive and legislative powers have been transferred from Westminster to Edinburgh. Today, at the time of writing this chapter, the Scottish National Party (SNP) is the strongest and largest political party in Scotland and has been continuously in government since 2007. The SNP continues campaigning for Scottish independence and supports the use of Scots and Scottish Gaelic in private and public life. In general, the movement for Scottish independence has seen an upward trend since the end of the last century even though a narrow majority of the Scottish people voted to remain in the United Kingdom in the 2014 independence referendum (Jackson 2020: 1 ff.).

Scotland's political status makes its standard variety difficult to classify with regard to the pluricentricity/pluriareality debate. Due to their history and culture, the Scottish people understand themselves as a nation and they have regained a great deal of political autonomy in recent decades. Yet, at the same time, Scotland is a constituent part of the United Kingdom and the main political power remains with its southern neighbor. It is therefore not possible to speak of Scotland as a fully-fledged nation state in a political sense, but it is likewise wrong to classify Scotland as a mere region of the United Kingdom. This makes Scotland a very interesting case as the pluricentricity/pluriareality debate has so far been applied to contexts of fully or almost fully independent nation states.

Yet, also Scotland's language situation is interesting for the pluricentricity/pluriareality debate. Apart from English, there are two other recognized languages spoken in the country, namely Scots and Scottish Gaelic.

Scottish Gaelic was once the predominant language in Scotland before the Anglian invasions during the seventh century AD (Stuart-Smith 2008: 49). However, the role of Scottish Gaelic continuously declined over the course of the centuries. Only recent years have seen a slight increase in the number of speakers among young age groups (National Records of Scotland 2015: 4) which is a result of the political promotion of the language. Today, the largest numbers of Scottish Gaelic speakers can be found in the Hebrides and Highlands in the northwest, more precisely in the council areas of Eilean Siar, Highland, and Argyll and Bute. Generally, these speakers are bilingual in Scottish Gaelic and English (Jones 2002: 2).

Scots derived from Northumbrian Old English and was introduced to the southeast of Scotland in the seventh century AD (McClure 1994: 23 f.). Scots surpassed Gaelic and became the kingdom's flourishing spoken and written language with a significant corpus of literature and poetry (Stuart-Smith 2008: 49). Thus, Scots was "the only Germanic variety in the British Isles besides Standard English ever to have functioned as a full language within an independent state (the Kingdom of Scotland) (...) (Johnston 2007: 105). It developed different dialects and underwent early stages of standardization (Johnston 2007: 105). This is also why Scots has been labelled the first national variety of English developed outside England (Leith & Jackson 1997). Yet, after the unification of crowns and parliaments, the role of Scots declined and gave way to Standard Southern English (Stuart-Smith 2008: 49). As of today, there are 1.5 million people in Scotland who can speak Scots and the largest quantities are found in Aberdeenshire, Moray as well as on Orkney and Shetland in the North East of Scotland.

The Scots language still plays an important part in the linguistic landscape of Scotland. While Scots and Scottish English are closely related and have a common origin, the relationship between the two is complicated. One factor that complicates the overall situation is the question whether Scots can be regarded as a distinct language or whether it is a northern dialect of English. This debate has not been settled and there are good claims on both sides of the argument (McArthur 1992: 104). Aitken (1979: 86) published an often-recited bipolar model with Scots-related expressions and words on the one side and their English equivalents at the other side of the spectrum (see Table 7.1).

In Table 7.1, the left columns 1 and 2 catalog lexical items originating from Early Scots. Correspondingly, the right columns 4 and 5 feature "later importations from southern English" (Aitken, 1979: 85). Scottish English speakers, thus,

Table 7.1 Bipolar model with Scots-related words and pronunciations on the left side and English equivalents on the right side. see Aitken (1979: 86) for a more detailed overview

Scots			English	
1	2	3	4	5
<bairn>	<mair>	<before>	<more>	<child>
<ken>	<hoose>	<name>	<house>	<know>

possess a choice between Scots-derived terms like <bairn> and <ken> (column 1), or their English counterparts, <child> and <know> (column 5). They also encounter options between Scots and English lexicons that exhibit structural similarities but differ in pronunciation and spelling, such as <mair> and <hoose> (column 2), and English <more> and <house> (column 4). Nevertheless, numerous items are common to both Scots and English, as outlined in column 3. Aitken (1979) observes that when speakers incorporate features from columns 1 to 3, their speech is identified as Scots. Conversely, employing only features from columns 3 to 5 designates their speech as English, or, as previously introduced, SSE.

Aitken described that most Scottish speakers can switch between the two ends of the spectrum with regard to the social context. That is to say that there are some Scottish people who, for instance, consciously implement English words and phrases in formal contexts whereas they use more Scots-related expressions in informal situations. These people are called *dialect-switchers* (Aitken 1979: 86). Aitken, however, also described that there are some speakers who "cannot or do not choose to control their styles in this way, but they do shift styles in a less predictable and more fluctuating way" (1979: 86). These people are called *style-drifters* as they drift along the bipolar linguistic continuum (Aitken 1979: 86). The example of this bipolar model demonstrates that the boundaries between Scots and Scottish English are not clear-cut. In contrast, they are rather fuzzy and overlapping in everyday speech. Speakers may therefore alternate between Scots and Scottish English in different situations.

In addition, the current definition of SSE is somewhat problematic. SSE is still defined by many linguists as "the variety of Standard English spoken in Scotland, [which] has few lexical and syntactic characteristics that set it apart from the Standard English used in England" (Giegerich 1992: 45 f.). Thus, it is assumed that, with regard to its lexis and grammar, SSE is roughly equal to Standard Southern British English (SSBE). In terms of phonology, however, SSE is similar to Scots (Johnston 2007: 112 ff.). Stuart-Smith (2008: 53), for instance, notes that Scots and SSE share the same vowel and consonant inventories. Yet, possibly due to this simplified definition, SSE has long been neglected in linguistic research

(Schützler et al. 2017: 274). Furthermore, "[d]ue to the particular situation of a Scots-English language continuum, more or less all grammatical variation that is not within the bounds of British standard grammar (…) is automatically categorized as Scots, and thus non-standard" (Schützler et al. 2017: 275). However, there may be features of Scots grammar that are also acceptable in SSE and there may be differences between SSE and SSBE that are outside the Scots-English continuum (Schützler et al. 2017: 275). Schützler et al. (2017) therefore compiled the ICE Scotland corpus as a tool to analyze the grammatical idiosyncrasies of SSE. This approach fits well into the pluricentricity/pluriareality debate. Instead of acknowledging the earlier normative definition of SSE, Schützler et al. (2017) intend to conceptualize the standard variety from a usage-based perspective with the help of a new corpus.

2.2 Vowel patterns in Scottish and British English

The SVLR, or Aitken's Law, is one of the most famous features in Scottish English phonology and is said to operate in both Scots and SSE (Aitken 1981: 135). It states that vowels are "long in stressed open syllables, before voiced fricatives and /r/, and before morpheme boundaries[,] and short elsewhere; with the two exceptions of /ɪ/ and /ʌ/ which are invariably short" (McClure 1977: 10). Therefore, following the SVLR, words like <fee>, <fear>, <freeze>, and <agreed> would exhibit long allophones in Scottish English. Whereas the rule historically affected all tense vowels and most diphthongs (McMahon 1991: 33 f.), most recent studies conclude that the patterns apply most consistently in the high vowels /i/ and /u/ as well as in the diphthong /aɪ/ (see e.g. Scobbie et al. 1999; Watt & Ingham 2000; Llamas et al. 2011).

Table 7.2 Long and short environments for the Scottish vowel length rule and the Voicing Effect. See Rathcke and Stuart-Smith (2016: 406) for a more detailed overview

Vowel length pattern	Postvocalic voiceless consonants	Postvocalic voiced plosives, nasals and laterals	Postvocalic voiced fricatives, /r/ and morpheme boundaries
Scottish Vowel Length Rule	short	short	long
Voicing Effect	short	long	long

Aitken's Law partially contradicts with the standard quantity alternation pattern present in most varieties of English, namely the Voicing Effect (VE) (Chen 1970). Whereas the VE generally triggers longer vowel realizations before all voiced consonants, the SVLR conditions a shortening of tense vowels before following laterals, nasals and voiced plosives. Consequently, while the VE leads to the lengthening of vowel allophones in words like <heed>, <lean>, and <heal>, these same words would feature shorter vowels in Scottish English as a result of the timing effects governed by the SVLR. In this respect, the vowel length patterns in Scottish English differ from most other varieties of English, including SSBE (see Table 7.2). There are some studies which noted that the language-external factors age and gender, and, in particular, an exposure to SSBE, lead to a weakening of SVLR patterns (Milroy 1995; Hewlett et al. 1999: 2159 f.; Watt and Ingham 2000: 222; van Leyden 2002: 14; Scobbie 2005: 5 f.). Yet, most recent studies suggest that language-internal factors, especially prosodic stress and phrasal position have a greater influence on durational patterns (Rathcke & Stuart-Smith 2016; Chevalier 2019). That is, increased levels of prominence and phrase finality significantly lengthen vowel durations (Rathcke & Stuart-Smith 2016: 415). High syllable and segment numbers, however, shorten vowel durations (Rathcke & Stuart-Smith 2016: 415) due to the effects of polysyllabic shortening (Turk & Shattuck-Hufnagel 2000) and intrasyllabic compression (Katz 2012). This means that words with many syllables tend to have shorter vowel durations than words with fewer syllables. Likewise, syllables with higher segment numbers have shorter vowel durations than syllables with lower segment numbers.

Even though several studies were carried out on Aitken's Law, there is contradicting evidence regarding its geographical scope, especially in SSE. Whereas some accounts claimed that the rule operates in most regions of Scotland (McClure 1977; Aitken 1981), newer case studies report less stable patterns, especially in the North East of Scotland (Lodge 1984; Agutter 1988; Watt & Yurkova 2007). Other studies found SVLR patterns in the north of England (Milroy 1995; Watt and Ingham 2000; Llamas et al. 2011). While most prior inquiries have been confined to specific cities or regions, the present study takes a country-wide approach toward the SVLR. The investigation aims to find out whether and to what degree vowel length patterns in 21st century Scottish English vary depending on a speaker's geographical background while controlling for other extralinguistic and intralinguistic factors. This investigation therefore implements the more recent approach of analyzing Aitken's Law in naturally occurring language while taking other suprasegmental factors into account (Rathcke & Stuart-Smith 2016; Chevalier 2019; Tanner et al. 2020). In contrast to recent studies, however, this study investigates Aitken's Law in formal language contexts (SSE). The present investigation represents a pilot study that was conducted at the beginning of a broader PhD project on Aitken's Law (see Weilinghoff, forthcoming, for the main publication). In contrast to the main project, the current investigation uses only a small subset of the data and discusses Aitken's Law against the background of the pluricentricity/pluriareality debate.

Scrutinizing the country-wide viability of the SVLR, a feature that has traditionally been assumed to be a characteristic national feature, sheds light on the pluricentricity/pluriareality debate from a Scottish perspective. This study aims therefore to answer the following research questions:

RQ1: In how far does the SVLR operate in 21st century spoken SSE?
RQ2: Can variation be best modeled from a national (pluricentric) or regional (pluriareal) perspective?

3. Method

3.1 Dataset

The dataset used for answering these questions was retrieved from the Scottish component of the International Corpus of English (ICE) (Schützler et al. 2017). ICE Scotland is the first one-million-word corpus of SSE and its spoken part includes manually corrected phonemic transcriptions on the segment level as well as sociolinguistic background information for most speakers. Out of the corpus, thirty-six read speeches from the category *broadcast talks* were retrieved for analysis. All chosen speeches are set in a comparable speech environment (mostly speeches in the Scottish Parliament) and all of them include detailed social background information (regional background, age, gender). The text type, *broadcast talks,* was chosen because it includes speakers from different regions of Scotland who are all reading a broadcasted speech in a highly formal context. Based on the available data, this study differentiated between four regions (East central, West central, North East, Highlands & Islands) and two genders. Out of the 36 speakers, 20 are female. The speakers' age could not be integrated as a continuous variable due to the lack of young speakers (mean age: 55,5 years). Thus, the study differentiated between two broad age groups (see Table 7.3).

Table 7.3 Overview of speaker sample

Speaker Total	Age group		Gender		Regional background			
	Younger (18–55)	Older (56–78)	Female	Male	West central	East central	North East	Highland
36	23	13	20	16	14	14	4	4

3.2 Data preparation

As the SVLR is said to apply most consistently in the high vowels and /aɪ/, this study analyzes duration patterns in the diphthong and in the high front vowel /i/ only. In order to account for the influence of suprasegmental factors, utterance- and syllable-level transcription layers were added semi-automatically to the ICE Scotland textgrids with the help of different Python scripts written by the author (more information can be found in Weilinghoff, forthcoming). The sound files and accompanying textgrids were then analyzed in Praat (Boersma & Weenink 2020) and prosodic stress (nuclear pitch accent vs. non-nuclear pitch accent) was added manually for all occurrences of /i/ and /aɪ/ with the help of auditory analyses.

A Praat script then extracted all phone labels and phone durations as well as other features that will be important for the analysis. This includes the correspondent utterance durations (excluding pauses), utterance syllable counts, word labels, word durations, word syllable counts, word phone counts, the following words as well as the previous and following phone labels of the phones. The word syllable number was considered to account for the effects of polysyllabic shortening (Turk & Shattuck-Hufnagel 2000) and the word phone number was also included to account for possible effects of intra-syllabic compression (Katz 2012).

Further intralinguistic factors which influence vowel durations were then calculated and added to the dataset in R (R core team 2020), including local speech rate (utterance syllable count / utterance duration), word type (content word or function word), phrase position (final or non-final) as well as the SVLR and VE contexts. The SVLR and VE coding follows the approach of Rathcke & Stuart-Smith (2016) and Chevalier (2019). Extralinguistic factors (regional background, age group and gender of speaker) were also added in R and the dataset was then filtered for the target vowels /i/ and /aɪ/. Due to the lack of clear acoustic boundaries, all hits with following vowels, semi-vowels and hesitations were excluded from the dataset (Turk et al. 2006: 5). As function words are frequently reduced in spoken language, they were excluded as well. Likewise, all hits without primary word level stress as well as duplicates and errors were removed, resulting in a final list of 1195 tokens for /i/ and 983 for /aɪ/ (see Table 7.4).

3.3 Statistical analysis

The statistical analyses were conducted in R with the lme4 and lmerTest packages and largely follow the approach of Rathcke and Stuart-Smith (2016) and Chevalier (2019). A preliminary analysis investigated the raw durations with respect to the

Table 7.4 Overview of the final dataset

Factor	Level	Token number /i/	Token number /aɪ/
Phrase position	final	358	260
	non-final	837	723
Prosodic stress	nuclear	256	322
	non-nuclear	939	661
SVLR	short	885	837
	long	310	146
VE	short	497	290
	long	388	547
	excluded	310	146
Gender	female	580	443
	male	615	540
Age group	younger	691	544
	older	504	439
Regional background	East central	471	390
	West central	469	391
	North East	161	84
	Highland	94	118
Total token numbers:		1195	983
Word syllable number (min-max)		1–5	1–6
Word phone number (min-max)		2–13	1–12
Local speech rate (min-max)		1.51–9.22	1.45–10.46

different factors represented in Table 7.4. Different plots were created to get a first overview of the overall distributions.

Linear mixed-effects modelling was then applied to control the variation of the target vowel durations on the fixed factors SVLR and VE environment as well as the extralinguistic (regional background, age group, gender) and intralinguistic factors (prosodic stress, phrase position, local speech rate, word syllable number and word phone number). Speaker and word label were treated as random effects concerning intercepts. The first model was run without any interactions to check which factors have significant main effects on vowel duration. Then, to avoid the effects of collinearity, separate models were run for the SVLR and VE effects for each vowel with two-way interactions for all language-internal and language-external factors. Due to the low token numbers, a three-way interaction between the SVLR contexts and the sociolinguistic background factors (regional background, age group, gender) could not be executed. Following the approach of Rathcke and Stuart-Smith (2016: 415), a backward fitting procedure was applied to account for model accuracy, and the best model fit was established through likelihood ratio tests and comparing the Akaike information criterion (AIC). Insignificant factors were eliminated step by step to obtain a better AIC.

4. Results

The durations of the diphthong /aɪ/ (overall mean: 148.46 ms) are on average 53 milliseconds longer than those of the vowel /ɪ/ (overall mean: 94.81 ms). Thus, the data suggests vowel intrinsic durational differences between the front high vowel and the diphthong. Both vowel durations are influenced by prosodic stress and the phrase position (see Figures 7.1 and 7.2).

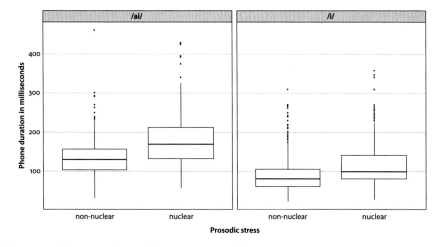

Figure 7.1 Influence of prosodic stress on vowel duration

The average of all vowel durations carrying nuclear prosodic stress are more than 45 milliseconds longer than those without nuclear stress (152.76 ms against 106.84 ms). Phrase-final lengthening does also apply as tokens in phrase-final position, as they are on average twenty-nine milliseconds longer than those in initial and medial position (139.83 ms against 110.79 ms). Moreover, the durations also suggest an influence of polysyllabic shortening and intra-syllabic compression (see Figure 7.3). The more syllables in a word and the more phones in a syllable, the shorter the vowel durations tend to be. Thus, the vowel /ɪ/ tends to be

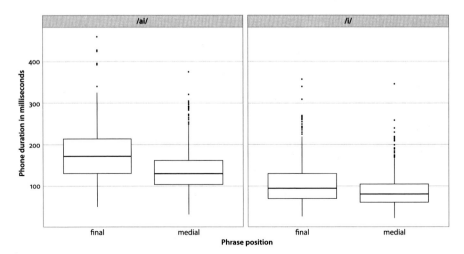

Figure 7.2 Influence of phrase position on vowel duration

longer in *speed* than in *speediness* (polysyllabic shortening) and longer in *seat* than in *streets* (intrasyllabic compression). The plots also show substantial differences in duration between the SVLR long and short contexts for both vowels and all dialect regions (see Figure 7.4). Vowels in SVLR long contexts (following voiced fricatives, /r/ and morpheme boundaries) are on average forty-six milliseconds longer than those in SVLR short contexts (155.75 ms against 109.32 ms). As there are similar vowel lengthening patterns across all dialect regions (see Figure 7.4), the influence of the regional background on Aitken's Law seems to be negligible. As for the VE, the vowels in long contexts (following voiced plosives, nasals and laterals) are on average eighteen milliseconds longer than the vowels in the short contexts (117.87 ms against 99.16 ms).

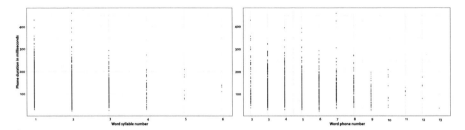

Figure 7.3 Vowel duration plots sorted for word syllable number (left) and word phone number (right)

The plots suggest that there are some differences between the different dialect regions and vowels (see Figure 7.5). Whereas the average vocalic durations for VE

Chapter 7. A Scottish perspective on the pluricentricity/pluriareality debate 153

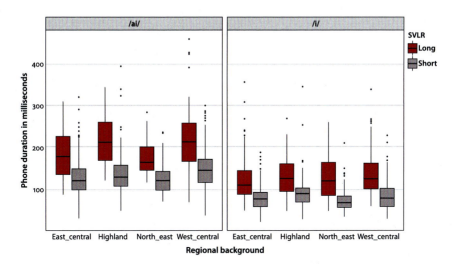

Figure 7.4 Vowel durations for /i/ and /ai/ in SVLR long and short contexts separated for the different dialect regions

long and short contexts are almost identical for the dialect regions East central and Highland, most other dialect regions display increased average vowel length in VE long contexts. Yet, on the whole, the durational differences between vocalic intervals in VE long and short contexts are not very pronounced. As the average durational differences are clearly greater between SVLR contexts than VE contexts, this suggests that Aitken's Law is in operation in 21st century SSE.

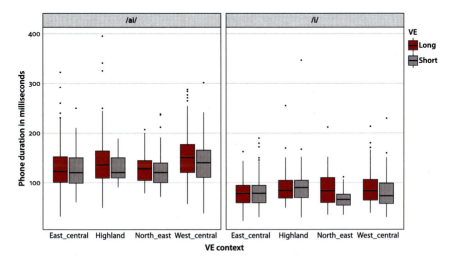

Figure 7.5 Vowel durations for /i/ and /ai/ in VE Long and short contexts separated for the different dialect regions

In order to test these observations, a first linear mixed effects model without any interactions was run to analyze which factors have significant main effects on vowel duration. As the SVLR and VE classifications partially overlap (*SVLR_long* and *VE_excluded* are identical), the VE context classification was omitted for this model. The dependent variable was phone duration and fixed factors included all suprasegmental variables (prosodic stress, phrase position, word syllable number, word phone number, SVLR contexts or VE contexts), all sociolinguistic variables (regional background, age group, gender) as well as the phone labels themselves (/i/ and /aɪ/). The word labels and the speakers were treated as random factors. The model outputs are summarized in Table 7.5.

Table 7.5 Linear mixed effects model outputs without interactions. (Intercept: SVLR_long, phone_label_/aɪ/, age_group_older, prosodic_stress_non-nuclear, phrase_position_final, regional_background_East_central, gender_female)

Random effects:			
Groups	**Name**	**Variance**	**std. deviation**
Word_label	(Intercept)	543.7	23.11
Speaker	(Intercept)	133.4	12.47
Residual		810.4	28.47
Number of obs: 2178, groups: Word_label, 556; Speaker, 36			

Fixed effects:				
SVLR model	**Estimate**	**std. error**	**p-value**	**Significance code**[*]
(Intercept)	261.70	6.99	<2e-16	***
SVLR_short	−53.93	2.97	<2e-16	***
phone_label_/i/	−59.22	2.67	<2e-16	***
age_group_younger	−8.95	3.91	0.0266	*
prosodic_stress_nuclear	22.95	1.91	<2e-16	***
local_speech_rate	−6.30	0.82	2.12e-14	***
phrase_position_non_final	−17.71	1.72	<2e-16	***
word_phone_number	−4.59	0.67	2.23e-11	***
regional_background_Highland	9.22	7.35	0.2203	
regional_background_North_east	−2.84	7.48	0.7067	
regional_background_West_central	−1.58	5.01	0.7548	
word_syllable_number	−0.58	2.40	0.8106	
Gender_male	−0.59	4.36	0.8931	

[*] Significance codes: $p<.001$ *** $p<.01$ ** $p<.05$ *

As seen in Table 7.5, almost all suprasegmental factors (prosodic stress, phrase position, local speech rate, word phone number as well as the SVLR context) have a significant effect on vowel duration when compared to the intercept. Only the number of syllables in a word did not show a significant influence on vowel length in the model output. The estimates show that SVLR short environments and non-final positions have negative effect sizes. Thus, the model estimates that these contexts account for shorter vocalic durations when compared to the intercept. Nuclear prosodic stress, however, has an estimate of 22.95 which indicates that vowels carrying nuclear prosodic stress are longer than those specified in the intercept. There is also a significant difference in vocalic duration between the two different age groups (age_group young compared to the intercept including age_group old) and between the phone labels themselves (/i/ compared to the intercept including /aɪ/). The phone label /i/ has a substantial negative effect size of −59.22, indicating shorter vocalic intervals. However, no significant influence on duration was detected for the other sociolinguistic variables (regional background, gender). Thus, when compared to the intercept, the regional background of speakers and the gender do not show a significant influence on vowel duration.

Even though the model outputs only provide an intercept-restricted overview, many results agree with the patterns that can be found in the previous plots. First, there are vowel intrinsic durational differences between the vowel /i/ and the diphthong /aɪ/. Second, vowel duration is significantly affected by prosodic stress, the phrasal position, the local speech rate, the word phone number as well as by the SVLR context when compared to the intercept. Thus, most suprasegmental features have a significant influence on vowel duration. Most sociolinguistic factors, however, do not significantly affect vocalic length. Only age-related variation could be detected in the model outputs.

As the vowel labels show significant durational differences, they will be analyzed further with separate models. At the same time, due to the overlap between SVLR and VE environments, a refined classification will be applied for the VE context modelling. That is, all specific SVLR long contexts (following voiced fricatives, /r/, and morpheme boundaries) are excluded in the VE model so that there is a sharp separation between VE effects and Scottish durational patterns. As this procedure created four highly complex models, the following paragraphs will only show the SVLR models and summarize the main findings.

4.1 Linear mixed effects modeling for /i/

The outputs of the best fit model with the SVLR classification for the vowel /i/ showed that the suprasegmental factors prosodic stress, phrase position, local speech rate, word phone number and SVLR short contexts are significant when compared to the intercept (see Table 7.6). Word syllable number, however, did not show a significant effect. The estimates show that a medial phrase position and SVLR short contexts account for significantly shorter vowel durations when compared to the intercept. Nuclear stress, however, has a positive estimate (53.22) indicating longer vocalic durations. There are significant interactions between the SVLR and the phrase position, the SVLR and prosodic stress, the SVLR and the local speech rate, prosodic stress and the word phone number, the phrase position and the word phone number as well as between prosodic stress and the phrase position in the model outputs. Despite different interactions and constellations, the model does not report a significant influence of the sociolinguistic factors (age group, gender, regional background) and there is no interaction between the latter and the SVLR.

Table 7.6 Best-fit linear mixed effects model with the SVLR classification for the vowel /i/ with interactions

Random effects:			
Groups	Name	Variance	std. deviation
Word_label	(Intercept)	342.0	18.49
Speaker	(Intercept)	117.0	10.81
Residual		611.4	24.73
Number of obs: 1195, groups: Word_label, 272; Speaker, 36			

Fixed effects:				
SVLR model	Estimate	std. error	p-value	Significance code*
(Intercept)	226.87	11.35	< 2e-16	***
SVLRshort	−76.83	10.91	3.27e-12	***
prosodynuclear	53.22	8.72	1.40e-09	***
Phrase_positionmedial	−63.14	6.70	< 2e-16	***
local_speech_rate	−9.35	1.65	1.73e-08	***
Word_phone_number	−7.36	1.17	5.24e-10	***
SVLRshort:prosodynuclear	−23.81	4.90	1.30e-06	***
SVLRshort:Phrase_positionmedial	22.76	4.44	3.38e-07	***
prosodynuclear:Phrase_positionmedial	10.63	4.21	0.011590	*
SVLRshort:local_speech_rate	5.20	1.84	0.004827	**
prosodynuclear:Word_phone_number	−4.83	1.39	0.000535	***
Phrase_positionmedial:Word_phone_number	5.65	1.14	7.91e-07	***

The best fit model for the VE classification showed a similar pattern. The factors prosodic stress, phrase position, local speech rate, word phone number have a significant effect when compared to the intercept. However, the VE itself does not have a significant influence. Thus, the VE short contexts are not significantly different from the values in the intercept which include the VE long contexts. There is, however, a significant influence from region Highlands. When compared to the intercept, which includes the region East central, the vocalic intervals from the Highlands are longer for the vowel /i/. Yet, there is no interaction between the region Highland and any other factor, indicating that the vowel durations generally tend to be longer in this area. Similar to the SVLR model, there is a significant interaction between the phrase position and prosodic stress, phrase position and word phone number as well as prosodic stress and word phone number in the VE model.

4.2 Linear mixed effects modeling for /aɪ/

The outputs for the best fit model with the SVLR classification for the diphthong /aɪ/ report a significant effect of the suprasegmental factors prosodic stress, phrase position, local speech rate, and the SVLR short contexts when compared to the intercept (see Table 7.7). Apart from that, there are interactions between the SVLR and the phrase position as well as between the SVLR and the local speech rate. There is also a significant interaction between prosodic stress and the word phone number, yet, the word phone number on its own did not have a significant effect on vowel duration. The model does also not report any significant effects for the sociolinguistic factors (regional background, age group, gender).

As for the VE classification, the best fit model reports significant effects for the factors prosodic stress, phrase position, local speech rate and age group. The estimate of the age group younger shows a negative effect size (−16.40) and this indicates that the younger speakers produce shorter vowels. However, no significant effect of the VE could be observed. Moreover, the regional background and gender of speakers do not have a significant influence on vowel durations when compared to the intercept. There are significant interactions between prosodic stress and phrase position as well as between prosodic stress and the word phone number.

Table 7.7 Best-fit linear mixed effects model for the SVLR classification for the diphthong /aɪ/ with interactions

Random effects:			
Groups	Name	Variance	std. deviation
Word_label	(Intercept)	671.3	25.91
Speaker	(Intercept)	319.6	17.88
Residual		793.2	28.16

Number of obs: 983, groups: Word_label, 285; Speaker, 36

Fixed effects:				
SVLR model	Estimate	std. error	p-value	Significance code*
(Intercept)	346.590	17.565	< 2e-16	***
SVLRshort	−170.381	17.288	< 2e-16	***
prosodynuclear	69.233	7.988	< 2e-16	***
Phrase_positionmedial	−36.814	6.198	4.01e-09	***
local_speech_rate	−22.910	3.260	3.97e-12	***
SVLRshort:Phrase_positionmedial	26.852	6.762	7.71e-05	***
SVLRshort:local_speech_rate	17.475	3.389	3.06e-07	***
prosodynuclear:Word_phone_number	−8.353	1.459	1.37e-08	***

5. Discussion

The results indicate that the durations of the vowel /i/ and the diphthong /aɪ/ are significantly influenced by prosodic factors (especially prosodic stress, phrase position, speech rate, word phone number and SVLR). Thus, words carrying nuclear prosodic stress and words in phrase-final position tend to be longer than those without nuclear stress and in medial phrase position. Furthermore, vowels tend to be longer if the speech rate and the word phone number are lower. These results are in line with recent investigations of the SVLR (Rathcke & Stuart-Smith 2016; Chevalier 2019) and highlight the influence of intralinguistic factors.

Whereas Aitken's Law has a significant influence on vowel duration, no significant effects could be reported for the revised VE context classifications. Thus, the SVLR operates in 21st century SSE in the vowel /i/ as well as in the diphthong /aɪ/ and there is no significant influence of the VE. Although some cross-varietal linguistic influence from SSBE has been reported, the vowel length patterns in SSE appear to be distinctively Scottish. A significant convergence towards SSBE vowel length patterns could not be detected in this study.

Some of the model outputs report a significant influence of the age group on vowel duration, and that vocalic intervals are longer for the vowel /i/ in the Highlands. Yet, these findings must be taken with caution as there is a high age range among the participants due to a lack of young speakers and the age group classification is generally very broad. Furthermore, the token numbers for the region Highland are relatively low, which might have an effect on the model outputs. The larger study on the SVLR (Weilinghoff, forthcoming) will provide more data and insights for these aspects. Nevertheless, the results of this investigation clearly show that language-internal factors tend to have a stronger influence on Scottish vowel length patterns than language-external factors (Rathcke & Stuart-Smith 2016; Chevalier 2019). However, it has to be noted that most speeches in this study were read in a very formal context (the Scottish Parliament). Speakers might avoid regional features in this public national setting.

The findings are also valuable for the pluricentricity/pluriareality debate and can be interpreted from different viewpoints.

From the pluricentric perspective, the lack of regional variation highlights that Scottish vowel length patterns apply on a national level. Even though there are some regions which are influenced by Scottish Gaelic (Highlands and Islands) and Scots (North East), no significant regional variation in the application of Aitken's Law could be detected. The speakers in this study further do not converge towards Southern British vowel quantity alternation patterns (VE). Taking into account the country's history as well as its current political situation, pluricentrists could therefore interpret the consistency of the SVLR patterns as a sign of national norm stabilization and diffusion and Scottish Standard English having achieved (epi-)center status. Due to Scotland's long period of independence, its language situation and the recently regained political autonomy, pluricentrists might argue that there is another influential center on the British Isles, both politically and linguistically. British English, one of the major English varieties, is usually equated with SSBE and Received Pronunciation (RP). This notion is clearly oversimplified and does not reflect the linguistic diversity of the United Kingdom (Schneider 2014: 198). Especially SSE can be addressed as another influential standard variety in the north of Great Britain which has retained distinctive and relatively stable pronunciation patterns.

Even though significant areal patterns could not be detected in the application of Aitken's Law, pluriarealists could still stress that Aitken's Law also operates in the north of England (Milroy 1995; Watt and Ingham 2000; Llamas et al. 2011). Thus, as previous studies have shown that SVLR patterns stretch across the Anglo-Scottish border, pluriarealists might follow the claim of Agutter (1988) and stress that Aitken's Law is not necessarily a Scottish national feature, but a regional pattern that can be found in the north of the Great Britain. The United Kingdom serves as a good example for regional diversity as it represents a union of four constituent countries: England, Scotland, Wales, and Northern Ireland. There is, of course, great linguistic variation within the constituent countries, for example, the FOOT-STRUT split, which separates the linguistic north and south of England (Wells 1982: 335). Hence, as linguistic variation does not follow political boundaries and as Aitken's Law stretches across Scotland and the north of England, pluriarealists might argue that it is therefore better to model variation in standard languages from a pluriareal perspective. In addition, proponents of pluriareality might also criticize that most of the speeches in this study were read in the Scottish Parliament. This highly formal and national setting could have suppressed the speakers' regional variation in pronunciation patterns.

Thus, the SVLR allows for both pluricentric and pluriareal interpretations. Both approaches can be useful to describe and model variation in standard languages in this context, stressing either the national (pluricentric) or areal (pluriareal) character of phonetic variation in standard languages. I would therefore argue that a mutual exclusion of the two approaches is neither necessary nor advantageous. The debate on the superiority of either concept is not useful as both approaches model variation against the background of geography; they just imply different perspectives and take different assumptions. The debate can also distract from other, far more important factors that influence language variation than the regional or national background of speakers. This may be especially the case in phonetic investigations. The debate about whether Aitken's Law is essentially a Scottish national (pluricentric) or non-Scottish regional (pluriareal) feature would distract from the fact that the pattern is strongly influenced by intralinguistic factors in connected speech. It is not only geography that plays a role when it comes to describing variation in standard languages. Researchers should prioritize a detailed analysis of the linguistic patterns themselves, meticulously examining their variations and interactions with other intralinguistic and extralinguistic factors. Thereby, scholars can gain deeper insights into the intricate dynamics of variation in standard languages.

6. Conclusion

The study in the present chapter has analyzed vowel length patterns in 21st century SSE against the background of the pluricentricity/pluriareality debate. Data was retrieved from ICE Scotland and linear mixed effects modelling was applied to account for variation in SVLR patterns with respect to prosodic factors as well as sociolinguistic variables. The results demonstrate that Aitken's Law operates in the vowels /i/ and /aɪ/ across all dialect regions. A significant convergence towards SSBE vowel patterns (VE) could not be observed. Furthermore, vowel duration patterns are strongly influenced by prosodic factors, especially speech rate, prosodic stress, the word phone number and the phrasal position. However, the influence of sociolinguistic variables (especially the regional background) on SVLR patterns are negligible. The findings of the study can be interpreted from both the pluricentric and pluriareal perspective. Pluricentrists might argue that the consistency of the SVLR patterns in SSE is a sign that the standard variety has achieved an epicenter status. Scotland can be seen as another center on the British Isles, both in terms of politics and linguistics. Pluriarealists, however, might stress that the patterns of Aitken's Law can also be found in the north of England, which underlines that the pattern does not follow political borders, thus demonstrating the pluriareal character of variation. As the findings of the present investigation can be interpreted from both the pluricentric and pluriareal perspective, I claim that a mutual exclusion of the two concepts is neither necessary nor beneficial. Both approaches can be used to model geographical variation, they just imply different perspectives and assumptions. Furthermore, a sole focus on geographical variation, be it from a pluricentric or pluriareal perspective, may leave out other, more important factors, such as prosody. Overall, Scotland provides an interesting perspective on the pluricentricity/pluriareality debate because it shows that the distinction between nation state and region (Scotland within the United Kingdom) as well as between language and dialect (Scots — English) is not always easy and clear-cut.

References

Agutter, Alex. 1988. The dangers of dialect parochialism: The Scottish vowel length rule. In Jacek Fisiak (ed.), *Historical Dialectology: Regional and Social*, 1–22. Berlin: De Gruyter Publishing.

Aitken, Adam Jack. 1979. Scottish Speech: A historical view, with special reference to the Standard English of Scotland. In Adam J. Aitken & Thomas MacArthur (eds.), *Languages of Scotland*. Edinburgh: W & R Chambers.

Aitken, Adam Jack. 1981. The Scottish Vowel-length Rule. In M. Benskin & M. L. Samuels (eds.), *So meny people longages and tonges: philological essays in Scots and mediaeval English presented to Angus McIntosh*. Edinburgh: Benskin & Samuels.

Ashby, Simone, Mário E. Viaro, Silvia Barbosa & Neuza Campaniço. 2012. Modeling phonetic variation in pluricentric languages: An integrative approach. *Dialectologia*, vol. 8, 1–26.

Boersma, Paul & David Weenink. 2020. *Praat: Doing phonetics by computer* [Computer program]. Version 6.1.38, Retrieved from: http://www.praat.org/

Chen, Matthew. 1970. Vowel length variation as a function of the voicing of the consonant environment. *Phonetica*, vol. 22. 129–159.

Chevalier, Florent. 2019. On sound change and gender: The case of vowel length variation in Scottish English. *Anglophonia*, vol. 27 [Online]. Retrieved from: https://journals.openedition.org/anglophonia/2204 (Date: 20.03.2020)

Clyne, Michael. 1989. Pluricentricity: National variety. In Ulrich Ammon (ed.), *Status and Function of Languages and Language Varieties*, 357–371. Berlin: De Gruyter.

Dollinger, Stefan. 2019. *The Pluricentricity Debate: On Austrian German and Other Germanic Standard Varieties*. New York: Routledge.

Elspaß, Stephan; Dürscheid, Christa & Arne Ziegler. 2017. Zur grammatischen Pluriarealität der deutschen Gebrauchsstandards – oder: Über die Grenzen des Plurizentrizitätsbegriffs. [Online]. Retrieved from: https://www.researchgate.net/publication/322481568_Zur_grammatischen_Pluriarealitat_der_deutschen_Gebrauchsstandards_-_oder_Uber_die_Grenzen_des_Plurizentrizitatsbegriffs

Giegerich, Heinz Joachim. 1992. *English phonology: An introduction*. Cambridge: Cambridge University Press.

Hewlett, Nigel, Ben Matthews & James M. Scobbie. 1999. Vowel duration in Scottish English speaking children. *Proceedings of the 14th International Congress of Phonetic Sciences*, 2157–2160. [Online]: Retrieved from: https://citeseerx.ist.psu.edu/viewdoc/download?doi=10.1.1.29.9645&rep=rep1&type=pdf

Jackson, Ben. 2020. *The Case for Scottish Independence: A History of Nationalist Political Thought in Modern Scotland*. Cambridge: Cambridge University Press.

Johnston, Paul. 2007. Scottish English and Scots. In David Britain (ed.), *Language in the British Isles*, 105–121. Cambridge: Cambridge University Press.

Jones, Charles. 2002. *The English Language in Scotland: An Introduction to Scots*. Glasgow: Tuckwell Press.

Katz, Jonah. 2012. Compression effects in English. *Journal of Phonetics*, vol. 40, 390–402.

Lanwermeyer, Manuela, Johanna Fanta-Jende Alexandra N. Lenz & Katharina Korecky-Kröll. 2019. Competing norms of standard pronunciation: Phonetic analyses on the ‹-ig›-variation in Austria. *Dialectologia et Geolinguistica*, vol. 27. 143–175.

Leith, Dick & Liz Jackson. 1997. The origins of English. In David Graddol, Dick Leith, Joan Swann, Martin Rhys & Julia Gillen (eds.), *Changing English*, 39–77. London and New York: Routledge.

Llamas, Carmen; Dominic Watt, Peter French & Lisa Roberts. 2011. Effects of the Scottish Vowel Length Rule on vowel quantity in Tyneside English. *Proceedings of the 17th International Congress of Phonetic Sciences*, 1282–1285. [Online]: Retrieved from: https://www.internationalphoneticassociation.org/icphs-proceedings/ICPhS2011/OnlineProceedings/RegularSession/Llamas/Llamas.pdf

Lodge, K. R. 1984. *Studies in the Phonology of Colloquial English*. London & Sidney: Croom Helm Ltd.

McArthur, Tom. 1992. The Scots – bilingual or just confused? *World Englishes* 11 (2/3). 101–110.

McClure, J. Derrick. 1977. Vowel duration in a Scottish accent. *Journal of the International Phonetic Association* 7(1). 10–16.

McClure, J. Derrick. 1994. English in Scotland. In R. Burchfield (ed.), *The Cambridge History of the English Language – Volume V English in Britain and Overseas: Origins and Developments*, 23–93. Cambridge: Cambridge University Press.

McMahon, April M. S. 1991. Lexical phonology and sound change: The case of the Scottish vowel length rule. *Journal of Linguistics*, vol. 27. 29–53.

Milroy, James R. D. 1995. Investigating the Scottish vowel length rule in a Northumbrian dialect. *Newcastle and Durham Working Papers in Linguistics*, vol. 4, 187–196.

Muhr, Rudolf. 1997. Zur Terminologie und Methode der Beschreibung plurizentrischer Sprachen und deren Varietäten am Beispiel des Deutschen. In Rudolf Muhr & Richard Schrodt (eds.), *Österreichisches Deutsch und andere nationale Varietäten plurizentrischer Sprachen in Europa: Empirische Analysen*. Wien: Hölder-Pichler-Tempsky.

National Records of Scotland. 2015. *Scotland's Census 2011 – Gaelic report (part 1)*. [Online]. Retrieved from: https://www.scotlandscensus.gov.uk/documents/analytical_reports/Report_part_1.pdf

Niehaus, Konstantin. 2015. Areale Variation in der Syntax des Standarddeutschen: Ergebnisse zum Sprachgebrauch und zur Frage Plurizentrik vs. Pluriarealität. *Zeitschrift für Dialektologie und Linguistik* 82(2). 133–168.

Rathcke, Tamara V. & Jane H. Stuart-Smith. 2016. On the Tail of the Scottish Vowel Length Rule in Glasgow. *Language and Speech* 59(3). 404–430.

R Core Team. 2020. *R: A language and environment for statistical computing*. [Computer program]. Version 4.0.3, Retrieved from: http://www.R-project.org/

Ruette, Tom, Dirk Speelman & Dirk Geeraerts. 2014. Lexical variation in aggregate perspective. In Augusto Soares da Silva (ed.), *Pluricentricity: Language Variation and Sociocognitive Dimensions*, 103–126. Berlin: De Gruyter.

Scobbie, James M., Nigel Hewlett & Alice Turk. 1999. Standard English in Edinburgh and Glasgow: The Scottish Vowel Length Rule revealed. In P. Foulkes & G. Docherty (eds.), *Urban Voices: Accent Studies in the British Isles*. London: Arnold Publishing.

Scobbie, James M. 2005. Interspeaker variation among Shetland Islanders as the long term outcome of dialectally varied input: Speech production evidence for fine-grained linguistic plasticity. *QMUC Speech Science Research Centre Working Paper WP2*, 1–9.

Schneider, Edgar W. 2014. Global diffusion, regional attraction, local roots? Sociocognitive perspectives on the pluricentricity of English. In Augusto Soares da Silva (ed.), *Pluricentricity: Language Variation and Sociocognitive Dimensions*, 191–226. Berlin: De Gruyter.

Schützler, Ole, Ulrike Gut & Robert Fuchs. 2017. New perspectives on Scottish Standard English: Introducing the Scottish component of the International Corpus of English. In Sylvie Hancil & Joan C. Beal (eds.), *Perspectives on Northern Englishes*. Berlin: De Gruyter.

Stuart-Smith, Jane H. 2008. Scottish English: phonology. In Bernd Kortmann & Clive Upton (eds.), *Varieties of English: The British Isles*. Berlin: De Gruyter.

Tanner, James, Morgan Sonderegger Jane H. Stuart-Smith & Josef Fruehwald. 2020. Toward "English" Phonetics: Variability in the Pre-consonantal Voicing Effect Across English Dialects and Speakers. *Frontiers in Artificial Intelligence*, vol. 3. 1–15.

Turk, Alice; Satsuki Nakai & Mariko Sugahara. 2006. Acoustic Segment Durations in Prosodic Research: A Practical Guide. In Petra Augurzky, Denisa Lenertova, Roland Meyer, Ina Mleinek, Sandra Pappert, Nicole Richter, Johannes Schließer & Stefan Sudhoff (eds.), *Methods in Empirical Prosody Research*, 1–28. Berlin: De Gruyter.

Turk, Alice & Stefanie Shattuck-Hufnagel. 2000. Word-boundary-related durational patterns in English. *Journal of Phonetics*, vol. 28. 397–440.

van Leyden, Klaske. 2002. The Relationship between Vowel and Consonant Duration in Orkney and Shetland Dialects. *Phonetica*, vol. 59. 1–19.

Watt, Dominic & Catherine Ingham. 2000. Durational evidence of the Scottish Vowel Length Rule in Berwick English. In Diane Nelson & Paul Foulkes (eds.). *Leeds Working Papers in Linguistics*, vol. 8. 205–228.

Watt, Dominic & Jillian Yurkova. 2007. Voice Onset Time and the Scottish Vowel Length Rule in Aberdeen English. *Proceedings of the 16th International Congress of Phonetic Sciences*, 1521–1524.

Weilinghoff, Andreas J. forthcoming. *Vowel Duration Patterns in Scottish English: The Scottish Vowel Length Rule in the 21st century*. Edinburgh: Edinburgh University Press.

Wells, John Christopher. 1982. *Accents of English 2: The British Isles*. Cambridge: Cambridge University Press.

CHAPTER 8

Revising the *Algemene Nederlandse Spraakkunst*
A pluricentric approach to diatopic variation in the grammar of Standard Dutch?

Arne Dhondt, Timothy Colleman & Johan De Caluwe
Ghent University, Belgium

> The third, fully revised version of the *Algemene Nederlandse Spraakkunst* (ANS), the main reference grammar of Dutch, aims to describe grammatical variation in the national standard varieties of Dutch. This paper investigates whether this pluricentric perspective is compatible with the geographical distribution patterns of Dutch grammatical variants. We provide an overview of the distribution patterns described in the second edition of the ANS and we check this description against frequency data from newspaper corpora for four selected variants which represent different distribution patterns. Although the observed distribution patterns do not always coincide with national borders, we argue that the pluricentric model does not (necessarily) conflict with linguistic reality and that it is the appropriate choice to meet the needs of Dutch language users.

Keywords: Dutch, pluricentricity, pluriareality, geographical variation, corpus linguistics, grammar, grammaticography

1. Introduction

In 2016, work started on a thorough revision of the second edition of the main reference grammar of Standard Dutch, the *Algemene Nederlandse Spraakkunst* (Haeseryn et al. 1997). This will be referred to as ANS2. The aim is to publish a fully revised online grammar, in what follows called ANS3, of which the first new, fully revised chapters became available in 2021. Among other reasons, this revision project was motivated by the need to bring the grammatical description up to date and in line with present-day norms and views about the status of variation within "standard" Dutch.[1] An important change vis-à-vis ANS2 is that ANS3 wants to implement a pluricentric perspective on Dutch. In other words, it aims to describe grammatical variation between the different national standard varieties of Dutch, viz. Standard Belgian (SBD), Standard Netherlandic (SND), and in a later stage once larger and more representative corpora of this variety will be available, also Standard Surinamese Dutch (SSD).

In Dhondt et al. (2020), we argue that, for this purpose, a systematic method should be developed for investigating national variation in the grammar on the basis of corpus data and translating the findings into a pluricentric grammatical description. We also reflected on a few challenges that would have to be overcome in order to arrive at such a method. However, a question that has not yet been addressed at length is whether it is actually fully justified to use the *pluricentric* model for the description of grammatical variation in Dutch: especially for German, some scholars have argued that the idea of *national* standard varieties does not adequately reflect linguistic reality and have instead advocated a *pluriareal* model (see the overview in e.g. de Cillia & Ransmayr 2019, Niehaus 2015). In this paper, we will therefore evaluate whether the pluricentric model is appropriate to describe diatopic grammatical variation in ANS3. More specifically, we focus on whether this model is compatible with the attested geographical distribution patterns of Dutch grammatical variants. Before we outline in more detail how we will address this question, the next sub-sections briefly introduce the pluricentric perspective on Dutch, show that diatopic variation is not described from this perspective in ANS2, and briefly summarize the arguments that have been put forward in the literature (mostly for German) for adopting a pluriareal rather than a pluricentric model to describe diatopic variation within standard varieties.

---

1. ANS3 can be consulted via https://e-ans.ivdnt.org/. The website also offers a description of (the aims of) the revision project. This article was originally submitted on 13 January 2021 and it is related to the PhD project of the first author, in which a method is developed to investigate and to describe diatopic grammatical variation in ANS3. From 2021 to 2024, the first author continued working on his PhD thesis, which was submitted on 24 January 2024. Some aspects of this article are dealt with more extensively in the PhD, e.g. the different arguments of Dürscheid et al. (2015: 209–10) against a plurinational perspective on German are discussed more thoroughly in relation to Dutch. For instance, with regard to the argument from variational linguistics, there is also attention devoted to the question to what extent previous research provides evidence that the Belgian-Netherlandic border has led to the divergence of (attitudes towards) language use on either side of the border.

1.1 The pluricentric perspective on Dutch

For the largest part of the twentieth century, a monocentric view prevailed in the linguistic literature on Dutch, which implied that the Dutch of (the west of) the Netherlands set the norm for the standard language and that all deviations from it (e.g. variants only used in Flanders, the Dutch-speaking part of Belgium) were to be considered non-standard, as discussed by Martin (2001: 709–710). From the 1980s or 1990s onwards, this monocentric perspective on "standard Dutch" was gradually replaced by a pluricentric perspective. Nowadays, the predominant view among linguists is that Dutch is a pluricentric language, i.e. a language which comprises "two or more standard varieties, each of which can be ascribed to, or is valid for, one center" (Ammon 2005: 1536) (cf. De Caluwe 2017, Martin 2001). In this definition, the notion 'center' can receive different interpretations, but most often it is taken to refer to different nations and states, so that *pluricentric* is often equated with *plurinational*.[2] For instance, the *Nederlandse Taalunie*, in its official policy on variation in Dutch, distinguishes three national standard varieties, viz. SBD, SND and SSD. These varieties share most of their lexical, grammatical, and pronunciation norms, but they also have some of their own, national norms (cf. Adviescommissie Taalvariatie 2019).[3]

1.2 The description of diatopic variation in ANS2

This pluricentric view has been adopted by (recent editions of) most of the main dictionaries of Dutch: e.g., the *Algemeen Nederlands Woordenboek*, *Prisma Handwoordenboek Nederlands* (Martin & Smedts 2009), and *Van Dale Groot woordenboek van de Nederlandse taal* (Den Boon & Hendrickx 2015).[4] Words and expressions do not only receive a label when they are typical of Belgian or Surinamese Dutch, but also when they are only used in the Netherlands. ANS2, however, does not yet offer a pluricentric description of Dutch grammar. ANS2 (0.6.2.1) holds the view that standard language "does not contain any elements or structures that clearly stand out as non-general [my translation, AD]" and when it comes to diatopic variation, ANS2 (0.6.2.3) distinguishes between *geografisch verschillende varianten* (lit. 'geographically differing variants', henceforth: variants with geographical variation) and *regionale varianten* (lit. 'regional variants'):[5]

---

2. In this paper, we will consider *pluricentric* and *plurinational* as synonyms.
3. The *Nederlandse Taalunie* ('Dutch Language Union') is an intergovernmental organization which develops policy on Dutch in the Netherlands, Flanders, and Suriname.
4. The *Algemeen Nederlands Woordenboek* is a dictionary that can be consulted online via https://anw.ivdnt.org/

- Variants with geographical variation are "elements and structures which are somewhat associated with a certain region, but which, for the majority of the language users, are not typical for the language in that region [my translation, AD]."[6] Therefore, they are part of Standard Dutch according to ANS2. For instance, in the whole Dutch language area, the strong imperfect *ervoer* 'experienced' can be used instead of the weak imperfect *ervaarde* 'experienced', but it is relatively more frequently used in the Netherlands as compared to Dutch-speaking Belgium.
- Regional variants are "elements and structures that, for many language users, are either characteristic of a certain part of the language area or unknown because they come from a different region [my translation, AD]."[7] Therefore, for ANS2, variants of this type do *not* belong to Standard Dutch. For instance, the use of the preposition *doorheen* 'through' is limited to Belgium and, hence, considered not to be a part of the standard language.

ANS2 thus does not take into account the possibility that the norms of Standard Dutch differ nationally: variants which are only used in a specific part of the language area by definition do not belong to Standard Dutch. ANS3 does want to implement a pluricentric perspective on Dutch, but as pointed out in the introduction, it is unclear whether a *pluriareal* model might perhaps not be a better choice for describing diatopic variation within Standard Dutch.

1.3 The pluriareal model

The pluriareal model differs from the pluricentric one in that it gives pride of place to regional differences *within* and *across* the different nations or states constituting a language area (Dürscheid et al. 2015: 209). The approach is nicely illustrated by the *Variantengrammatik,* a reference work which aims to describe diatopic grammatical variation within the German written *standard of use* on the basis of corpus data (see Dürscheid et al. 2015; Elspaß et al. 2017; Niehaus 2015). The *Variantengrammatik* does not start from the assumption that there are different national varieties of Standard German (e.g. Swiss, Austrian and German

---

5. "de taal waarin geen elementen of structuren voorkomen die duidelijk opvallen als niet-algemeen" (ANS2 0.6.2.1). Note that, when referring to ANS2, we will refer to paragraph numbers and not to specific pages.

6. "elementen en structuren die wel enigszins streekgebonden zijn, maar voor de meerderheid van de taalgebruikers niet kenmerkend voor de taal in een bepaalde regio." (ANS2 0.6.2.3.i)

7. "Elementen en structuren die voor veel taalgebruikers kenmerkend zijn voor een bepaald deel van het taalgebied, of onbekend omdat ze afkomstig zijn uit een andere regio" (ANS2 0.6.2.3.ii).

German), but describes grammatical variation between different *regions* within the German language area. For this purpose, frequency data are compiled from a digital corpus of roughly six-hundred million words, which contains articles from sixty-eight regional newspapers from all parts of the German language area, as newspaper data are taken to reflect the standard of use (Niehaus 2015: 141–144). The corpus is subdivided into fifteen subcomponents based on the national *or* regional origin of the articles. Some of the subcomponents cover countries (e.g. Switzerland or Luxembourg), whereas others cover regions within countries (e.g. north-west-Germany or middle-Austria).

Dürscheid et al. (2015: 209–210) put forward three arguments against the adoption of a plurinational model for the grammatical description of German. First, there is a language-political argument: nation states do not constitute a solid basis to distinguish varieties, as they can dissolve. The authors exemplify this by referring to the reunification of Germany, after which there was according to them no longer any reason to distinguish 'DDR-Deutsch' from 'BRD-Deutsch'. A second argument is related to linguistic perception: for the German language, research would show that Swiss, German and Austrian laymen do not perceive national varieties (yet), so that — at least for German — this concept merely seems to exist in the minds of linguists. It is unclear, however, whether both arguments stand up to scrutiny for German. With regard to the language-political argument, one could for instance object that the existence of two states was a valid reason to discern two varieties *before* the reunification, and that the varieties would probably not have disappeared overnight after the reunification. Moreover, with regard to linguistic perception, recent research by De Cillia & Ransmayr (2019: 224–225) has found for Austria that a majority of German teachers and secondary school pupils *do* recognize the existence of national variation within Standard German and the existence of an Austrian Standard German.

The third argument against pluricentricity comes from variational linguistics: according to Dürscheid et al. (2015: 209–210), the distribution patterns of supposedly national variants frequently cross national borders and it remains unclear whether one can find more differences between nations than within nations. This last argument is further elaborated in Elspaß et al. (2017: 72–73), where it is claimed that the pluricentric approach creates the impression that we are dealing with relatively uniform national standard varieties. According to Elspaß et al. (2017), this does not correspond to a linguistic reality for German, as data from different projects on diatopic variation within Standard German (e.g. the *Variantengrammatik,* the *Atlas zur Aussprache des deutschen Gebrauchsstandards* (Kleiner 2011ff) and the *Variantenwörterbuch des Deutschen* (Ammon et al. 2016)) show that there is only a minority of variants that are specific, i.e. used in one country only, and that are used in an absolute manner within that country, i.e.

that do not compete with equivalents that potentially have a broader geographical scope. Elspaß et al. (2017: 72–73) state that most diatopic variants are non-specific: their distribution patterns cross national borders and more often seem to coincide with borders of traditional dialect areas. Moreover, in most cases they are relative variants, i.e. they are not the *only* variant used in a given region, but are used next to equivalents. For instance, the word *ambitiös* 'ambitious' is not only used in Luxembourg, but also in Switzerland, and in both countries, it is used next to its equivalent *ambitioniert*. True national variants, i.e. specific and absolute variants, are mainly found in official language use, e.g. the word *Klassensaal* 'classroom' only occurs in Luxembourg and does not have an equivalent in Luxembourgish German.

1.4 Aim and overview

If we want to evaluate whether the pluricentric approach is adequate for describing diatopic variation in ANS3, the question arises to what extent the arguments against the adoption of a plurinational perspective briefly discussed in the previous subsection also hold for Dutch. As the revised ANS3 aims to describe national variation on the basis of production data, the question about the geographical distribution patterns of variants in production data becomes especially prominent: to what extent do these patterns coincide with national borders in the Dutch language area and are we dealing with absolute or relative variants? In this paper, we will therefore investigate what distribution patterns can be observed for Dutch grammatical variants. In Section 2, we take stock of the variants for which ANS2 indicates diatopic variation and investigate whether specific or non-specific and absolute or relative patterns are described. In Section 3, we will select four variants which represent different patterns of diatopic distribution according to the grammatical description in ANS2 and investigate how they are actually distributed in newspaper corpora. In Section 4, we will then return to the question of whether the pluricentric model is adequate for ANS3: we will evaluate whether the observed distribution patterns in Dutch are compatible with the aim of ANS3 to describe Dutch grammar from a pluricentric perspective, and we will then also revisit the language-political argument and the perception argument and briefly discuss them in relation to Dutch. As ANS2 only provides information on Dutch in Europe, and as there are at present no good electronic corpora available for Surinamese Dutch, we will leave this national variety aside for now and focus on Belgian and Netherlandic Dutch.

2. Geographical distribution patterns of grammatical variants described in ANS2

To arrive at an overview of the different geographical distribution patterns of grammatical variants described in ANS2, we first made an inventory of all variants for which ANS2 describes some kind of diatopic variation, i.e. containing both 'geographically differing' and 'regional' variants. Moreover, in order to estimate whether these variants are in relative or absolute use in the areas in question, we also checked whether ANS2 mentions alternative expressions for the variants. Alternative expressions are here defined broadly, as alternative phrasings which are referentially/truth-conditionally similar to the variant under focus (see Section 3 for examples). Table 8.1 summarizes the distribution patterns we found.[8,9]

In the overview in Table 8.1, we find different types of distributional patterns:

- Specific variants are those to which the label 'regional' is assigned in ANS2 and for which it is specified that they are (mainly) used either in Belgium or in the Netherlands. We find sixty-four regional variants for Belgium and a mere four for the Netherlands, a skewed distribution which probably results from the monocentric history of Dutch.
- Non-specific variants are variants for which the diatopic distribution does not coincide with national borders. We distinguish three subtypes:
  A. The variants with geographical variation, which are used in the whole of Belgium and the whole of the Netherlands (forty-seven cases).
  B. Those variants which are labelled as 'regional' and for which it is specified that they are used either in the whole of Belgium and parts of the Netherlands, in the whole of the Netherlands and parts of Belgium, or in parts of Belgium and parts of the Netherlands (ten cases).
  C. Those variants that are used only in *parts of* Belgium or *parts of* the Netherlands according to ANS2 and which thus get a label 'regional' (five variants for Belgium, and sixteen variants for the Netherlands).
- The inventory also includes ten variants which cannot readily be categorized as specific or non-specific variants. They are labelled as 'regional' in ANS2, but either no further information about their diatopic distribution is given, or the grammar only states that they are used in the south, west, east or north of the language area, without reference to countries.

---

8. We took into account all variants for which ANS2 indicates diatopic variation, even when these variants are lexical or phonetic rather than grammatical variants.

9. In the last column, we mention between brackets for how many of these cases alternative expressions are given.

Table 8.1 Overview of distribution patterns found in ANS2

Type of distribution	Type of diatopic variation according to ANS2	Geographical distribution according to ANS2	Number of cases of this type of distribution in ANS2
specific	regional	Belgium	64 (5)
specific	regional	the Netherlands	4 (1)
non-specific	geographical variation	whole language area	47 (1)
non-specific	regional	(i) Belgium and parts of the Netherlands, (ii) the Netherlands and parts of Belgium or (iii) parts of Belgium and parts of the Netherlands	10 (0)
non-specific	regional	parts of Belgium	5 (0)
non-specific	regional	parts of the Netherlands	16 (2)
uncategorized	regional	no (clear) specification	10 (2)

We thus find both specific and non-specific patterns in ANS2. For most variants, ANS2 mentions alternative expressions, so that it is at least possible that these variants are used next to (more general) equivalents in the part of the language area where they occur, i.e. that they are relative variants. The overview in Table 8.1 should be handled with caution, however, as the labels in ANS2 have frequently been assigned intersubjectively by the editors and not on the basis of e.g. corpus data (ANS2 0.6.2.1). Moreover, we do not know how much this overview tells us about the variation within *Standard* Dutch in the pluricentric sense. After all, on the basis of the description in ANS2, we do not know which regional variants belong to SBD and SND; it is for instance quite possible that some of the specific variants are restricted to non-standard varieties.

In the next section, we investigate whether the description in ANS2 matches the actual distribution pattern of the variants in standard language contexts: we of course cannot investigate all variants, but, by way of a case study, we selected a number of variants which represent different types of distribution patterns. We present frequency data for these variants, collected from the Belgian and Netherlandic newspaper components of the SoNaR Dutch Reference Corpus (Oostdijk et al. 2013) and we check to what extent these frequency data corroborate the distribution patterns described in ANS2. Following the *Variantengrammatik*, we consider newspapers to be standard language contexts, so that these data can be considered indicative of how common the use of the variants is in standard language. The selected cases are presented in Table 8.2; the non-specific variants are subdivided into types A, B and C, according to their geographical distribution. Further details about the variants will be given in Section 3.

Table 8.2 Selected variants for the corpus-based investigation

Type of distribution	Type of diatopic variation according to ANS2	Geographical distribution according to ANS2	(Pair of) variant(s)
specific	regional	Belgium	preposition *doorheen* 'through'
non-specific (type A)	geographical variation	whole language area	*komen* 'to come' + infinitive/past participle
non-specific (type B)	regional	parts of Belgium and parts of the Netherlands	*zo'n* 'such' + plural or non-count nouns
non-specific (type C)	regional	parts of Belgium	*beginnen* 'start' + bare infinitive

3. Case studies

3.1 Specific variant: The preposition *doorheen* 'through'

A specific variant only used in Belgium, according to ANS2, is the complex preposition *doorheen* 'through', e.g. in *doorheen de eeuwen* 'through the ages', which is labelled as 'regional' in ANS2 (9.3.4) and is presented as the equivalent of the circumposition *door...heen* 'through' (e.g. *door de eeuwen heen* 'through the ages').

We checked the distribution of *doorheen* and *door...heen* in the Belgian and Netherlandic newspaper component of SoNaR. In both components, we searched for

- the word *doorheen*, used in a sentence, and preceded or followed by zero to one-hundred words (1,928 hits for Belgium and 812 hits for the Netherlands);
- the combination of the word *door* followed within ten words by the word *heen*, with both forms occurring in the same sentence and the combination preceded or followed by zero to one-hundred words (1,426 hits for Belgium and 1,554 hits for the Netherlands).[10]

---

10. It was specified for practical reasons that *doorheen* or *door...heen* had to be used in a sentence and also what range of words could precede or follow the term: only when this specification is added, is one allowed to export enough context from SoNaR.

All double and irrelevant hits were deleted. Table 8.3 shows the absolute and normalized token frequency of *doorheen* in the Belgian and Netherlandic newspaper components. The absolute token frequency significantly differs between the components ($\chi^2 = 571.65$, $df = 1$, $p < 0.0001$) and the normalized token frequency shows that the complex preposition *doorheen* is almost exclusively used in Belgian newspapers, so that the specific distribution pattern described in ANS2 is confirmed.[11] Even though the preposition is by no means rare in Belgian newspapers, it remains difficult to estimate on the basis of absolute and normalized token frequency exactly how common the variant is in SBD.

Table 8.3 Absolute and normalized token frequency of *doorheen* 'through' in SoNaR Newspapers

Component	Absolute token frequency of *doorheen*	Total number of words in component	Normalized token frequency of *doorheen*
Belgian Dutch	1500	152 288 524	9.8497 tokens/million words
Netherlandic Dutch	5	59 381 224	0.0842 tokens/million words

To get a better idea of this, one could check in what percentage of cases this preposition is chosen over its supposed equivalent *door...heen*. However, a first inspection of the dataset suggests that the variants are less "equivalent" than assumed by ANS2, as they are definitely not interchangeable in all contexts: the circumposition seems the only possibility in certain lexical environments (e.g. *door zijn voorraad/krachten heen zitten* 'have no supplies/strength left', *door het dolle heen zijn* 'to be beside oneself') and perhaps also syntactic contexts (e.g. in combination with personal pronouns only the circumposition occurs in our dataset, e.g. *door mij heen* 'through me'). Moreover, it is unclear to what extent their meanings overlap (viz. in what semantic contexts they are interchangeable). More research is thus needed on the differences between the variants if we want to contrast the figures and determine whether *doorheen* is a relative or absolute variant in Belgian Dutch.[12]

---

11. For all case studies, chi-square tests were used if at least 80% of the expected cell frequencies were equal to or larger than 5. If not, Fisher's exact test was used. Note that chi-square tests might, in our case studies, result in a higher likelihood of Type I errors, as the assumption of independent observations might be violated (our data likely contain more than one observation per author and per newspaper). However, we cannot easily apply multivariate methods which take into account the effects of author and newspaper, as data on the author and newspaper are either not available or cannot be automatically exported from the corpus.

3.2 Non-specific variant (type A): *Komen* 'to come' with an infinitive or a past participle

A pair of non-specific variants which occur in both the whole of Belgium and the whole of the Netherlands are the infinitive vs. the past participle used with *komen* 'to come' to indicate the manner of coming, as illustrated in (1). According to ANS2 (18.5.3), the past participle is preferred in the southern part of the language area, viz. in Belgium and to a lesser extent also the southern provinces of the Netherlands, whereas the infinitive is more often chosen in the northern part, especially in the west.

(1) En daarvoor *komt* hij nou viermaal in de week naar Nijmegen *gereden/rijden*!
 (ANS2 18.5.3)
 'And for that reason, he is driving (lit. he comes driven/driving) to Nijmegen four times a week!'

Both variants are not interchangeable in all syntactic, lexical, and semantic contexts (cf. Dhondt et al. 2020). One context in which they *are* interchangeable (subtle semantic differences left aside) is sentences that are not in the perfect tense and in which the combination expresses a spatial movement (e.g. in 1).

To check the distribution of infinitives and past participles after *komen* in Belgian and Netherlandic Dutch, we therefore limited ourselves to combinations with the verbs in (2), which usually express a spatial movement.[13]

(2) *fietsen* 'to cycle', *lopen* 'to run', *rennen* 'to run', *rijden* 'to drive', *vliegen* 'to fly', *wandelen* 'to walk'

The Belgian and Netherlandic newspaper components of SoNaR were queried for sentences containing

- a finite verb form of the lemma *komen*, in the same sentence preceded or followed by the past participle of the verbs in (2) within a twenty-five-word span;
- a finite verb form of the lemma *komen*, in the same sentence followed by the infinitive of the verbs in (2) within a twenty-five-word span.

---

12. Dhondt (2024) contrasts the figures for *doorheen* and *door…heen* in different lexical, syntactic, and semantic environments, and in doing so, examines to what extent these adpositions are interchangeable.

13. Separable complex verbs based on these simplex verbs were also included in the dataset, e.g. *aanvliegen* 'fly towards' and *oprijden* 'drive up'.

All irrelevant and double hits were deleted.[14] This yielded the results in Table 8.4.[15] When the verbs in (2) are combined with *komen*, the distribution between infinitive and past participle significantly differs between Belgian and Netherlandic Dutch newspapers ($\chi^2 = 401.54$, $df = 1$, $p < 0.0001$, Cramer's $V = 0.5827$): there is a strong preference for the past participle in Belgian Dutch, and a weaker preference for the infinitive in Netherlandic Dutch. The distribution pattern described by ANS2 (18.5.3) is thus confirmed. Both variants are used in the whole of the language area, so that they are relative variants.

Table 8.4 Absolute and relative token frequencies of infinitive and past participle of the verbs in (2) in combination with *komen* 'to come' in SoNaR Newspapers

Component	Infinitive	Past participle	Total
Belgian Dutch	105 (10.3%)	917 (89.7%)	1022 (100.0%)
Netherlandic Dutch	132 (76.3%)	41 (23.7%)	173 (100.0%)
Total	237	958	1195

3.3 Non-specific variant (type B): The demonstrative pronoun *zo'n/zulke* 'such' with plural or non-count nouns

According to ANS2 (5.6.6), the demonstrative pronouns *zo'n* 'such' and *zulk(e)* 'such' are in complementary distribution in Standard Dutch:

– *zo'n* is used with singular nouns that can be combined with the indefinite article *een* 'a'
  e.g. *zo'n man* 'such a man'
– *zulk(e)* is used in all other cases, viz. with plural or non-count nouns
  e.g. *zulke mannen* 'such men', *zulk vee* 'such cattle'

---

14. For *fietsen* 'to cycle', two hits that did not express a spatial movement were left out, too. For *aanvliegen* 'fly towards', one such result was left out.

15. Even when we normalize the token frequencies, the construction with *komen* is more frequent in Belgian Dutch (6.71 constructions/million words) than in Netherlandic Dutch (2.91 constructions/million words). When looking at the individual verbs, this seems largely due to constructions with *rijden* 'drive', which are much more frequent in Belgian Dutch (665 tokens, 4.17/million words) than in Netherlandic Dutch (55 tokens, 0.93/million words). It is not clear why constructions with *rijden* 'drive' are more frequent in Belgian Dutch, but possibly the national corpora are not evenly balanced in terms of topic. In any case, even when leaving out *komen*-constructions with *rijden* 'drive', this does not substantially change the relative frequencies of infinitives and participles in Belgian and Netherlandic Dutch, so that this verb does not seem to distort the results.

However, ANS2 indicates that *zo'n* can also be combined with plural or non-count nouns in regional language use, more specifically in a large southeastern part of the Dutch language area. This description does not necessarily imply that the variant is used in Belgium *and* the Netherlands, but we assume that this is what is meant, as ANS2 seems to have based its description of the diatopic distribution on De Rooij (1989: 198). De Rooij observes that *zo'n* can be combined with plural or non-count nouns in the dialects of a large southeastern part of the Dutch language area, and specifies that this refers to the eastern provinces of Belgium (Flemish Brabant, Antwerp, and Limburg) and the southeastern provinces of the Netherlands (the eastern part of Northern Brabant and Netherlandic Limburg). For that reason, we see this variant as a non-specific variant which occurs both in *parts of* Belgium and in *parts of* the Netherlands.

Note, however, that *zo'n* can also be combined with a non-count noun in standard language according to ANS2 (5.6.6), but only if it has an intensifying instead of an identifying sense. The use of *zo'n* in (3) thus belongs to standard language according to ANS2, whereas the use of *zo'n* in (4) does not.

(3) Hij had *zo'n* pijn dat hij er niet van kon slapen. (ANS2 5.6.6)
 'He had so much pain that he could not sleep.'

(4) Huiskamertoneel of theater in de living is het nieuwste concept in de theaterwereld en ook wij zagen **zo'n huiskamertoneel** wel zitten.
(SoNaR, Belgian Newspapers)
 'Living room theatre or theatre in the living room is the newest concept in the theatre world and we also liked the idea of such living room theatre.'

To check the geographical distribution of *zo'n* and *zulke* with plural and non-count nouns, the Belgian and Netherlandic newspaper components of SoNaR were searched for *zo'n* and *zulk(e)* immediately followed by a noun, which yielded 29,595 hits for Belgian Dutch and 16,881 for Netherlandic Dutch. For both varieties, a random sample of two-thousand tokens was created, from which we retrieved all combinations with plural nouns and all combinations of identifying *zo'n* or *zulk(e)* with a non-count noun.[16] The results of this procedure for plural nouns and non-count nouns are shown in Tables 8.5 and 8.6, respectively.

Both for plural nouns ($\chi^2 = 101.17$, $df = 1$, $p < .0001$, Cramer's $V = 0.3842$) and for non-count nouns (two-tailed Fisher's exact: $p < .001$), the distribution between *zo'n* and *zulk(e)* significantly differs between Belgian and Netherlandic Dutch newspapers: in both contexts, *zo'n* (almost) exclusively seems to occur in the Belgian sample. Even though ANS2 suggests that the combination of *zo'n* with plural

---

16. We labelled a non-plural noun as non-count if it cannot be combined with the indefinite article *een* 'a' in the sentence in which it is used.

Table 8.5 Absolute and relative token frequency of *zo'n* and *zulk(e)* in combination with plural nouns in a sample of two-thousand hits from SoNaR Newspapers

Component	Zo'n	Zulk(e)	Total
Belgian Dutch	104 (27.8%)	270 (72.2%)	374 (100.0%)
Netherlandic Dutch	1 (0.3%)	325 (99.7%)	326 (100.0%)
Total	105	595	700

Table 8.6 Absolute and relative token frequency of identifying *zo'n* and *zulk(e)* in combination with non-count nouns in a sample of two-thousand hits from SoNaR Newspapers

Component	Zo'n	Zulk(e)	Total
Belgian Dutch	7 (46.7%)	8 (53.3%)	15 (100.0%)
Netherlandic Dutch	0 (0.0%)	23 (100.0%)	23 (100.0%)
Total	7	31	38

and non-count nouns has a non-specific distribution pattern, the corpus data thus show a specific distribution pattern (at least in newspapers). In Belgium, *zo'n* is a relative variant as it is used next to *zulk(e)* in these combinations. Combinations with *zo'n* seem common in SBD, as they are used in a quarter to a half of all relevant cases in Belgian newspapers.

3.4 Non-specific variant (type C): *Beginnen* 'start' with a bare infinitive or *te*-infinitive

A non-specific variant that is used only in parts of one country is described in ANS2 (18.5.4.20). In the western part of Belgium, *beginnen* 'start' (either as a finite verb, as an infinitive or as an *infinitivus pro participio*) can be combined with a bare infinitive (as in 5) instead of a *te*-infinitive (as in 6) in the verbal end group.[17]

(5) Ik *moet* eens *beginnen werken*. <regional>   (ANS2 18.5.4.20)
    'I have to start working.'

(6) Ik hoor dat Jan zijn viool al *is beginnen te stemmen*.   (ANS2 18.5.4.20)
    'I hear that Jan has already started tuning his violin.'

---

17. When the verb *beginnen* is used in the perfect tense (i.e. in the complement of a perfect auxiliary *hebben* 'have' or *zijn* 'be') and occurs in the final verb cluster followed by the main verb of the clause, as in (6), it does not appear as a past participle, but as an infinitive, the so-called *infinitivus-pro-participio*.

To check the geographical distribution of bare infinitives and *te*-infinitives after *beginnen* in the verbal end cluster, we searched the Belgian and Netherlandic newspaper component of SoNaR for the word *beginnen*, followed by an infinitive within a span of zero to two words. The infinitive and *beginnen* had to occur in the same sentence and the combination could be preceded or followed by zero to twenty-five words. For Belgian Dutch, this yielded 5,444 hits, for Netherlandic Dutch only 563 hits. For Belgian Dutch, a random sample of 563 hits was put together, so that equal numbers of hits were processed for both varieties.[18] All double and irrelevant hits were deleted. Table 8.7. presents the results.

Table 8.7 Absolute and relative token frequency of bare infinitives and *te*-infinitives after *beginnen* 'start' in the verbal end group in SoNaR Newspapers

Component	Bare infinitive	*te*-infinitive	Total
Belgian Dutch	315 (67.2%)	154 (32.8%)	469 (100.0%)
Netherlandic Dutch	1 (0.6%)	161 (99.4%)	162 (100.0%)
Total	316	315	631

The distribution of bare infinitives and *te*-infinitives after *beginnen* significantly differs between the Belgian and Netherlandic components ($\chi^2 = 210.64$, $df = 1$, $p < .0001$, Cramer's $V = 0.5814$). The distribution pattern described by ANS2 is confirmed in the sense that bare infinitives after *beginnen* (almost) exclusively occur in the Belgian data. On the basis of national corpora, we cannot conclude anything about differences within countries, but the large preference for bare infinitives in Belgian newspapers makes it unlikely that this variant would be characteristic of a smaller region *within* Belgium. Further research is necessary to verify whether we are dealing with a specific variant, but this remains difficult so long as no regionally stratified corpora of written Standard Dutch are available. In Belgium, the combination of *beginnen* with a bare infinitive is a relative variant, as it is used next to combinations with a *te*-infinitive. The bare infinitive after *beginnen* seems common in SBD, as it is the preferred variant in two thirds of all cases in Belgian newspapers.

---

18. We used a sample because the query for Belgian Dutch yielded too many examples to check manually in the context of this paper. By using a sample, however, the likelihood of Type II errors increases.

3.5 Summary

Table 8.8. summarizes the findings of the corpus research. It shows which distribution patterns were found for the different variants included in the investigation and indicates whether the distribution patterns of ANS2 were confirmed.

In at least one, and possibly even two, of the four investigated cases, the distribution patterns described in ANS2 were not corroborated by the corpus data: these variants were non-specific according to ANS2, but we found a specific geographical distribution. For the combination of *beginnen* 'start' with a bare infinitive, we cannot really be sure that the distribution pattern is specific. For the combination of *zo'n* 'such' with a plural or non-count noun, it is not clear why we do not find a non-specific pattern. As was already pointed out, it is uncertain whether the regional distribution patterns described by ANS2 reflect the use of variants in *standard language* contexts: it is, for instance, possible that we would find a non-specific distribution pattern for these variants if we considered other registers than newspapers. Whatever the case may be, these findings show that we cannot simply assume that the distribution patterns described by ANS2 are representative of how the variants are actually distributed in Standard Dutch corpus data.

Table 8.8 Summary of the findings of the corpus research

(Pair of) variant(s)	Distribution pattern in newspaper component of SoNaR	Distribution pattern ANS2 confirmed?	Relative or absolute use in newspaper component of SoNaR
preposition *doorheen* 'through'	specific (Belgium)	yes	?
komen 'to come' + infinitive/past participle	non-specific (type A)	yes	relative in Belgium and the Netherlands
zo'n 'such' + plural or non-count nouns	specific (Belgium)	no	relative in Belgium
beginnen 'start' + bare infinitive	specific (Belgium) (?)	no (?)	relative in Belgium

For two, possibly three variants, we found a specific distribution pattern: the variants are only used in SBD. All three variants seem fairly common in Belgian newspaper data, even though this is difficult to tell for *doorheen* 'through' as we only have absolute and normalized token frequency at our disposal. To decide whether the variants are sufficiently common to be considered part of Standard Dutch, we could define frequency criteria, i.e. threshold values which the variant should cross to be considered part of the standard variety. It is unclear, however, whether it is justified to use such threshold values and, if so, how high these should be; see Dhondt et al. (2020) for a more elaborate discussion of the problems related to the use of frequency criteria for determining the normative status of variants.[19]

4. Discussion

4.1 Pluricentric or pluriareal distribution patterns?

At the beginning of this paper, we raised the question of whether the pluricentric approach is an appropriate perspective from which to describe diatopic grammatical variation in ANS3. We discussed three arguments given by Dürscheid et al. (2015: 209–210) against a pluricentric description of German and zoomed in on their argument from variational linguistics: Elspaß et al. (2017) state that a pluricentric description creates the impression of uniform national varieties and they claim that this does not correspond to linguistic reality, as most German variants displaying diatopic variation are not 'national' variants, i.e. their distribution patterns often do not coincide with national borders and, usually, the regionally marked variants are used next to equivalents with a broader geographical distribution. They therefore advocate a pluriareal perspective on German.

In this paper, we investigated what distribution patterns we find for Dutch grammatical variants, in order to evaluate whether these patterns are compatible with the aim of the revised ANS3 to provide a pluricentric description of Dutch grammar. For that purpose, we made an overview of the distribution patterns that can be observed for Dutch grammatical variants on the basis of an inventory of variants for which ANS2 describes diatopic variation. This overview shows that we find both specific and non-specific patterns. Moreover, there are indications that most variants are in relative use, i.e. in the area where they occur, they are used next to equivalent variants which potentially have a broader geographical scope. As a closer look on four variants with diatopic variation has shown, the grammatical description in ANS2 does not always give a completely accurate picture of the use of these variants in standard language contexts and the patterns should thus be checked on the basis of corpus data.

As is the case for German, a lot of grammatical variants in Standard Dutch could thus be said to show a *pluriareal* distribution. As such, we might conclude

---

19. Dhondt (2024) proposes a method for determining the normative status of variants on the basis of frequency data.

that ANS3 should describe diatopic variation from a pluriareal perspective and should reject the idea of national standard varieties of Dutch. We believe, however, that it would be mistaken to conclude that ANS3 should take a pluriareal perspective: in the remainder of this paragraph, we will not only show that Dürscheid et al.'s (2015) argument from variational linguistics can be questioned, but we will also revisit the other two arguments against a pluricentric conception of German, and show that they do not (entirely) apply to the Dutch situation.

4.2 The argument from variational linguistics

First, we believe Dürscheid et al.'s (2015) argument from variational linguistics is questionable, as we might not necessarily need "national" (i.e. specific and absolute) *variants* to be able to speak of national *varieties*. On the basis of a literature review, Ghyselen & De Vogelaer (2018) come to a set of criteria for variety status that can be empirically tested. According to them, "whether a type of language can be considered a variety is a matter of degree, depending on the number of variety characteristics displayed by that language use" (Ghyselen & De Vogelaer 2018: 16). A first characteristic of a variety is that it is a set of co-varying language features that are used with similar stylistic functions by multiple speakers. Another characteristic is that this set of features has emic category status, i.e. language users "should also perceive that type of language use as a separate category" (Ghyselen & De Vogelaer 2018: 5). Ghyselen & De Vogelaer (2018: 5) add that language variants that are limited to one variety (also called 'idiovarietary features') can be taken as a characteristic of variety status, but they add that these "are usually not considered *essential* for variety status [my emphasis, AD]." As such, national (i.e. specific and absolute) variants do not seem a prerequisite to speak of national varieties. In order to verify whether there really exist national varieties of Standard Dutch, it should thus be investigated whether the criteria of covariance and emic category status are met. Ghyselen & De Vogelaer (2018) show how this may be done, viz. by studying both production and perception patterns, on the basis of both quantitative and qualitative data.

A pluricentric description in ANS3 would thus not necessarily be at odds with the distribution patterns we found. From a practical point of view as well, the existence of non-specific and/or relative patterns of distribution does not preclude ANS3 from taking a national perspective as such patterns can also be described from a plurinational point of view, e.g. by using gradual labels. For the use of a past participle in combination with *komen* 'to come', one could say that it is used both in Belgian and in Netherlandic Dutch, but that it is chosen in the majority of the cases in Belgian Dutch while, in Netherlandic Dutch, it is fairly common in use as well but not the most frequently chosen variant. The combination of *zo'n* with plural and non-count nouns could receive the label Belgian Dutch, and by means of gradual labels, it could be shown to what extent *zo'n* and *zulk(e)* are used in these combinations in Belgian Dutch. In fact, such a labelling system is not all that different from the one the Variantengrammatik is using to describe the distribution of grammatical variants over different regions.

4.3 The argument from perceptional linguistics

Next to the argument from variational linguistics, Dürscheid et al. (2015: 209–210) also raised two other arguments against a pluricentric conception of German: speakers of German would not perceive national varieties, and nation states would not constitute a solid basis to discern varieties. These arguments, however, do not seem to hold (entirely) for Dutch.

With regard to the perception argument, it has to our knowledge not yet been (extensively) investigated whether laymen discern national standard varieties. For Netherlandic speakers, it seems beyond doubt that they are aware of their own norm (even though they might not recognize that Netherlandic Dutch is not the only standard variety). For Belgian Dutch, one can safely assume that speakers are aware that there is an own pronunciation norm, but does this also hold for grammar and lexis? The existing research does not seem entirely conclusive. In his exploratory research, De Schryver (2015) found that nearly 60% of the interrogated linguistic professionals (e.g. lawyers, journalists, actors, teachers) agrees that Netherlandic Dutch cannot function as the standard language model for Flanders. On the other hand, still nearly 40% did agree that the written media in Flanders should strive towards one Standard Dutch for the whole Dutch language area. De Schryver (2015) also asked his respondents to rate forty sentences which contained lexical and grammatical items that are typical of Dutch in Belgium, and it turned out that many of them were accepted by the majority of the respondents. As the participants do not reject Belgian items, it is at least possible that an own Belgian norm exists in their minds, but the results cannot be taken as evidence for the awareness of such a norm, as the participants might not realize that these variants are limited to Belgium. Perhaps, the research of Impe (2010) might constitute indirect evidence for the awareness of a Belgian standard language, as she found through a questionnaire that Flemish people rate SBD higher in terms of beauty than SND. Further research, however, seems necessary to check to what extent the perceptional argument applies to Dutch.

4.4 The language-political argument

Nevertheless, when it comes to the political argument, we believe that national boundaries *do* provide an important basis for distinguishing standard varieties in the case of Dutch, as the states that make up the Dutch language area in Europe (Flanders and the Netherlands) could be considered to constitute separate language communities: domains such as education, public administration and the media are organized on a *national* level in the Netherlands and in the Dutch-speaking part of Belgium, which implies that a great deal of the spoken or written texts in standard language (e.g. newspapers, radio programs, legal texts, coursebooks) is aimed at a nation-specific audience.[20] As a matter of fact, this probably is the reason why there are currently only large *national* corpora of standard language use available for Dutch.

As so many of the texts in standard language are aimed at the national level, it is especially useful for speakers of Dutch that reference works describe what belongs to the national standard (and not what is used in standard language contexts in a region *within* Dutch-speaking Belgium or the Netherlands), perhaps even regardless of whether there truly exist national standard 'varieties' in the sense of Ghyselen & De Vogelaer (2018). Of course, this argument is specific to the Dutch language area, which consists of fairly small countries, both geographically and demographically speaking, and in which, for instance, education, public administration, and the media, are therefore largely organized on a national level. Possibly, regional standard variation is of bigger importance in geographically larger language areas, where the regional level is likely to be more important in these domains.

5. Conclusion

In conclusion, the arguments against a pluricentric conception of German do not seem to hold for Dutch (even though research is needed into the perception of variation within Standard Dutch). We believe the pluricentric model is appropriate to describe diatopic grammatical variation in ANS3. The distribution patterns do not always coincide with national borders, but this does not imply that it is practically unfeasible to describe this variation pluricentrically in ANS3 nor that a pluricentric description conflicts with linguistic reality. The description of grammatical variation in ANS3 should in the first place meet the needs of the language users, and from their perspective, the pluricentric model seems the appropriate choice.

---

20. Strictly speaking, education and the media are not organized on a national level in Belgium. In the Dutch-speaking part, the Flemish (and not the federal) government is responsible for these domains.

References

Adviescommissie Taalvariatie. 2019. Visie op taalvariatie en taalvariatiebeleid. Visietekst van de Adviescommissie Taalvariatie in opdracht van het Algemeen Secretariaat van de Taalunie. http://taalunieversum.org/sites/tuv/files/downloads/Visietekst%20taalvariatie%20-%20februari%202019.pdf

Ammon, Ulrich. 2005. Pluricentric and divided languages. In Ulrich Ammon, Norbert Dittmar, Klaus J. Mattheier & Peter Trudgill (eds.), *Sociolinguistics. An international handbook of the science of language and society*, 1536–1542. Berlin/New York: Walter de Gruyter.

Ammon, Ulrich, Hans Bickel & Alexandra N. Lenz. 2016. *Variantenwörterbuch des Deutschen. Die Standardsprache in Österreich, der Schweiz, Deutschland, Liechtenstein, Luxemburg, Ostbelgien und Südtirol sowie Rumänien, Namibia und Mennonitensiedlungen.* Berlin: de Gruyter Mouton.

De Caluwe, Johan. 2017. Van AN naar BN, NN, SN… Het Nederlands als pluricentrische taal. In Gert De Sutter (ed.), *De vele gezichten van het Nederlands in Vlaanderen. Een inleiding tot de variatietaalkunde*, 121–141. Leuven: Acco.

de Cillia, Rudolf & Jutta Ransmayr. 2019. *Österreichisches Deutsch macht Schule: Bildung und Deutschunterricht im Spannungsfeld von sprachlicher Variation und Norm.* Wien: Böhlau.

De Rooij, Jaap. 1989. Zo'n dingen zeggen ze hier (niet). Regionale verschillen in het gebruik van zo'n en zulk(e). In Siegfried Theissen & Joseph Vromans (eds.), *Album Moors. Een bundel opstellen aangeboden aan Joseph Moors ter gelegenheid van zijn 75ste verjaardag*, 181–201. Liège: CIPL.

De Schryver, Johan. 2015. Hoe Vlaams is het Standaardnederlands van taalprofessionelen. *Over Taal* 54(1). 6–9.

Den Boon, Ton & Ruud Hendrickx. 2015. *Van Dale Groot woordenboek van de Nederlandse taal.* Utrecht/Antwerpen: Van Dale Uitgevers.

Dhondt, Arne. 2024. Pluricentrisme in de praktijk. Naar een methode voor de codificatie van grammaticale verschillen tussen Belgisch Nederlands en Nederlands Nederlands. Gent, BE: Universiteit Gent PhD dissertation.

Dhondt, Arne, Timothy Colleman, Johan De Caluwe & Gauthier Delaby. 2020. Naar een pluricentrische *Algemene Nederlandse Spraakkunst*. Het gebruik van productiedata voor de beschrijving van nationale variatie. *Handelingen van de Koninklijke Zuid-Nederlandse Maatschappij voor Taal – en Letterkunde en Geschiedenis*, vol. 73, 85–133.

Dürscheid, Christa, Stephan Elspaß & Arne Ziegler. 2015. Variantengrammatik des Standarddeutschen. Konzeption, methodische Fragen, Fallanalysen. In Alexandra N. Lenz & Manfred M. Glauninger (eds.), *Standarddeutsch im 21. Jahrhundert: theoretische und empirische Ansätze mit einem Fokus auf Österreich*, 205–233. Göttingen: V&R Unipress.

Elspaß, Stephan, Christa Dürscheid & Arne Ziegler. 2017. Zur grammatischen Pluriarealität der deutschen Gebrauchsstandards – oder: Über die Grenzen des Plurizentrizitätsbegriffs. *Zeitschrift für deutsche Philologie*, vol. 136, 69–91.

Ghyselen, Anne-Sophie & Gunther De Vogelaer. 2018. Seeking systematicity in variation: theoretic and methodological considerations on the "variety" concept. *Frontiers in Psychology*, vol. 9, artikel 385.

Haeseryn, Walter, Kirsten Romijn, Guido Geerts, Jaap de Rooij & Maarten van den Toorn (eds.). 1997. *Algemene Nederlandse Spraakkunst*. Groningen/Deurne: Martinus Nijhoff/Wolters Plantyn.

Impe, Leen. 2010. Mutual intelligibility of national and regional varieties of Dutch in the Low Countries. Leuven, BE: Katholieke Universiteit Leuven PhD dissertation.

Kleiner, Stefan. 2011ff. Atlas zur Aussprache des deutschen Gebrauchsstandards. http://prowiki.ids-mannheim.de/bin/view/AADG/

Martin, Willy. 2001. Natiolectismen in het Nederlands en hun lexicografische beschrijving. *Revue Belge de Philologie et d'Histoire* 79(3). 709–736.

Martin, Willy & Willy Smedts. 2009. *Prisma Handwoordenboek Nederlands. Derde, herziene druk*. Houten: Het Spectrum.

Niehaus, Konstantin. 2015. Areale Variation in der Syntax des Standarddeutschen. Ergebnisse zum Sprachgebrauch und zur Frage Plurizentrik vs. Pluriarealität. *Zeitschrift für Dialektologie und Linguistik* 82(2). 133–168.

Oostdijk, Nelleke et al. 2013. The construction of a 500 million word reference corpus of contemporary written Dutch. In Peter Spijns & Jan Odijk (eds.), *Essential speech and language technology for Dutch: Results by the STEVIN-project*, 219–247. Berlin: Springer.

CHAPTER 9

Pluricentricity AND pluriareality
Building the case for complementarity

Ryan Durgasingh[1,2] & Philipp Meer[2,3]
[1] Ruhr University Bochum, Germany | [2] University of Münster, Germany |
[3] University of Campinas, Brazil

> Moving beyond the contention which has characterized the pluricentricity and pluriareality debate, this summative chapter draws together the argumentative strands in the chapters in this volume to build the case for their complementarity. We show the various ways in which terminological differences, of geography and of sociolinguistics, have somewhat obscured the underlying similarities of these models, and highlight many of the key findings of this book's contributors in doing so. The chapter ends by highlighting how some of the issues related to the pluri-concepts might lie in the different assumptions and foci of different linguistic paradigms, and with a request that further work on pluricentricity and pluriareality view the models as flexible constructs which can work together towards mutual benefits.

Keywords: pluricentricity, pluriareality, complementarity, epicenter, language variation, standard

In keeping with the titular opening promise of this volume's introduction to lay out the pluricentric/pluriareal debate, the contributions herein have systematically tackled the thorny issues surrounding modeling standard variation through these conceptual lenses. In so doing, some of the authors have more-or-less adhered to one or the other of these models, while others have attempted to complicate the picture by highlighting either blind spots or areas of unexplored overlap. All of them have added much needed discussion and nuance to a contentious issue within the field of variation studies, especially as it pertains to issues of standardness in English, German, and Dutch linguistics. In this conclusion, we will bring together some of the defining arguments that have been laid out by the collection's chapters, and attempt to fulfil the other promissory part of our introduction's title: build a nascent case for the underlying complementarity of pluricentricity and pluriareality.

To begin, at a foundational level, we have seen that the two models share at least an agreement that variation and standardness are not mutually exclusive. There is the assumption in both camps that variation exists at the standard level of usage (Clyne 1992; Leitner 1992; Ammon 1995, 1998; Scheuringer 1996), even if there is disagreement on how best to explain this. Some of the literature reviewed in the early sections of our introduction explores the development of these models (with pluriareality being a later, related response to pluricentricity) during the course of the 20th century, highlighting that this focus came about because of a perceived need to conceptualize how standardness in particular could be discussed within the developing sociolinguistic turn towards *language and society* around the 1960s. By agreeing on variation in standards, the two also implicitly agree on the equality of these standards from a sociolinguistic perspective — that is, that the standard-speaking person will most likely use those particular variants which are standard for them within, for instance, formal domains. Lastly, and perhaps most importantly as a basis for both of these models, is a focus on geography. Both pluricentricity and pluriareality focus on the traditional distinction of lectal variation as being delimited by areal patterns. In the main, these models focus on borders, though how borders are or are not defined forms a central part of their divergence.

It is this latter point that has focused much of the contentious debate surrounding the use of the two labels in particular. Pluricentricity finds utility in political borders (Ebner 2014: 8; Dollinger 2019a: 44, 2019b: 100); the nation state as a dialectal boundary in relation to standard variation has played a defining and growing role in, especially, World Englishes research since the 1980s (e.g. Kachru 1985; Schneider 2018; Mair 2021). Conversely, pluriareality points out that standard variation need not follow hard-and-fast political borders, but may rely more on traditional dialect boundaries (described by socio-historical or geographical limits), particularly in cases of contiguity as is the case for standard German language use (Wolf 1994; Scheuringer 1996). Some of the contributions here have tackled this issue in particular, to mixed findings. Schneider comes to two key conclusions as it pertains to English worldwide and geographical boundaries: there is (1) little evidence of distinct national varieties in terms of specific features but cross-varietal differences in general usage tendencies, and that (2) there is considerable evidence of overlap in areal language production patterns within and across national borders (Schneider, this volume). Dhondt et al. concur in their contribution, but do not advocate for an outright pluriareal reading in their chapter, either. Their findings also show that the patterns of distribution do not always coincide with national borders, but argue that the observed patterns are not necessarily at odds with a pluricentric view, especially when focusing on general usage tendencies rather than the question of variety-exclusive variants (Dhondt et al., this volume). For Dhondt et al., as we will see frequently in this concluding chapter, the debate between pluricentricity and pluriareality often comes down to terminological differences, rather than actual linguistic reality.

A defining difference between pluricentricity and pluriareality has been the focus on nation states — very important for the former, and argued to be overemphasized by adherents to the latter. But, as we explored briefly in the introduction, pluricentricity does not completely rule-out the role of regional variation for standards. "Regional pluricentricity" or "second level pluricentricity" have both been put forward as terms which, by their definitional basis, accommodate the idea of variation within and outside of the nation state (Auer 2014: 44; Muhr 2018: 40–42). A sticking point between the pluri-concepts on this level is the relatively high or low amount of variation that may exist within particular national borders (or which spill over them). Pluriarealists point to a large amount of standard variation within (especially larger) countries as evidence that purely national standards do not exist, with many pluricentrists arguing that this is simply evidence of regionally and socially conditioned variation at the national level.

A related geographically contentious point has been the role of epicenters in the ongoing debate. In the pluriareal stance, separate epicenters for different standard variants may exist within a single nation, or they may radiate across national borders in contiguous states (cf. Elspaβ, this volume, Figures 2.2 and 2.3). However, the assertion by Auer (2014: 22) that pluricentricity, when equated with plurinationality (and related to the Schneider's "weak reading" of pluricentricity in this volume), does not focus on epicenters or variant radiation, does not quite hold when applied to much of the work done in the World Englishes paradigm. While often not explicitly cited as "epicentric influence," work on the development of Outer Circle Englishes, and in particular postcolonial varieties, in the past decades has indeed made this a focus of research (e.g. Hoffmann et al. 2011; Hundt 2013; Schneider, 2014; Gries & Bernaisch 2016; Heller et al. 2017; Peters et al. 2019). Whether or not a postcolonial variety exhibits features of endonormative stability, or may have more or less exonormative orientations, is still a fruitful area of World Englishes research (Schneider 2007). Schneider's (this volume) strong reading of pluricentricity, shows exactly that national standards (either of the postcolonial or referent variety) are well supported in the current research on standards — with the question of whether or not new(er), more demographically powerful varieties exert influence on others (Hundt 2013), or if old/Inner Circle varieties continue to exert influence on developing standards, still being important and sometimes central. The case, then, that this geographically-related argument highlights an opposition between pluricentricity and pluriareality seems to have been overblown by the use of terms which are not shared between the models. Conceptually, at least, both pluri-concepts are invested in the relative spread of features from epicenters to peripheries.

The intranational versus transnational focus on variation comes with experimental ramifications that may have similarly obscured the complementarity and complexity underlying the sociolinguistic factors which pluricentricity and pluriareality wish to capture. As demonstrated, for instance, in Elspaß (this volume) pluriareal approaches to language variation start from the local/regional level of language use (often using corpora which have been compiled across national borders) and move outwards — exploring the range of standard variants outside of political borders. The focus here is on the prevalence of features and their distribution, irrespective of socio-political definitions. Pluricentricity's focus, on the other hand, has been top-down in its assumption of national standards. In much of the work on World Englishes in the last few decades, there has been an underlying and taken-for-granted assumption of pluricentricity in relation to ESL and/or postcolonial varieties (cf. e.g. Leitner 1992; Mair 2009). English corpora, such as some of those analyzed in Schneider (this volume) and Weilinghoff (this volume), show the tendency to come at the issue of variation from the "nation-first" perspective and to compare national varieties against each other. As with pluriareal analyses, feature analyses are driven by frequency measures, but the focus here is delimited by socio-political borders and explanations for differences are argued for or against their prevalence in terms of cross-linguistic influences. Niehaus's contribution in this book has highlighted one possible way in which both pluricentricity and pluriareality can be united regarding this phenomenon in the form of enregisterment: "Regiocentric 'core' areas either are the cause or the consequence of enregisterment. So, the idea of enregisterment will more easily appeal to speakers who perceive that their language use almost universally corresponds with the 'core' area usage, a perception of salient features which in turn influences speaker's attitudes" (Niehaus, this volume: 75). As Niehaus points out in his preliminary modeling of (geographic) standard German, neither pluricentricity nor pluriareality need lay claim to absolute correctness, but, rather, play to their methodological strengths in order to understand the variation at work.

Added to this, enregisterment and similar theories which help to account for the sociological realities of language use can help to clarify the exact limits of pluricentricity and pluriareality in terms of another aspect of their research focus. A major strand of pluricentric research has been the language attitude study, with many respondents of German and English studies seemingly agreeing with the idea of national standard varieties. Although the presence of the same variants across borders may capture one aspect of standard variation, the specific perceptions of speech communities related to their identity-forming functions is nonetheless an important factor of sociolinguistic identity, one for which the idea of pluricentricity seems particularly apt. Perhaps the overt focus on national borders has rather obscured the fact that both of these models, in their intent and analyses, seem to largely be investigating different aspects of language use, rather than opposed ones. On one hand, as Elspaß (this volume) argues, the pluriareal model's focus on production seems to be suitable to describe variation across lects that are geographically contiguous, such as is the case with varieties of German. On the other hand, Ransmayr's contribution on metalinguistic awareness and perception in students and teachers in Austria found a large tendency to conceptualize German in accordance with the pluricentric model. While this division may seem to neatly capture the two realities — one model for perception, one for production — the picture is nonetheless complicated by overlap: Ransmayr's findings also suggest fine-grained understandings and perceptions of pluriareal variation within Austrian standards. The overall picture, then, is a complicated one that might not lead to a completely binary understanding of standard variation, but different understandings of language in society as summed up by Schneider's argument that pluricentricity and pluriareality need not exclude each other, but may be seen as capturing different aspects of the complexity of variation, with varying emphasis on patterns of perception and production, respectively.

This complexity of variation in geographical space has underpinned much of the back-and-forth debate between pluricentricity and pluriareality. Several authors in this collection have made the observation that the distinctions between the two models might actually be those of terminological differences and that the research foci above may actually be better accommodated by shifts in definitional focus. Elspaß, for instance, suggests that the models may be seen as complementary insofar as each is likely to be more appropriate for different kinds of standard language scenarios: pluricentricity in the case of varieties across dispersed territories, pluriareality in contiguous areas. This contention dovetails with Ransmayr's position that pluricentricity might better account for variation at the (socio)political level, while pluriareality might best account for regional variation. Indeed, the two may even benefit from one another's experimental orientations as Ransmayr argues that pluricentric and pluriareal views may, in fact, build on each other: meticulous pluriareal accounts of the distribution of variants may be used as a foundation for further pluricentric exploration and theorizing of aspects beyond geographical variation. A further mixed case is provided by Weilinghoff, with his results showing that variation in the SVLR in Scottish Standard English is primarily conditioned by language-internal (prosodic) factors; the SVLR seems to operate relatively homogenously at a national level and mostly independently of geographical factors. At the same time, previous studies have shown that the alternation pattern is observed in Northern England. The mixed findings here suggest aspects of sociolinguistic reality that can be captured on some levels by pluricentricity, while others can be best accounted for by pluriareality, depending on how much weight one puts on either feature frequency or their social meaning(s).

Niehaus's suggestion of enregisterment in this volume is just one way in which related sociolinguistic theories can bridge the gap between these models. In his proposal of a new theoretical framework for the modeling of standard German (and potentially standards in other languages) that combines the pluriareal concept of areas in terms of high (aggregate) density in frequency of variants with the issue of social meaning of variation (often emphasized in pluricentric accounts), he makes the compelling case for an integrationist approach towards modeling variation. This argument is further reinforced by Buschfeld's (this volume) contention for global Englishes (but other languages as well) that the two models are not mutually exclusive, and each do indeed account for separate (and sometimes overlapping) areas of sociolinguistic reality. Her discussion on Standard Singaporean English (SSE):

> shows how language policies, attitudes and perceptions have contributed to the shaping of SSE and its preference over CSE/Singlish in at least the official domains of language use. ... this notion of an existing homogenous standard lends itself to a pluricentric interpretation. On the other hand, actual feature use is much fuzzier and seems to be more typologically, "sprachbund" motivated than determined by national boundaries. ...Therefore, the one thing that can be safely concluded from the above observations is that only a joined perspective combining pluricentric and pluriareal aims, perspectives, and methodologies can shed conclusive light on the current debate. (Buschfeld, this volume: 132)

Finally, because of this volume's wide-ranging contributions — authors working in the linguistic traditions of English, German, and Dutch — an unforeseen point of contention has presented itself as a striking issue in the pluri-debates: different paradigms seem to begin from different definitional starting points. Perhaps as a function of how/when the field of World Englishes was first conceptualized (after centuries of colonization and settlement activities), much of the work in English variation has taken non-contiguous dispersion of English varieties for granted. Kachru's Three Circles of English Model (1985), a major turning point in the development of the field, for instance, followed socio-historical patterns of settlement and use, tracing the development of Englishes across the globe. By contrast, and due to its own socio-history, German linguistics especially has not placed as large of an emphasis on dispersed varieties outside of Western Europe. In this vein, we have seen a division between some of the Anglicist chapters — Schneider (Chapter 5) and Buschfeld (Chapter 6) — and mainly the German-focused ones. The English-focused chapters have approached the pluri-concepts with a redefining focus rooted in the interests of the World Englishes paradigm – offering: a "strong" and/or "weak" approach to pluricentricity (Schneider), readings which incorporate non-standard features (Schneider and Buschfeld), or questions related to the need for the debate at all in a globalized world (Buschfeld, and Schneider to a lesser degree). The German and Dutch entries, by contrast, have more-or-less retained the definitions that have been especially important in talking about contiguous versus non-contiguous standard variation. We point this out here, not because we wish to side with either camp, or because we think that this division invalidates the major points of complementarity that our contributors have made, but to suggest that theorizing of this nature needs to also first acknowledge the particular historical foci of the field and how past or present trends may affect our research. As we have pointed out above, some definitional refocus on our theories in light of actual data – perception and use – may offer much needed clarity.

The benefits of such theorizing in the heated and ongoing pluri-debates cannot be overstated. While we have built a case in this summative chapter for pluricentric and pluriareal complementarity, we hope to have also highlighted that some of the contention may be due to underlying assumptions within different linguistic fields and/or definitions. We also hope to stress, like several of our chapters, that pluricentricity and pluriareality are best treated as flexible orientations, useful for their experimental and descriptive power, but offering insights into different dimensions of overall sociolinguistic realities. Rigid arguments which attempt to silo these models may actually work against the scientific fields to which they are both attempting to contribute. We believe that this collection, with its breadth of coverage – across three related Germanic languages and various methodological orientations – has shown the way forward for the debates surrounding these polarizing models, and for mapping the state of variation in standards in the 21st century.

References

Ammon, Ulrich. 1995. *Die deutsche Sprache in Deutschland, Österreich und der Schweiz*. Berlin: De Gruyter.
Ammon, Ulrich. 1998. Plurinationalität oder Pluriarealität? Begriffliche und terminologische Präzisierungsvorschläge zur Plurizentrizität des Deutschen – mit Ausblick auf ein Wörterbuchprojekt. In Peter Ernst & Franz Patocka (eds.), *Deutsche Sprache in Raum und Zeit*, 313–323. Wien: Edition Praesens.
Auer, Peter. 2014. Enregistering pluricentric German. In Augusto S. d. Silva (ed.), *Pluricentricity: Language variation and sociocognitive dimensions*. Berlin: De Gruyter.

Clyne, Michael G. (ed.). 1992. *Pluricentric languages: Differing norms in different nations.* Berlin: De Gruyter.

Dollinger, Stefan. 2019a. *The Pluricentricity Debate.* London: Routledge.

Dollinger, Stefan. 2019b. Debunking "pluri-areality": On the pluricentric perspective of national varieties. *Journal of Linguistic Geography* 7(2). 98–112.

Ebner, Jakob. 2014. Österreichisches Deutsch: Ein Klärungsversuch. In Bundesministerium für Bildung (ed.), *Österreichisches Deutsch als Unterrichts — und Bildungssprache*, 7–9. Vienna.

Gries, Stefan T. & Tobias Bernaisch. 2016. Exploring epicentres empirically: Focus on South Asian Englishes. *English World-Wide* 37(1). 1–25.

Heller, Benedikt, Tobias Bernaisch & Stefan T. Gries. 2017. Empirical perspectives on two potential epicenters: The genitive alternation in Asian Englishes. *ICAME Journal* 41(1). 111–144.

Hoffmann, Sebastian, Marianne Hundt & Joybrato Mukherjee. 2011. Indian English — An emerging epicentre? A pilot study on light verbs in web-derived corpora of South Asian Englishes. *Anglia* 129(3–4). 258–280.

Hundt, Marianne. 2013. The diversification of English: Old, new and emerging epicentres. In Daniel Schreier & Marianne Hundt (eds.), *English as a contact language*, 182–203. Cambridge: Cambridge University Press.

Kachru, Braj B. 1985. Standards, codification and sociolinguistic realism: The English language in the outer circle. In Randolph Quirk & H. G. Widdowson (eds.), *English in the world: Teaching and learning the language and literatures*, 11–30. Cambridge: Cambridge University Press.

Leitner, Gerhard. 1992. English as a pluricentric language. In Michael G. Clyne (ed.), *Pluricentric languages: Differing norms in different nations*, 179–237. Berlin: De Gruyter.

Mair, Christian. 2009. Corpus linguistics meets sociolinguistics: Studying educated spoken usage in Jamaica on the basis of the International Corpus of English. In Thomas Hoffmann & Lucia Siebers (eds.), *World Englishes — problems, properties and prospects: Selected papers from the 13th IAWE conference*, 39–60. Amsterdam: John Benjamins.

Mair, Christian. 2021. World Englishes: From methodological nationalism to a global perspective. In Britta Schneider, Theresa Heyd & Mario Saraceni (eds.), *Bloomsbury World Englishes Volume 1: Paradigms*, 27–45: Bloomsbury Academic.

Muhr, Rudolf. 2018. Misconceptions about pluricentric languages and pluricentric theory — an overview of 40 years. In Rudolf Muhr & Benjamin Meisnitzer (eds.), *Pluricentric languages and non-dominant varieties worldwide: New pluricentric languages — old problems*, 17–56. Frankfurt: Peter Lang.

Peters, Pam, Adam Smith & Tobias Bernaisch. 2019. Shared Lexical Innovations in Australian and New Zealand English. *Dictionaries: Journal of the Dictionary Society of North America* 40(2). 1–30.

Scheuringer, Hermann. 1996. Das Deutsche als pluriareale Sprache: Ein Beitrag gegen staatlich begrenzte Horizonte in der Diskussion um die deutsche Sprache in Österreich. *Die Unterrichtspraxis / Teaching German* 29(2). 147–153.

Schneider, Edgar W. 2007. *Postcolonial English: Varieties around the world.* Cambridge: Cambridge University Press.

Schneider, Edgar W. 2014. Global diffusion, regional attraction, local roots? Sociocognitive perspectives on the pluricentricity of English. In Augusto S. d. Silva (ed.), *Pluricentricity: Language variation and sociocognitive dimensions*. Berlin: De Gruyter.

Schneider, Edgar W. 2018. World Englishes. In Mark Aronoff (ed.), *Oxford Research Encyclopedia of Linguistics*. Oxford University Press.

Wolf, Norbert R. 1994. Österreichisches zum österreichischen Deutsch. Aus Anlaß des Erscheinens von: Wolfgang Pollak: Was halten die Österreicher von ihrem Deutsch? Eine sprachpolitische und soziosemiotische Analyse der sprachlichen Identität der Österreicher. *Zeitschrift für Dialektologie und Linguistik* 61(1). 66–76.

Index

A
American English 96–102, 106, 111, 121, 133
Asian Englishes 4–5, 103–104, 107–109
Australian English 4, 92, 100–104, 121, 133, 142
Austrian German 7, 21–22, 28, 30, 33–34, 37, 47, 49–60, 71, 79–83, 93–94, 191

B
British English 2, 96–102, 128, 144–145, 159
Belgian Dutch 9, 166–168, 171–180, 182–183
Belgian German 21, 28–29, 32, 35, 37, 70, 73–74

C
complementarity 1, 4–6, 7, 9, 15, 40, 45–46, 60, 66, 68–69, 72, 76–77, 131, 187–191, 193
contiguity 2, 4–5, 7, 15–21, 27, 32, 39–40, 134, 188–189, 191–193
corpora 4–5, 16, 24, 26–27, 34, 93, 98–102, 110, 124–126, 148, 169–172

D
diatopic variation 166–177, 181
debate 1–3, 6–8, 21, 61, 66–68, 74, 90–92, 94, 96–97, 113, 118–121, 132–135, 141–144, 147, 187–189, 191–193
Dynamic Model 121

E
enregisterment 5, 8, 18, 40, 66, 68–69, 72–73, 75–84, 190
epicenter 4, 6, 21, 39, 84, 90–92, 112, 119–122, 125–128, 130–131, 133, 161, 189–190

epicentric influence See *epicenter*

G
German German 2, 22, 25, 47–48, 55–56, 80, 91, 94, 119
globalization 110, 121–122, 134

I
indexicality 38, 68–69, 72, 75–77
Indonesian English 125–126

L
language attitudes 4, 7, 16, 46, 50–51, 55, 60, 67–68, 71–72, 76, 79–80, 83, 94–95, 126–127
language ideologies 8, 16–17, 22, 25, 39, 47, 61, 66, 68–69, 73–78, 81–84, 93, 119–120, 123, 135
language-external factors 147, 150
language-internal factors 147, 150, 191
Luxembourgish German 21–22, 24, 29, 32, 35, 37, 40, 70, 73, 78, 120, 169, 170

M
Malaysian English 92, 104, 107–108, 120, 122, 124, 126
multilingualism 6, 82, 107, 119, 123

N
national identity 4, 46, 71, 72, 73, 80–82, 83, 113, 143
Namibian English 121, 127–130, 134
national variants 22, 26, 67, 169, 170, 181
Netherlandic Dutch 2, 167–168, 170, 174–180, 182, 183, 184

New Zealand English 100, 101, 104, 121, 133, 142

P
perception 4–5, 16, 21, 24, 26, 36, 39, 60, 67–68, 70–72, 77, 78, 91, 99, 111–112, 113, 130–132, 135, 169, 182, 183, 184, 190–192, 193
plurinational 18–25, 38–40, 74, 167
production 4–5, 68, 91, 99, 111–113, 131, 135, 170, 182, 188, 191

R
register 20, 27, 55, 72–73, 75–76, 80, 180
relative variants 34, 35, 48, 60, 170–172, 174, 176, 178–179

S
Scottish English 144–147
Scottish Vowel Length Rule (SVLR) 142, 146–148, 151–155, 158–161
Singaporean English 92, 101, 103, 104, 107, 108, 119–134, 142, 192
South African English 121, 128–132, 142
Surinamese Dutch 166, 167, 170
Swiss German 58, 71, 82, 169

T
Three Circles Model 189, 192

W
World Englishes 2, 3, 6, 39, 83, 92, 99–103, 108–110, 122–130, 134